Mission Driven Bureaucrats

ADVANCE PRAISE FOR *MISSION DRIVEN BUREAUCRATS*

"*Mission Driven Bureaucrats* is a love letter to bureaucrats cunningly disguised as an analysis of organizational management. Honig gives voice to bureaucrats who do the spadework of making our societies work and provides a highly readable yet sharply incisive look at how to build organizations that help bureaucrats— and, hence, our communities—flourish."

—Hahrie Han, Professor of Political Science and Director, SNF Agora Institute, Johns Hopkins University

"Dan Honig is a voice crying out in a wilderness of popular, but fundamentally misguided attempts to make the organizations and agencies of governments work better. Everyone working in and around government will benefit from his views that are both evidence based—and wise. Honig performs the near impossible balancing act of standing on the shoulders of giants, not just of one discipline, but of many academic disciplines and of the unacknowledged giants of practice. Honig lays out a persuasive case for a bold new approach to improving people's lives by empowering bureaucrats to do their job."

—Lant Pritchett, Development Economist

"I am thrilled by the publication of Dan Honig's *Mission Driven Bureaucrats: Empowering People To Help Governments Do Better*. The book is a welcome addition to our stock of knowledge about what makes a difference in how governments perform. Honig provides readers with the detailed architecture of how successful bureaucracies and the bureaucrats that populate them build the higher purpose that makes a difference for so many. The book is a coherent, accessible, and effective guide to the meaning of mission in the lives of people who make bureaucracies work and those they serve."

—James L. Perry, Distinguished Professor Emeritus, Paul H. O'Neill School of Public and Environmental Affairs, Indiana University

"*Mission Driven Bureaucrats* offers a fresh rethink of how governments can enable public sector workers to be more effective. Grounded in extensive engagement with committed public servants in a remarkably wide range of settings and sectors around the world, the analysis frames the author's own original mixed methods research with a masterful synthesis of cutting-edge social science. The analysis convincingly counterposes 'management for compliance' with 'managing to empower,' making the case that managers can inspire public servants to serve the public better if they act more as coaches than overseers. Think team-building vs punching the clock—Ted Lasso vs Frederick Taylor."

—Jonathan Fox, American University

"This deeply researched book provides a fresh understanding of why empowerment and motivation can catalyze *Mission Driven Bureaucrats* to drive broad positive changes via their effects on their peers. Written with verve, its path-breaking findings challenge dominant compliance-based principal-agent models by placing unobservable performance as key to improving public sector bureaucracies to better meet the needs of their citizens."

—Devesh Kapur, Johns Hopkins School of Advanced International Studies

Mission Driven Bureaucrats

Empowering People to Help Governments Do Better

DAN HONIG

WITH CONTRIBUTIONS FROM SARAH THOMPSON

OXFORD
UNIVERSITY PRESS

Oxford University Press is a department of the University of Oxford. It furthers the University's objective of excellence in research, scholarship, and education by publishing worldwide. Oxford is a registered trade mark of Oxford University Press in the UK and certain other countries.

Published in the United States of America by Oxford University Press
198 Madison Avenue, New York, NY 10016, United States of America.

© Oxford University Press 2024

Library of Congress Cataloging-in-Publication Data
Names: Honig, Dan, 1981– author.
Title: Mission driven bureaucrats : empowering people to help governments
do better / Dan Honig.
Description: New York, NY : Oxford University Press, [2024] |
Includes bibliographical references.
Identifiers: LCCN 2023043013 | ISBN 9780197641200 (paperback) |
ISBN 9780197641194 (hardback) | ISBN 9780197641224 (epub)
Subjects: LCSH: Civil service—Personnel management—Cross-cultural studies. |
Civil service—Recruiting—Cross-cultural studies. |
Employee motivation—Cross-cultural studies.
Classification: LCC JF1601 .H644 2024 | DDC 352.6—dc23/eng/20231208
LC record available at https://lccn.loc.gov/2023043013

DOI: 10.1093/oso/9780197641194.001.0001

Paperback printed by Marquis Book Printing, Canada
Hardback printed by Bridgeport National Bindery, Inc., United States of America

MIX
Paper from
responsible sources
FSC® C103567

In Memory of David Robert Shanaman (1981–2019)
For all those whose work holds less meaning than it should; for all citizens
who could benefit from more Mission Driven Bureaucrats in their
government—every citizen of every country.

CONTENTS

PREFACE

The seed of *Mission Driven Bureaucrats* came from my wife Özsel, who had just returned from a work trip as an international education consultant. Özsel was telling me about meeting a mid-level education ministry bureaucrat from a government whose political ideology both of us strongly oppose. She couldn't help marveling at this particular bureaucrat's dedication, considering the conditions in which he worked. He had not received his salary in months and the ministry's facilities were dreadful; during their short meeting, the electricity in his office went out multiple times. Yet despite the obvious challenges, this capable and hardworking bureaucrat produced work of truly excellent quality.

I had met many similar dedicated bureaucrats in my work around the world. Bureaucrats who care deeply about and work hard at improving the lives of their fellow citizens, despite seemingly dysfunctional circumstances. I wondered aloud about their motivation. Why do some people do such great work despite highly challenging environments? In the absence of financial incentives or rigid oversight, what drives these bureaucrats?

"I don't know if it's that complicated," replied Özsel, who is Turkish. "It's like AKP's [the Islamist political party that has been in power in Turkey since 2002] early motto, *Halka hizmet Hakka hizmettir*—'serving the people is serving Allah.' This bureaucrat doesn't need electricity, supplies, or even supervision to work as hard as he possibly can. He is serving a higher purpose."

Of course, I thought, with the shock of something that is perfectly obvious once said, but nonetheless novel. It didn't apply only, or particularly, to religious conviction either; we could have been talking about any bureaucrat whose internal compass is aligned with their organization's mission.

This in turn got me thinking about the approaches to management I'd seen in the countries in which I've worked. In many contexts there is still no effective way to monitor and control many government employees—was this the best approach for these Mission Driven Bureaucrats? As I thought about it, I could come up with a number of examples of controls and processes meant to improve performance in fact getting in the way of these types of bureaucrats doing good work.

Thinking about this also made me reflect on my own experience with a demotivating workplace. I found myself thinking again and again about the summer of 1998, sitting in a vacant apartment filled with broken ceiling fans.

My friend Dave and I were doing maintenance work for an apartment management company in our hometown, Detroit. We planted trees, repainted walls, and did basic plumbing and electrical. The work was varied and interesting, and I felt that we were helping folks, doing good work.

But then came the ceiling fans. The management company had installed the same defective fan in hundreds—maybe thousands—of apartments. When the fan was run for an extended period in high heat—which, of course, is precisely when one turns on one's fan—a metal bracket near the motor often melted slightly and began to touch the rotating bit of the assembly, causing an irritating noise.

When temperatures rose in July, dozens and then eventually hundreds of fans broke in the same way at the company's apartment complexes. We found ourselves doing the same thing over and over—take the fan down; disassemble it; pound down the broken bracket; slather on some heat-resistant putty; reassemble it. It took a few tries to get right—to find the precise position where the reworked bracket would not hit the blade assembly. But once Dave and I got the hang of it, we could each fix a fan in a little less than an hour. Rather than teach other employees to fix this minor system-wide problem, the company's approach was essentially "let Dave and Dan deal with it."

Doing this repetitive job over and over was unpleasant enough on its own, but soon we increasingly had to deal with another issue: angry tenants. Since we could be in only one apartment complex on a given day, many people had to wait several weeks until we made it to their apartments. They were annoyed—and rightly so, as the noise was extremely irritating. We came to consider it a good day if only a few residents swore at us as we left, delivering some (usually expletive-enhanced) version of "Why'd I have to wait weeks for something that only takes you jokers an hour to fix? Get off your lazy butts and work harder!"

I was offended because we weren't lazy—at least not in the beginning. We did our best to fix each fan as fast as we could. Eventually, we asked to work from vacant unit in each apartment complex, with other staff bringing the fans to us. This arrangement spared us the bad interactions but also deprived us the occasional thanks offered by grateful residents. Soon enough—alone in our vacant unit—we noticed that the company didn't really care how fast we fixed the fans. So, why should we?

As the weeks dragged on, Dave and I started taking longer and longer breaks, smoking and talking. At some point Dave remarked that I thought about everyday stuff in unusual ways—"you should definitely go to college, man" (I'd been on the fence, thinking I'd just finish high school); "Or maybe even teach it or something someday." "Yeah," I remember saying, "that could be cool. Ain't going to happen, but you never know."

Whatever benefits those chats might have had on my long-term career trajectory, they didn't do much for the ceiling fans. Over time our combined output fell from a couple dozen fans to maybe ten fans a day.

I like to think of myself as hardworking and dedicated. But that summer in Detroit taught me a lesson that in many ways informs this book: my motivation and work ethic are influenced by my work environment. They depend on the task at hand and how I am treated by my employer, my coworkers, and the people my work is meant to benefit. In the end, those angry residents were right; my laziness had prolonged their exposure to that annoying noise. But I think that had more than a little bit to do with how we were treated (by the company, but also perhaps by the people we were meant to help), which in turn affected our motivation.

The last time I saw Dave was in 2009, back home after the first semester of my PhD studies. Our lives had taken different paths. Dave was doing some real estate work and talking about starting his own cleaning company; he was tired of working for other people, he explained. As we caught up, I brought up those broken fans from the summer a decade before. I chuckled over the distant memory of this pointless job, having gone on to find work I really loved. Dave just looked at me intensely. "It's all like that," he said. "Every job I've ever had. *None of it matters.*"

We more or less lost touch after that. Another decade later—around noon on April 8, 2019—Dave died by suicide. I'm more than a little ashamed to say I only learned of it a year later; out of perhaps morbid curiosity, I consulted my Google calendar to determine where I was during Dave's final moments. I had been eating lunch at a Thai restaurant in Washington, DC, with George Washington University's Jennifer Brinkerhoff, a wise and kind public administration scholar. I could even remember what we'd discussed over our noodles and curry. In what strikes me as a strange and tragic coincidence, given my last conversation with Dave, we had been talking about academic theory related to employee motivation.[1]

Of course, I know nothing about the deeper reasons why Dave is no longer with us. But this book is dedicated to him. Our experience together during the summer of 1998 taught me how bad management could demotivate us both. I feel sadness and anger when I think about everything that Dave's mind, hands, and good heart could have accomplished.

In my early conversations about Mission Driven Bureaucrats, I was in search of academic research exploring the particulars (the when and why) of something I think virtually everyone who's ever had a job would agree with: good work happens when good, capable people who care about getting the work done well are in a work environment that encourages and supports them in doing that work. Almost all of the scholars I spoke with—experts in a wide range of fields, from sociology to public management to economics to organizational behavior—helpfully informed me of relevant theories and empirical findings. But when I looked at the literature they recommended, no single theory or set of empirics combined all the elements I suspected mattered. To improve things, I felt we really needed to know when focusing on attracting, supporting, and retaining Mission Driven Bureaucrats was likely to lead to the best possible performance.

Having now done the research and written the book, I believe that cultivating Mission Driven Bureaucrats will help the governments they work for deliver more to their publics—all of us. This book is in no small part my way of asking, and hoping, for your help in making it so.

PART I

WHEN SHOULD WE EXPECT A FOCUS ON MISSION DRIVEN BUREAUCRATS AND EMPOWERMENT-ORIENTED MANAGEMENT TO IMPROVE PERFORMANCE?

1

The Mission of Bureaucrats, and of This Book

> What is it about the people who are doing the jobs in government that make them want to do it? . . . If you worked for Apple and the CEO every day got up and said how horrible Apple was and how horrible the people who worked at Apple were, and [he] only went looking for people who made mistakes at Apple. . . . And then those people were pilloried. And anybody who did really good things inside of Apple and made it better got no attention whatsoever. What is it about these people—who are these people who will not just go to work in these conditions but work and embrace these big challenges?
> —Michael Lewis, on US Government bureaucrats[1]

> Bureaucrats have preferences . . . among them is the desire to do the job.
> —James Q. Wilson, *Bureaucracy*[2]

In March 2020 I was on sabbatical in Dakar, Senegal, doing research for this book. As COVID-19 spread Senegal reacted quickly, closing its borders and canceling all commercial flights. It set up public quarantine and contact tracing, established a curfew, and implemented rules for wearing masks and gloves on public transportation. Senegal did all this well before the United States or the United Kingdom had initiated any of these policies.

When I say that "Senegal" reacted quickly I really mean individual Senegalese people. Policy direction came from President Macky Sall, but actual execution relied on tens of thousands of individuals acting in the name of the state. Bureaucrats—employees from the Ministry of Health, doctors on the state's payroll, police officers—were the "Senegal" who did contact tracing, treated the infected, and enforced the curfew and border closures designed to minimize the spread of the virus. As March turned to April, the US State Department organized an evacuation flight from Dakar, urging Americans to take the opportunity to return home.[3] A few days later, my wife, our son, and I joined 150 or so other Americans at Dakar's very empty airport. Many were sad to leave

Mission Driven Bureaucrats. Dan Honig, Oxford University Press. © Oxford University Press 2024.
DOI: 10.1093/oso/9780197641194.003.0001

Senegal and quite afraid of what lay ahead in America. Once everyone received a medical check, we entered a repurposed cargo plane operated by the US State Department Operations Medicine team. A man named Joseph, wearing a full protective suit, addressed us from the front of the plane.

"Listen up!" Joseph had to shout, as cargo planes do not come with speakers. "This isn't a normal flight and we're not flight attendants. We're medical professionals and our job is to get you home safely." He told us there were sandwiches and water in the back of the plane. "Please clean up after yourselves— we will only have a few hours on the ground in the US and we'll need every minute we can get."[4]

One of the passengers asked how long the crew had been doing this—flying back and forth every day across thousands of miles to evacuate Americans during a global emergency.

"Almost a week," Joseph replied, looking exhausted. "We were in Liberia yesterday, and somewhere else the day before. Another place tomorrow."

A different passenger shouted from the back of the plane, "Are you getting overtime for this?"

Joseph laughed. "No," he said. "We're government employees. This is our job." He paused for a moment. "I'm proud to do this—I'm honored to help y'all get home."

Then, something remarkable happened. One person started clapping, then another, and soon enough, everyone in the plane had joined the applause. We were thanking Joseph for helping us, but we were also applauding his sacrifice. We were applauding our government for employing people like Joseph. At that moment, when no one knew how long the pandemic would last, Joseph and his team gave us hope that America might just get through the pandemic.

COVID-19 was not the first time that bureaucrats stepped up when duty called. While their stories are rarely remembered or celebrated, the history of the United States—and indeed the entire modern world—is replete with examples of bureaucrats going above and beyond what was expected of them. In late 2018, US President Trump and Congress could not agree on a budget. Given the arcane requirements for public spending in the United States, that meant a "government shutdown" with nearly a million government bureaucrats officially "furloughed"—told they would not be paid and instructed not to come to their offices.

Yet, *hundreds of thousands* of US bureaucrats still showed up to work. Workers who showed up were ineligible for unemployment benefits, unlike those who followed orders and stayed home.[5] Many employees chose to work and not be paid—when the other option was being paid not to work. Why?

The executive vice president of the National Air Traffic Controllers Association explained:

We've taken an oath.... We know we're important to the United States economy and we are going to work. We're just not getting paid. So even if this drags on, people will come to work.[6]

A senior official from the American Federation of Government Employees, the largest US federal workers union, said:

Federal employees are extremely devoted to the mission of their agencies ... [bureaucrats] don't just fall into these jobs. They believe in public service, they believe in what they do.[7]

Those bureaucrats were individuals, making individual decisions to come to work. But their decisions were also driven by their connections to others—to citizens, who would have suffered if they hadn't shown up; to their colleagues, whom they sought not to let down; to their managers, who helped them feel valued in the workplace.

Those influences could have worked in the "other" direction, too. They could have snuffed out those bureaucrats' motivation. They could have ensured that bureaucrats saw their jobs as meaningless process, where it wouldn't have mattered at all whether they'd shown up.

What This Book Is About

This is a book about Mission Driven Bureaucrats, why citizens need them, and how the public service can cultivate more of them. Mission Driven Bureaucrats are individuals who work in the bureaucracy and who want to serve their organization's laudable mission of helping citizens.[8] They do their jobs because they believe in them, not because a bunch of rules or incentives force them to act in ways that they otherwise would not.

I argue that in many cases, the public sector would benefit from a managerial approach I call *managing for empowerment*. This is an approach that allows autonomy, cultivates competence, and creates connection with peers and purpose.[9] Managing for empowerment seeks to support bureaucrats in exercising judgment, trusting them to forward their mission with their managers' support. Managing for empowerment is the managerial style that I suspect most readers of this book would personally prefer, and that many of us—particularly those of us in "white collar" professional jobs—already enjoy.

Managing for empowerment can help attract and retain Mission Driven Bureaucrats.[10] Management practice that supports employees rather than constrains them, that seeks to empower bureaucrats rather than control them, will also frequently induce greater mission motivation in the workforce.[11] More mission motivation will, this book will argue, frequently lead to better performance, to a state that can better serve its citizens' and residents' needs.

In contrast, current public sector management is often typified by what I call *managing for compliance.* Compliance-oriented management's primary goal is, as the name suggests, to induce employees to do things they would not otherwise do. Compliance-oriented management can take the form of setting rules whose violation leads to sanction. It can also take the form of target-setting, where employees are rewarded for meeting those goals.[12]

Compliance-oriented management is heavily dependent on monitoring. Managers must be able to observe quite accurately when employees are performing well or badly so that rewards and sanctions can be dispensed. This accurate monitoring is often very difficult to do in ways that actually induce bureaucrats to fulfill the mission of their agency. Compliance-oriented management is not universally bad, and empowerment-oriented management is not universally good. But this book argues that many governments at present overuse compliance tools and underuse empowerment tools in managing bureaucrats, to the detriment of public sector performance.

By "bureaucrats" I mean any individual who receives their pay from the government. While the term "bureaucracy" has grown to encompass large or hierarchical firms in the private sector, I mean here to refer solely to the public sector.

My discussion of devoted, hardworking bureaucrats has probably already raised some eyebrows. Bureaucrats don't have the best reputation. The *Oxford English Dictionary* notes that the term "bureaucrat" is "frequently depreciative."[13] Its first recorded appearance, back in 1832, was in a magazine decrying "those enormous frauds of the Bureaucrats, for which history affords no parallel."[14]

The negative reputation of the bureaucrat is a bit of a paradox. When most of us think of individuals we personally know who work as social workers, or public school teachers, or firefighters (who are, of course, all bureaucrats), we generally think of good people who are very mission-driven. But when we think of bureaucrats as a whole, we suddenly see them as lazy, greedy, and uncaring. This book will seek to prove that this collective stereotype is untrue. Rather, many bureaucrats are, or have the potential to be, extremely motivated to do their jobs.

Given the baggage that accompanies the word "bureaucrats," I could have chosen to call bureaucrats "civil servants" or "public servants." But this is not a book about a few exceptionally wonderful people who are employed by the government. Instead, it's about normal people with characteristics that are true of the majority of public sector employees, from the employees in the school district office, to emergency hotline responders, to the middle managers who supervise them. This is what the word "bureaucrat" means—that which is typical of people who work in a bureaucracy. I hope to convince you that the word "bureaucrat" should have the positive connotation that I believe it deserves.

Every citizen of every country wants and needs to access government services. We want our kids to go to the best public schools and the best public hospitals. We want our air to be clean and our markets to be suitably regulated. We want social programs to be efficient and to help the less fortunate. The best way to achieve these aims is to attract, retain, and engage public servants who genuinely desire to care for citizens. A mission-driven bureaucracy is not a distant dream but something that is in our hands to create.

The Road from Here

So, where is this story actually going? Chapter 2 develops the theory undergirding this book. We'll take a closer look at the connections between missions, management, and motivation, and when we should expect managing for empowerment to lead to better performance.

Chapter 3 dives into evidence. I first explore the effects of management practices on the mission motivation of individuals. Managing for empowerment can alter individual motivation, orientation, and even identity. People are not fixed types. Mission Driven Bureaucrats can be made and un-made by the actions of management.

Chapter 4 explores the relationship between management practice and employee recruitment and retention. Managing for empowerment can help attract and retain the most mission-motivated employees.

"Management" is not only the actions of individual managers. Chapter 5 explores the role of broader factors that can influence a bureaucrat's motivation, including her peers, their norms, and the broader organizational climate. Chapter 5 also explores how missions are set, and how they can be changed when they are not serving the public interest.

Chapter 6 explores how and when managing for empowerment can help governments achieve what citizens want most—better public services. Managing for empowerment improves performance by cultivating mission motivation in employees.

It is of course true that not every bureaucrat should be trusted and empowered. Chapter 7 addresses common concerns about managing for empowerment, accountability, and the prevention of corruption. It argues that managing for compliance is not necessarily the most effective path to minimize malfeasance. Empowerment-oriented approaches to accountability deserve greater consideration.

When it comes to public sector performance, there is no exact recipe for success—but there *is* a common set of ingredients. Chapter 8 proposes strategies that managers, organizational leaders, and bureaucrats can adopt to foster empowerment-oriented management.

The final chapter, Chapter 9, focuses on you. I say "you" with confidence because whoever you are, I'm pretty confident that you are a citizen. Citizens do better when the people who work for government perform better.[15] The behavior of the people who work for government is ultimately shaped by what you—what all of us—think about and expect from those people.

Ultimately, our opinions about the bureaucracy shape what the public sector will provide us. We, the public, tend to act as though a single instance of fraud in the government is fatal, while overlooking the performance gains that go unrealized from a public service that fails to empower its employees. Blaming bureaucrats instead of management systems or flawed policy for bureaucratic failings is costly—costly to bureaucrats and, more important, costly to *all of us*.

When we focus on atypical bureaucrats for being lazy or greedy, we're telling policymakers that we want more compliance-oriented management. But though compliance-oriented strategies might minimize the bad actions of a few bureaucrats, these strategies also get in the way of *beneficial* work by other bureaucrats. This often leaves citizens sicker, students less equipped for their futures, and streets less safe than they otherwise would be.

Standing on the Shoulders of Many Who Have Come Before

I did not invent the idea of empowering employees or tension between empowerment and compliance. This fundamental tension appears as early as the writings of Han Feizi in the third century BCE, as the Chinese state grew in scale. As Han Feizi put it, "When a sage rules a state he does not count on people doing good on their own but rather takes measure to keep them from doing wrong."[16] In the Anglophone study of public administration, the clash emerged dramatically in the 1940s, in a heated debate between Carl Friedrich and Herman Finer. Friedrich argued for greater discretion for employees on the ground, as they often had better and more up-to-date knowledge of the key facts about the work. Finer in contrast argued for tight control from the top: "a relationship of obedience to an external controlling authority."[17] More recently, a number of scholars have explored the relationships between motivation, mission, and performance in the public and private sectors.[18]

This book synthesizes and builds upon existing scholarship. In making my argument I draw from public management, political science, public policy, economics, sociology, organizational behavior, and beyond.[19] I will also draw on empirical projects I've been involved in directly.

This book will take you to rural Thailand, where officials deliver excellent public services despite decades of political upheaval and objectionable instructions from Bangkok. It will take you to my hometown of Detroit, where mission-motivated social workers leave the Child Protective Service *not* because of the difficulty of their work, but because compliance-oriented management prevents them from doing the work they long to do. It will take you to Liberia and Ghana, where fast-stream civil service programs attract the mission-motivated. It will take you to a government agency in Dhaka, Bangladesh, where managing for empowerment supports employees who would have all preferred to work somewhere else. It will take you through millions of observations from new and existing surveys.

This book also taps on a great deal of empirical evidence generated by others that speaks to this book's themes. Randomized controlled trials, observational studies, ethnographies, and field experiments all point toward the critical role of Mission Driven Bureaucrats and the importance of management practice in supporting bureaucrats to achieve good outcomes. This body of evidence spans the globe and a variety of public sector work.[20] To my knowledge, this evidence has never been gathered into a cohesive whole. This book aims to do just that. Referring to the broader universe of existing studies also puts the findings from my own empirical work into a richer context. This work variously supports and explores the limits of a empowerment-oriented approach, suggesting when and where it is likely to be most beneficial to performance.

What Makes the Public Sector Distinct?

Much of this book's argument could absolutely apply to private sector firms. Many private sector firms have valuable missions and mission-driven employees. Management practice is also certainly important for improving their motivation. So why does this book focus on the public sector in particular?

First, public sector missions are nearly always in the public interest. As Goodsell puts it: "The public agency is ideally energized by an article of faith that goes beyond marketing. At its best, the mission is a fundamental, institution-specific, purposeful commitment to the larger society."[21] Management that forwards these missions will almost certainly make citizens' lives better and is thus all the more worthy of investment and attention.[22]

Because their missions are so obviously laudable, public agencies tend to be more "attractive" to those aspiring to do good in the world. That's great news, since various civil service protections make it difficult to terminate poorly performing employees. This means that a poorly managed public agency can end up with an unmotivated workforce of scope and scale that is much less likely in the private sector. Public sector managers should worry all the more about the departure of Mission Driven Bureaucrats.

Performance is also harder to measure and monitor in the public sector. Unlike the private sector, managers can't simply refer to balance sheets or profit statements. They must often rely on their own judgment to determine if their mission is being fulfilled. As I will argue later in this book, these difficult-to-monitor contexts are those in which managing for empowerment will reap the greatest benefits.[23]

Perhaps most important, the private sector has *already begun* to employ management for empowerment. Despite all the reasons to believe management for empowerment would work better in the public sector than the private, it's in the private sector that this approach has been most well-regarded.[24]

The public sector is the place where management for empowerment has been least utilized but could be most impactful. It seems to me that scholars, managers, and the general public alike currently think more deeply about the workplace empowerment and motivation of tech workers and telemarketers more than we do the empowerment and motivation of public servants.[25] That seems a great shame; by empowering public servants we all can benefit from better public services.

Mission Driven Bureaucrats Are All Around

While the Mission Driven Bureaucrats described in this chapter's opening absolutely deserve our praise, America is typical, not exceptional, in having a cadre of mission-driven public servants. I've met Mission Driven Bureaucrats everywhere I've lived and worked—a list that includes the United States, United Kingdom, Thailand, India, East Timor, Somalia, South Sudan, Liberia, and the Netherlands.

Countries differ from one another in many ways, but these are differences in degree, not kind. We're just plain wrong about some of the systematic differences we normally ascribe to relatively poor countries as compared to relatively rich ones. The idea that bureaucrats in the developing world are systematically different kinds of people from those in developed countries is a stereotype with little factual support. Chapter 4 will tackle this more directly.

I like to say I support my favorite sports team, baseball's Detroit Tigers, whether they win or lose, and on any day that ends in "y" (that is, all of them). I think the argument in this book is relevant to all countries whose names begin with a capital letter. Each and every one. That's because this is a story about the people who work for a government. It is therefore relevant to all countries—every country has individuals who work for the state and contribute to their nation's development.

The existence of Mission Driven Bureaucrats and potential benefits of managing for empowerment isn't exclusively a rich country or poor country story. It's not a story particularly about countries run by Europeans and their descendants or particularly about those that aren't; nor is it particularly about big countries or small countries. The management practices that will unlock the best public service delivery will differ in different settings. However, the evidence suggests that the answer has less to do with a country's name or status, but with the nature of its work, employees, and organizational systems.

In the pages to come, I will draw on evidence suggesting the existence of Mission Driven Bureaucrats in countries that collectively house over two-thirds of the world's citizens. I'll also bring in profiles of real-life Mission Driven Bureaucrats from around the world whom I've come across in my journey, written in collaboration with Sarah Thompson.[26]

The first Mission Driven Bureaucrat you'll meet immediately after this chapter is Joseph Roberts, the gentleman on my evacuation flight from Dakar to DC. You'll learn what brought him to the work, what drives him, and what sustains him in a very difficult job.

Joseph and the other Mission Driven Bureaucrats in the pages to come have been specifically selected and profiled because of their dedication to their work. But while those profiled are not average bureaucrats, their devotion to their mission is not exceptional. We live in a world where Mission Driven Bureaucrats are all around.

Public Services at Their Best

I want you to take a moment and think about a time when you enjoyed truly excellent public services. I've posed this question to a lot of people, and not one of them has replied with an answer about their government producing stellar numbers or quantifiable outputs. Every answer has been about a human being—usually a teacher, nurse, social worker, and so forth—exercising judgment and care to personally support another citizen.

None of these individuals can do it alone. They exist as part of a larger system that can enable or obstruct those on the frontlines to do their jobs. For a bureaucrat to excel in their work, that system must trust, empower, and uplift them.

One of the clearest descriptions of exceptionally high-performing public services in prior research comes from Ceará, Brazil. A quarter-century ago, Judith Tendler documented excellent public services in the sectors of agricultural extension, health, procurement, and employment support—all within one of Brazil's poorest and historically least well-governed states. How was this possible?

Tendler described Ceará's good performance as typified by "greater worker discretion and autonomy," as well as excellent cooperation and trust between workers, management, and citizens.[27] Bureaucrats "demonstrated unusual dedication to their jobs," working alongside managers who "created a strong sense of 'calling' and mission." Workers were offered the autonomy to carry out tasks "in response to their perception of what their clients needed, and out of a vision of the public good," and "wanted to perform better in order to live up to the new trust placed in them."[28]

This describes managing for empowerment. *This* is what best facilitates a Mission Driven Bureaucrat to provide the kind of care that typifies virtually every example of a thriving public service that I've ever heard about from citizens.

If management does not trust and empower bureaucrats, it is difficult in turn for those bureaucrats to trust citizens. Treating bureaucrats as individuals who must be made to comply tends to force them to treat citizens similarly.

Bureaucrats around the world have the potential to be agents of social and economic justice. They can transform lives. Without them, the state is just an idea—to *do* anything, it needs bureaucrats who act in the state's name. The prevailing approach to public sector management too often does not inspire, cultivate, reward, or attract mission-driven people. There are many Mission Driven Bureaucrats, and more can be done to nurture them.

A world with Mission Driven Bureaucrats is one with public servants who feel supported and empowered, not controlled and monitored.

A world with Mission Driven Bureaucrats is one with citizens who feel seen, heard, and supported.

A world with Mission Driven Bureaucrats is one with flourishing citizens, better schools, safer streets, and healthier humans.

This world is possible. In fact it already exists—in pockets. This book is about how to expand those pockets to include the rest of the world. All that's needed is time and care from managers, organizational leaders, junior staff, politicians, and citizens—you and me. Let's get going.

Profile: Casey Joseph Roberts

Mission Driven Bureaucrats in US State Department
Operations Medicine (Guardian)

"If I didn't feel like I was accomplishing anything here and I didn't feel like I was trusted, I probably wouldn't be long for this job. No one would."

Joseph, whom I met on the evacuation flight from Senegal described in Chapter 1, is a "guardian" for the Operational Medicine (OpMed) team within the US State Department. He has an easy smile and is the kind of person who can talk to anybody.

Joseph was a bit hesitant to have this conversation. Getting permission from the State Department to interview him was a complex process, in no small part because of the importance he attributed to the collective nature of the team's achievements. As Joseph repeatedly stressed, "There's nothing I've done in COVID response that I did by myself. Nothing."

What were the sources of his impressive motivation, we wondered? Where did his drive to help others come from? "I would say, my dad . . . my dad was always there to help whoever. We had little old ladies living around us, so we were always going over to help here and there with the neighbors. It's just something we've always done." This commitment to help others has characterized every job Joseph has ever held. It's part of his identity.

Joseph joined the US Marines seven days after he graduated from high school in Zion, Illinois. The decision was a no-brainer. "It was just something I always was going to do, didn't even think twice about it." After his enlistment in the Marine Corps, he joined the US Army Special Forces (Green Berets) as a medic.

He holds a Purple Heart, a medal awarded to those wounded or killed in US military service, as did his father and grandfather. It took time and reflection over the last decade for Joseph to realize that "traumatic brain injury, anxiety,

PTSD, depression, all that stuff [that was] going on" with him was "not normal" and needed treatment. Joseph explained, "in our world, it's just normal because, I don't know, feels like all my friends have been shot at one point or another, or had some horrible traumatic thing in combat. It's just, you know, I was twenty years old when the towers fell, so my whole adult life's been preparing for combat, going to combat."

When he was able to work again, Joseph became a representative for the Special Operations Command Care Coalition, supporting anybody from Special Operations who was wounded and sent to San Antonio, where he was based. "I was your guy on the ground. You know, doing whatever I could to help you out, whatever you needed, whatever your family needed. You had the hospital and they're doing a great job treating patients, and we were just that extra guy on the side."

The job involved coordinating the support for others wounded in the military. It came with "crazy long hours" and Joseph did it while he, too, was still a patient. But he remembers it as a time when he was able to help others—when he was "accomplishing something." For example, he'd work with "a guy who just lost both his legs yesterday [and] is arriving at the hospital today at midnight. I'd pick up his mom and dad at the airport and [take] them [to] the hospital in Texas, getting the family all settled in so they can see their kid who just had the most traumatic thing happen to him." It was emotional and tough, but "it felt good. It felt right." Being able to help patients and their families motivated him immensely. That feeling of purpose and connection to beneficiaries is what motivates Joseph to return to tough work environments over and over again.

Joseph completed his training in emergency management at the State Department in March 2020, just a few months before the pandemic erupted and the first evacuation flights took place. He knew when he took the job that at some point, "the world's going to explode; it doesn't matter how it explodes, be it an earthquake, a volcano, a terrorist attack . . . if it goes wrong, we're there to try to help and figure out solutions." Joseph's unit steps up when duty calls. That's one of the reasons why he sought out his job at the State Department in the first place.

His current role has been among the most "rewarding" because he has been connected to the purpose of his actions—he has been able to see exactly how his work helps citizens. When COVID hit, Joseph and his team worked around the clock to evacuate Americans from countries shutting their borders. Yet, his eyes light up when he talks about this time because they were "bringing American citizens home from places that don't have the medical support for COVID. That was huge." The "relief on their faces" when the plane took off, or eventually landed back on US soil, motivated him to keep going. "Everything I've done since COVID started, . . . bringing the medical supplies, delivering all that, and it's just like, I know this is going to where it needs to be." As with so many bureaucrats, helping citizens in need sustained Joseph's mission motivation despite challenging work environments.

Joseph was also clear to acknowledge the central role played by the management practices of agency leaders. He felt fortunate; "in my career, I've had, for the most part, very good leadership." At the height of the COVID response, Joseph's current manager, Dr. Walters, was "there at the craziest hours; you'd walk in and [see him] writing on the whiteboard with everyone else."

Dr. Walters's willingness to roll up his sleeves is not the only leadership quality that reinforces Joseph's mission motivation. Dr. Walters supports Joseph's team every step of the way. "You can reach out to him twenty-four hours a day, no matter what. . . . I know I can call the boss. Would I ever call Doc Walters directly? No. I'm gonna go up through the levels. But I know I can call my top boss and I know he'll pick up. And that's awesome to know . . . it's huge." Dr. Walters managed his team by letting hierarchy fade into the background and actively offering his support and guidance.

Joseph's team relies on a strong culture of trust between leadership, bureaucrats, and their peers. Joseph explained that "being able to trust your team players, your coach, your teammates" was incredibly important to him. "Especially in a time of need. . . . You know the need is there and then you see one guy step up, one gal steps up, and then another one steps up, and then you step up, and everybody's helping each other at two o'clock in the morning. . . . You know, this is why I'm here."

In Joseph's view, a team needs to be managed in a way that allows autonomy and creates connection to impact. For mission-driven people to do the difficult work that is asked of them, they need to see the fruit of their labor. Mission Driven Bureaucrats need to feel empowered, trusted, and impactful. "If I didn't feel like I was accomplishing anything here and I didn't feel like I was trusted, I probably wouldn't be long for this job. No one would." Luckily, State OpMed is just such a place. "That's the great part about our organization, we're given the opportunity to make decisions."

It seems that Joseph's innate optimism, his calmness in the face of risk and tragedy, and his desire to serve will keep him in places "where crisis is happening." The supportive management and trusting work environment he's found will keep Joseph and his peers at the State Department. And the citizens who benefit from their service are all the better for it.

Empowerment-Oriented Management, Mission Motivation, and Performance

> If we look at government agencies around us that stand out as "best,"
> we will find they consist of cohesive groups of women and men who
> are "turned on" by something. But by what? Not their paychecks, nor
> the latest reform gimmicks, but by *the very work they are doing*: stopping
> child abuse, fighting forest fires, battling epidemics.
>
> —Charles Goodsell, *Mission Mystique*[1]

> In those situations in which it is assumed that most subordinates con-
> form and obey not because they have internalized the norms of the
> dominant, but because a structure of surveillance, reward, and punish-
> ment makes it prudent for them to comply.... Any weakness in surveil-
> lance and enforcement is likely to be quickly exploited; any ground left
> undefended is likely to be ground lost.
>
> —James Scott, *Domination and the Arts of Resistance*[2]

We live in a world typified by compliance-oriented management. As Erin
McDonnell puts it in a recent book about public sector performance, "currently
dominant approaches to state reform . . . seek to limit discretion," focusing instead on top-down control and monitoring.[3] This rings true to my experiences
in almost every country I've lived and worked in—conventional wisdom
dictates that compliance-oriented management is the best way to manage our
governments.[4]

But when does this "wisdom" lead us astray? When, and why, can managing
for empowerment be a better path? This chapter will outline the theoretical
foundations for the rest of this book's argument.

This chapter describes the nature of organizational missions and mission-
motivated action. It will lay out two stylized strategies to improve performance

Mission Driven Bureaucrats. Dan Honig, Oxford University Press. © Oxford University Press 2024.
DOI: 10.1093/oso/9780197641194.003.0002

in the public sector: empowerment-oriented Route E and compliance-oriented Route C. Finally, it will examine the circumstances in which managing for empowerment might indeed be worth our investment.

Mission Points

The de facto purpose of any organization—the shared understanding of what the organization is striving to achieve—is what I call its "mission point."[5] In the public sector, an agency's mission point typically involves serving the public in some way.[6] Unlike many private firms, a public agency's mission is not the means to a profitable end. It's the end in itself.[7]

Many organizations have an overarching mission point focused on improving some aspect of citizens' welfare, with sub-units having distinct mission points that contribute to this larger goal. A country's ministry of health might have the mission point of promoting citizens' health, for example, with one unit of the ministry devoted to reducing diabetes in the population.

Mission points are not quite the same as mission statements. An agency could outwardly claim to serve a particular mission but in practice aim at another. Nevertheless, mission statements can be useful to articulate and define an agency's mission. They often help to organize an organization's "internal ethos," orienting the behaviors of leaders, senior managers, and more junior staff.[8] The Michigan Department of Environment Quality, for instance, "promotes wise management of Michigan's air, land, and water resources to support a sustainable environment, healthy communities, and a vibrant economy."[9] The Singapore Ministry of Education aims to give children a "balanced and well-rounded education, develop them to their full potential, and nurture them into good citizens."[10] The Punjab (India) Department of Water Supply and Sanitation "endeavors to provide safe drinking water and sanitation facilities to rural habitations on a sustainable basis."[11]

Most readers would agree that these statements describe laudable missions. A few may even wish to serve these missions, seeking out jobs that can contribute to these goals. This reaction highlights the second important role that mission points play—they attract those who share that mission and want to work toward it. These individuals are what this book considers "mission-motivated." They are drawn to fulfill a mission for reasons entirely of their own. Importantly, mission motivation is specific to context, not generalizable across all public sector jobs.[12] A mission-driven nurse and a mission-driven teacher would not necessarily be equally committed if they exchanged jobs. Mission-motivated employees will often be quite dedicated, particularly where they come to adopt what public administration scholars term "high mission valence."[13] This means that they not only believe that their mission is important, but that their individual actions are meaningfully contributing to it.

Mission points are not fixed, unchangeable features of agencies.[14] As Goodsell reminds us, government agencies are "social organisms that carry values and persist over time while also evolving as circumstances unfold."[15] However, mission points are self-reinforcing. Employees with divergent views tend to leave an agency, while those who remain are often socialized to adopt the current mission point of the agency as their own personal mission point. When this happens, an agency will evince what Goodsell calls "mission mystique"—an organization's mission and their employees' personal commitment to it will reinforce one another.[16]

Unsurprisingly, public agencies with well-established mission points are often those that perform at their best. As Merilee Grindle highlights in a study of public servants from twenty-nine organizations in six countries, high-performing agencies have "well-defined missions that were widely ascribed to by employees."[17] Mission points can also stimulate good performance by acting as a basis for accountability. Employee performance can be assessed by whether it is in service of the organization's mission point.[18]

Mission-Driven Action Is Not Just Doing What Supervisors Demand

Scholars frequently think of bureaucracies as a series of principal-agent chains. These are vertical links between someone who is "above" (the principal) and someone who is "below" (the agent). In this framework, lower-level bureaucrats are agents of their managers, managers to ministers, and ministers to legislators.[19] This view has often informed efforts to improve the functioning of public organizations. As McDonnell puts it, "current [reform] approaches advocate for abstract monitoring systems that can monitor across large scales and at a distance, assuming only a pinnacle principal can be trusted to monitor his interests."[20]

Principal-agent theory is often an extremely useful way of thinking about bureaucracies. However, it won't be the primary theoretical building block of this book. This book is instead focused primarily on whether a given bureaucrat, wherever they are in the chain, is forwarding their agency's mission point and ultimately serving public welfare. This is consistent with a principal-agent framework, in that the *ultimate* principal in a public agency is the public. As commonly used, however, principal-agent models tend to take for granted that management is "right" and a given bureaucrat is potentially "wrong."[21] Jon DiIulio summarizes this nicely:

Principal-agent models of bureaucratic behavior have considerable value. But they are far better at explaining why bureaucrats shirk (goof off on the job), subvert (commit acts of administrative malfeasance), or steal (use public office for private gain) than they are at explaining why bureaucrats behave as "principled agents"—workers who do not shirk, subvert, or steal on the job even when the pecuniary and other tangible incentives to refrain from these behaviors are weak or nonexistent.[22]

Mission Driven Bureaucrats will seek to promote the public interest even when their managers or politicians might not.[23] Employees can take steps to advance their mission points even when their supervisors oppose them. "Whistleblower" laws protect employees who expose acts of corruption, waste, or fraud by their superiors.[24] The existence of these laws illustrates that employees carry out actions in support of their mission, even when these conflict with their superiors' wishes. Research suggests that employees who are more mission-motivated are also more likely to do exactly that.[25]

The actions of management need not be *illegal* to obstruct public welfare. Anyone who has ever had a boss will understand that their instructions can often differ greatly from what might actually serve their mission. The actions of a supervisor, politician, or even head of state can become unmoored from an agency's mission point—and ultimately from the mission of the public sector.

A case in point comes from one of the most oft-maligned US agencies: the post office. The unofficial motto, and arguably the mission point, of the US Postal Service is "nothing stops the mail."[26] It is perhaps no surprise, then, that bureaucrats resisted when operational changes in late 2020 threatened to delay mail-in ballots for the presidential election. This was commonly understood as a move by then-President Trump to thwart Democratic mail-in voters. As the *Washington Post* reported:

> Mechanics in New York drew out the dismantling and removal of mail-sorting machines until their supervisor gave up on the order. In Michigan, a group of letter carriers did an end run around a supervisor's directive to leave election mail behind, starting their routes late to sift through it. In Ohio, postal clerks culled prescriptions and benefit checks from bins of stalled mail to make sure they were delivered, while some carriers ran late items out on their own time. In Pennsylvania, some postal workers looked for any excuse—a missed turn, heavy traffic, a rowdy dog—to buy enough time to finish their daily rounds. "I can't see any postal worker not bending those rules," one Philadelphia staffer said.[27]

It seems that nothing can stop the mail even when the people trying to stop it are the politicians ultimately in charge. This illustrates the power of mission points and employees' belief in them. If actions that bend the rules are done in fulfillment of an agency's mission point, then these are mission-driven actions.[28] Mission Driven Bureaucrats are motivated to fulfill their agency's mission, not their boss's particular interpretation of that mission.[29]

Two Stylized Routes to Performance Improvement: Compliance-Oriented "C" vs. Empowerment-Oriented "E" Management

Mission Driven Bureaucrats don't require tight oversight. They truly care about their jobs, so they will seek to serve their mission regardless of whether they are being watched by their bosses. This insight is at the core of foundational management scholarship dating back at least to 1960, when MIT Professor Douglas McGregor wrote a book called *The Human Side of Enterprise*.[30]

McGregor depicted two broad equilibria for organizations. A "Theory X" organization has tight, top-down management and workers who will only do what they are supervised and externally induced (with sanctions or rewards) to do. "Theory Y" based on trust and a healthy degree of autonomy, with management that guides and supports employees. Theory Y organizations have mission-motivated employees who *want* to accomplish the organization's goals. Y-type employees would not be interested in working for an organization that employs Theory X management.

McGregor's model highlights two key ideas that undergird this book. First, different managerial approaches suit different employees and circumstances. Second, management practices do not simply respond to a workforce, but shape that workforce. Figure 2.1 describes two stylized paths to improve an organization's performance using managerial reforms: managing for empowerment and managing for compliance. These adapt the logic of McGregor's X and Y equilibria into performance improvement strategies.

Compliance-oriented Route C, depicted at the bottom of Figure 2.1, emphasizes the role of managers to align their employees' actions with their organization's mission point. Route C could also be described as hierarchical or top-down management because it uses tools that come from "above" employees to coerce or control them.[31] Superiors monitor or collect data about their subordinates' activities. They then reward or discipline them accordingly. Route C depends heavily on this ability of managers to monitor their employees.

Figure 2.1 Route E and Route C —Two routes to improving performance via changes in management practices

Empowerment-oriented Route E, depicted at the top of Figure 2.1, encourages employees to exercise a self-directed desire to fulfill their organization's mission. Rather than coming from "above," empowerment-oriented management comes from "behind." It seeks to support employees, providing structures that develop the employees' own judgment and mission motivation.

The distinction between empowerment and compliance is not about *whether* employees are held accountable for their actions. It's about what accountability means in practice. Are employees driven to do their jobs only because of external incentives or sanctions? Or are they held to account by a genuine commitment and connection to their beneficiaries?

Empowerment-oriented management builds on psychology's Self-Determination Theory (SDT).[32] SDT theorizes the foundations of mission-driven motivation. It argues that motivation stems from the fulfillment of innate human needs for autonomy, competence, and relatedness.

An empowerment-oriented managerial approach is one that

(1) *Allows autonomy*: Bureaucrats are given a zone of independent action in which to make judgments and see themselves as causal agents.
(2) *Cultivates competence*: Bureaucrats are encouraged to foster a sense of skill and capability, a confidence in their own abilities to further their agency's mission.
(3) *Creates connection to peers and purpose*: Bureaucrats are encouraged to connect and feel valuable to other humans through their work, most frequently to coworkers and beneficiaries.

Autonomy is the feeling that one is a "causal agent," possessing the independent ability to make decisions. Autonomy incorporates discretion, which is the specific granting of authority from a superior to a subordinate, but also goes beyond it. It encompasses an employee's entire independent "decision latitude," whether or not this is explicitly or formally delegated.

Competence is the feeling that one is skilled and capable at work. This does not simply mean being praised, but also feeling as though one is increasing in competence—learning and growing on the job. Competence implies some degree of agency and exercise of judgment. If an individual is so tightly managed that they perceive themselves to make few if any independent decisions, they will not perceive themselves as exercising competence. Employees must believe it matters that they, rather than someone else, are doing their job.

Connection to peers and purpose reframes Self-Determination Theory's third element, "relatedness." Relatedness is the "need to feel belongingness and connectedness with others."[33] It is used in the broader management literature most frequently to refer to connection to coworkers. These connections are extremely valuable for public sector employees, as we will see. But for many Mission Driven Bureaucrats, there is an additional, special form of connection at play. This is the employee's connection to the citizens who benefit from their work. This might be a direct interaction, as for a so-called street-level bureaucrat, but it may also simply mean witnessing the positive impact that one's actions make upon the lives of citizens.

The profile that follows this chapter will introduce you to Florence Kuteesa, formerly budget director of the Ugandan Ministry of Finance. Florence's mission motivation, and that of her team, was indeed reinforced by a work environment characterized by autonomy, competence, and connection. When those things changed, so did her team's mission motivation.

The specific management practices that allow autonomy, cultivate competence, and create connection will depend heavily on context. Empowerment-oriented practices must be uniquely tailored to the task, environment, employees, and resources of managers.

An Idea as Old as Time ... or at Least the 1970s

This discussion about Route E and Route C might sound technical—but it needn't be. The key dynamics are surprisingly well captured by pop music.

Consider the Beatles' "Baby You Can Drive My Car," Aladdin's offer to show Princess Jasmine "A Whole New World," or Lil Peep's promise that he could "make you rich" in "Save That S**t." All three offer material benefits to the object of their affection. They clearly utilize an incentive-driven Route C approach.

Route C management works quickly. Offering someone a ride in your car is easy and may initially be effective at winning someone over. But once the target has been showered with riches, ridden in fancy cars, and seen the world, what then? Incentives need constant supply—compliance-oriented management will stop having its desired effect in the absence of continued monitoring and rewards.

In contrast, 1970s rockers (and I believe unappreciated philosophers of organizational studies) Cheap Trick in "I Want You to Want Me" articulate a different approach. This song's protagonist doesn't offer conditions or propose rewards. He sings, "If you want my love, you got it / when you need my love, you got it." His approach is simply to be available, and in so doing encourage his sweetheart to *want* to be with him. The protagonist has a strategy: be there. Be supportive. Be open, engaged, responsive. This typifies an empowerment-oriented managerial approach.

Route E takes effect more slowly. It requires patience and commitment. But there is much to recommend about Cheap Trick's decidedly Route E approach to romance. It is arguably more ethical and respectful. It also far more sustainable. The Route E approach doesn't promise one's lover anything more than quiet support, and hence garners a love based on trust.

Route E is built on, and reinforces, trust. In an agency that manages for empowerment, mission-driven employees, much like Cheap Trick's imagined lover, are unlikely to stray.

The Many Mission Motivations of Bureaucrats

You might rightly be wondering what "mission motivation" actually *is*. Mission motivation is specific to context, not generalizable across all public sector jobs.[34] Helpfully, in *Motivating Public Employees*, Esteve and Schuster provide a schema of public employees' motivations that I reproduce here as Figure 2.2.[35]

The framework makes clear that public employees, like all people, can be driven by extrinsic and intrinsic motivators. Extrinsic motivators are circumstances outside the self, often generated by outcomes. They include salaries or promotions, but also the desire to change the world for the better. To be extrinsically motivated, individuals must simply be driven by something outside of themselves. Intrinsic motivators are the internal psychological states induced by various activities. Intrinsic motivators include, for instance, the "warm glow" one receives from doing good work. They might also include enjoyment of the work itself.

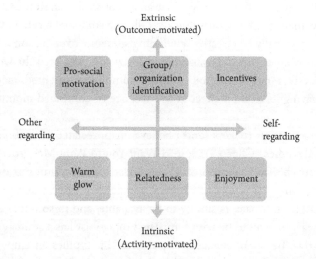

Figure 2.2 Esteve & Schuster's (2019, p. 14) schema of work motivators in the public sector

A mission motivation causes people to act in service of a mission, even when not forced to do so.[36] All intrinsic motivators are mission motivators. Some extrinsic motivators—those that are "other-regarding," or relate to helping others—are *also* mission motivators. Yes, they are about an individual's "internal" desire to achieve them—but they are coming from the outside, they're extrinsic drivers of performance. Extrinsic motivators such as prosocial motivation or identification with an organization's goals are very important for many Mission Driven Bureaucrats.[37]

So, what *isn't* a mission motivator? Rules and controls. If a rule is required to prompt an employee to do something, that employee is acting out of fear of sanctions, not out of commitment to her mission.

Incentives are also not mission motivators.[38] Incentives are carrots and sticks—they coerce employees to act in ways that they otherwise would not. They require an effective system to monitor employees in order to be allocated accordingly. This requires setting up a system of controls to check "who is doing what," or ensure employees are behaving.

A pay-for-performance scheme is a common example of an incentive in action. This type of scheme provides financial rewards to employees for specific actions.[39] However, incentives don't always have to be about money. Promotions are also a kind of incentive. Firms can use the prospect of moving up the hierarchy to induce employees to engage in actions they otherwise would not. This is why I also describe compliance-oriented management as hierarchical management—it pulls an employees' attention up the hierarchy.

Ultimately, there are many varieties of mission motivation, and it is not necessary for all employees at an agency to share the same motivator. Mission Driven Bureaucrats are those who want to get the job done even if management isn't looking. It's this desire, not the particular reason why an individual has that desire, that matters most.[40]

The Mission-Motivated and Motivateable: Bina, Samir, and Peter

Not all bureaucrats are equally mission-motivated. Nor can all bureaucrats become mission-motivated. Let me introduce three types of bureaucrats to help us think about this: mission-motivated Bina, mission-motivateable Samir, and unmotivateable Peter.

"Bina" is relentlessly devoted to her agency's mission, even in the most difficult contexts.[41] Binas are the type of people you know you can always count on—whose inherent, glowing motivation is not likely to be decreased by external circumstances. You might think that such apparent angels are rare. But the evidence suggests that Binas are more commonly found than you think.

Accountability Lab, an NGO operating in a dozen countries in Sub-Saharan Africa and South Asia, runs a competition called "Integrity Idol" (patterned loosely on the TV show *American Idol*) to "highlight the good people in the system"—the Binas.[42] They find many, many applicants. No matter how difficult or demotivating the terrain, Binas maintain their mission motivation. Part II of this book will have much more to say about the frequency of Binas and what it takes to retain them in an organization.

"Peter" is the exact opposite of Bina.[43] You can count on Peter to give as little effort as possible to keep his job. Nothing that managers or leaders or anyone else could do would make Peter a Mission Driven Bureaucrat.[44] Peters absolutely exist, though Part II will suggest there are often fewer of them than we think—or at least many fewer than I thought before examining this question closely.

"Samir" is everyone between Bina and Peter.[45] As American singer Dolly Parton (may have) once said, "Some of us are saints; some of us are sinners; but for all the rest of us, it sure does depend."[46] If Bina's the saint and Peter is the sinner, Samir is all the rest of us. Under the right empowerment-oriented environment, Samir can be a Mission Driven Bureaucrat, behaving nearly identically to Bina. However, in a managerial environment that does not sufficiently allow autonomy, cultivate a sense of competence, or create connection to peers and purpose, Samir will behave like Peter. Consistent with Parton's view, Samirs are often the largest group. People who initially appear to be Peters in fact reveal themselves to be Samirs over time.

Binas and Peters are who they are, but Samirs change in response to management practice. The more Samirs an agency has, the more it is worth considering using management for empowerment to increase mission motivation and promote mission-driven behavior. Management for empowerment will also support Binas in pursuing the organization's mission. An agency with many Binas and Samirs—which the evidence in Part II suggests is most agencies—also needs to worry that too much compliance-oriented management will prompt them to walk out the door.

Is More Compliance Always Less Empowerment?

Compliance-oriented management is by no means always a bad thing. Few workplaces will perform well with *no* compliance-oriented management. Many rules and controlled processes are welcome features of the bureaucracy. A tax examiner needs guidance on what should be included in a proper return and how to engage citizens. A police officer needs clear procedures for the storage of their service weapon, or for the collection and storage of evidence. A nurse needs instructions for how to collect patient information. In these situations, compliance-oriented rules are very helpful. But few workplaces perform at their best under extreme compliance, when compliance-oriented management constitutes most or all of managerial practice.[47]

A Route C tool is much like a screwdriver—perfect for some tasks, useful to have in every toolkit, but terrible for changing a tire. We currently live in a world where many people use compliance-oriented screwdrivers for changing tires. This reflects an error on the user's part, not an inherent flaw within screwdrivers. Route C strategies just have to be used in the right conditions.

Managers typically don't choose between compliance or empowerment, but rather "more or less" of one or the other. Management is a continuum, not a light switch with two settings—"on" and "off." Most agencies perform at their best under some combination of compliance-oriented and empowerment-oriented practices. To illustrate this, we can situate the extent to which an agency employs compliance-oriented management practices on a simplified spectrum. Figure 2.3 illustrates a hypothetical Agency A. At 0, imagine an agency with no hierarchy, monitoring, or controls at all. It's essentially a free-for-all environment at work. At 100, imagine that every action taken by employees is heavily controlled by bosses. Most agencies should, and usually do, lie somewhere in the middle.

Figure 2.4 illustrates a similar spectrum for the amount of empowerment-oriented management practices in a given agency. Empowerment-oriented management is not defined by the absence of controls. It is instead typified by the *presence* of practices that support and nurture mission motivation. At 0, employees are offered little autonomy, are unable to develop competences, and are disconnected from their peers and impact. At 100, employees are fully empowered by management practices that encourage them to forward their agency's mission point.

Though compliance and empowerment might seem like opposites in theory, they don't have to be in tension. More E doesn't always have to mean less C. A manager looking to improve her system could turn up one of these levers

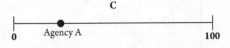

Figure 2.3 Compliance-oriented management spectrum

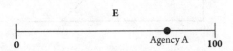

Figure 2.4 Empowerment-oriented management spectrum

and not the other. For instance, she could integrate more Route C tools like rewards for good performance, moving along the C spectrum, but leaving the Route E lever unchanged. The opposite also applies. She could manage in ways that allow her employees to connect more to peers and purpose, moving her along the E spectrum, while leaving the C lever unchanged. One way to manage for empowerment may be to reduce compliance-oriented practices, but it's not the only way.

Figure 2.5 puts the E and C spectra together to demonstrate the positions where an agency's managerial environment might sit. Below the diagonal black line, Figure 2.5's frontier, C and E strategies are not necessarily in tension; more of one need not necessitate less of the other. An organizational leader at point A could choose to invest in more C and *not* E, moving horizontally from A to B. This leader could also choose to move from A to D, increasing her use of both compliance and empowerment-oriented managerial tools simultaneously. In my experience most workplaces are in practice in this situation, operating well below the frontier.

However, Figure 2.5's frontier illustrates that there is ultimately a limit to the compatibility of C and E. When an agency is operating on the frontier, for instance at point D, it is no longer possible to increase both C and E tools simultaneously. Trade-offs begin to appear. No agency could ever reach the hypothetical point K, where an agency is seemingly under both extreme compliance and extreme empowerment. The autonomy to exercise judgment, a key element of empowerment-oriented management, is in tension with extreme compliance-oriented management. A system where every little action by employees is dictated by managers simply cannot be one that also allows autonomy or cultivates a sense of competence in bureaucrats. All agencies must thus exist either on or below the frontier.

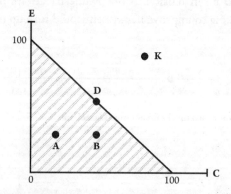

Figure 2.5 Managing for compliance and empowerment are sometimes (but not always) in tension.

Most workplaces that I have observed operate far below the frontier. Why? Many agencies are simply undermanaged—they lack sufficient *thoughtful* management of any kind. This means that it's often possible to invest in empowerment-oriented management without reducing compliance. In fact, many agencies would benefit from doing so.

From Management Practice to Performance

The graphs above are two-dimensional, focusing on the ratio of E vs. C in a particular context. But most policymakers and citizens aren't primarily concerned about the type of management used in the public service, but rather its impact on *public performance*. They're interested in how we can save more lives, improve education, and keep citizens safe.

Performance is, in graphical terms, a z-axis, or a third dimension of the graph depicted in Figure 2.5. How a given set of managerial practices translates into performance is fundamental to the all-important question of whether to pursue a particular managerial strategy.

I'm not going to actually draw three-dimensional graphs incorporating performance here. In part this is because I don't have a precise "function" or answer to the question of how management practice translates into performance. However, we can think systematically about the circumstances that influence the shape of this hypothetical graph. When would agencies perform better under empowerment-oriented management? I think there are two key factors to consider here: the monitorability of the work or tasks and the motivation of workers.

Monitorability of the Work

Compliance-oriented management rewards or punishes employees according to their performance. It relies on the ability of managers to observe employee performance using measurable outputs. This is sometimes relatively straightforward—but it often is not.

Consider the differences between a vaccine delivery team and a team of social workers, perhaps employed by the same public health system. The performance of the former can be easily measured by the number of vaccines delivered per day, which modern technology (GPS, RFID chips, etc.) has made easier than ever before. But what about the social worker? Few facets of a social worker's job can be monitored frequently and reliably. We could try to observe the outcomes of the social workers' clients. But it would still incredibly difficult to determine the extent to which those outcomes were shaped by a social worker's actions, and not any other factors.

When organizations can't measure employee performance reliably, compliance-oriented regimes end up monitoring things that are related to good outcomes, but not the same as them. This often boils down to employees' compliance with arbitrary rules or processes. A social worker's performance might end up being measured by the number of cases they clear a day, instead of the quality of their service. This is an example of incomplete monitoring of performance, or as I call it, "good but not great" monitoring.

Good but not great monitoring is most commonly seen when jobs involve making subjective judgments or incorporating information that cannot be explicitly observed. It can lead employees to focus only on those elements of their job that are being monitored, even if these are not the only or most important ones.[48] As employee effort in other aspects of their job declines, the monitored metric may become an even worse indicator of performance.[49] As a scholarly classic puts it, we need to worry about "The Folly of Rewarding A, While Hoping for B."[50] Mission-motivated Bina might still perform those unmonitored or "invisible" tasks that are important for performance. But Samir and Peter may not.

When "invisible" tasks, qualities, or expertise are essential to performance, compliance-oriented management will be less effective at encouraging employees to forward their mission point.[51] To illustrate the impact of these "invisible" qualities, consider the phenomenon of so-called work-to-rule strikes. Employees "strike" not by refusing to come to work, but by refusing to do anything that is not explicitly required by their contracts. Such a strike might not have much impact on jobs that have clear processes and measurable outputs. For many other jobs, such a strike would be extremely disruptive.

Good but not great monitoring can also actively obstruct performance by pulling attention "up" to targets rather than "down" to citizens. This is a version of what management scholar Ethan Bernstein calls the "transparency paradox": that more transparency can in fact undermine employee performance by keeping employees focused on strict compliance to the expense of productivity-enhancing behaviors.[52] Nobel laureate Jean Tirole and Philippe Aghion describe a similar trade-off between "principal control" and "agent initiative" in economics. When managerial oversight increases, employees devote less effort toward tasks that are not codified and observed by managers. This trade-off can prevent employees from developing practical skills and garnering contextual knowledge.[53] Philosopher Thi Nguyen in "Transparency Is Surveillance" calls similar managerial interventions "epistemic intrusions," in which monitoring "curtail[s] the ability [of experts, including bureaucrats] to apply the full powers of expertise."[54] Social scientists Karl Polanyi and James Scott have likewise argued that hard-to-codify knowledge—that which can only be acquired through practical experience—is important for the production of good outcomes.[55]

Fairly comprehensive data suggests that "great monitoring" is possible only for a minority of what governments do. Imran Rasul, Dan Rogger, and Martin Williams set out to figure out what proportion of tasks performed by the Government of Ghana can be well monitored, drawing on standard performance reports required for virtually all tasks the Government of Ghana performs. The researchers assess whether it was clear before the task started what would constitute good performance ("ex-ante clarity," as they call it), and for that same task whether it was clear afterward from what could be monitored and documented if the task had in fact been done well ("ex-post clarity").[56] Looking at 3,620 tasks across a range of agencies, they find that less than 30 percent score above 4 on a 5-point scale in both dimensions; only 11.2 percent score a perfect 5 on both.[57] Imperfect "good but not great" monitoring is very frequently the best form of monitoring available.

The consequences of good but not great monitoring affect managers as well as employees. Imperfect monitoring limits the information managers receive about employees, making it harder for them to identify which managerial strategies lead to good performance. In an organization where monitoring is pretty great (e.g., the vaccine delivery team), monitoring data is likely to be useful in identifying shortcomings and implementing changes. In organizations with good but not great monitoring (e.g., our social work agency), managers are far less likely to figure out what drives or impedes performance. As a result, organizations that could benefit most from managing for empowerment are often the least likely to adopt them. Managers reliant on bad monitoring simply *don't notice* the underlying problems and potential improvements from strategic change. If the information managers receive is poor, their responses to those inputs will be poor as well.

For Route C to work well, monitoring must not only be technically possible but also *actually implementable* in a given context. Managers often explain poor results by saying something like, "Well, if the monitoring tool had functioned as designed, it would have worked great." But when a monitoring system is not functioning quite well, compliance-oriented management simply will not work. In my experience, this non-functioning is often the result of factors that are unlikely to be resolved, including environmental limitations, technical lacunae, or vested interests.

An almost-working monitoring system is one that is not, in fact, working—and may never do so. If monitoring can't be implemented effectively, a compliance-oriented managerial approach is not likely to result in optimal performance. In these cases, we are often better off using a different approach entirely.

Motivation of Workers

Another key factor is the current and potential mission motivation of a workforce. This refers to an agency's proportion of Binas, Samirs, and Peters. An agency's mission motivation is like a sports team's talent. It can be improved with good management. But it's also useful for a workforce to have substantial mission motivation even before management acts upon it. It's thus important to attract mission-motivated people to apply, to hire them when they do, and to keep them from leaving. In Chapter 4, I'll explore evidence that compliance-oriented management often repels the mission-motivated, while empowerment-oriented management attracts and retains them.

When current employees are highly mission-motivated or motivateable, empowerment-oriented management will be most beneficial. Unlike Peters, mission-motivated Binas and motivateable Samirs are not likely to use additional autonomy to shirk or engage in corruption. They will use every opportunity to forward their agency's mission. They do so best in empowerment-oriented environments that kindle that motivational fire and support them in fulfilling their mission point.

This doesn't mean that an agency with Peters should write off Route E entirely. It is true that some Peters might take advantage of the autonomy that Route E offers. It might then be a good idea to dismiss or reassign them to tasks suited for Route C management. But even when Peters are present, it is still possible that performance can be improved by Route E reforms. The gains from helping Binas and Samirs do their jobs better can offset the losses from Peters, resulting in net performance gains.

People can reasonably disagree about what "better" performance is, of course. If an agency's managerial reform leads some citizens to receive better service, but other citizens encounter receive the same (lack of) care they did in the past, is this better performance (because some citizens are doing better) or worse performance (because treatment is not equitable)? These are ultimately broader societal and political questions, which Chapter 7 touches upon.[58]

Monitorability and motivation are still far from the only factors that influence how management practice translates into performance. Other important elements include the extent to which a task requires local information and the exercise of judgment to be performed well; the political environment; agency risk appetite; and whether a task offers potential personal benefits to corrupt employees. Not all managerial strategies can even be plausibly implemented in a given agency. As Part III of this book will describe, political considerations and public opinion can limit the strategies that are available to managers. Nevertheless, monitorability and motivation are good places to start to design reforms that enable employees to thrive.

The Long-Run Dynamics between Management and Motivation

In the long run, management practice can meaningfully shape a workforce. We can model the effects of C and E management on different workforces in Table 2.1.

In the language of game theory, there is no strictly dominant strategy here. If a job can be easily monitored, or if a workforce is not and cannot become mission-driven, performance is best under relatively compliance-oriented management. The ideal outcome in such an organization would be the bottom-left cell of Table 2.1. If a job is difficult to monitor and employees are or can become mission-driven, performance is best under relatively empowerment-oriented management. The ideal outcome would then be the top-right cell of Table 2.1.

In my experience, many agencies find themselves with a great deal of compliance-oriented management even when that is not suitable for their

Table 2.1 **Management practice and individual motivation**

Current Employee Mission Alignment	Management Practice	
	Mostly Managing for Compliance	*Mostly Managing for Empowerment*
Currently Mission-Motivated	Management may deplete employees' mission motivation, devolving to the square below.	An equilibrium at which management supports, attracts, and retains Mission Driven Bureaucrats to forward their agency's mission point with managerial practices that allow autonomy, cultivate competence, and create connection.
Currently Not Mission-Motivated	An equilibrium in which employees will do only what they are monitored and coerced to do, and employees who are mostly not mission-motivated. This is fine if monitoring is complete, but problematic if not.	Management can increase the mission motivation of current employees and/or attract the mission-motivated and transition to the square above. However, a stable culture of shirking and malfeasance may also be reached; organizations can get "stuck" here.

workforce and tasks. There are many reasons this might be so. To start, we live in an era where many assume that the products of compliance-oriented management (clear and countable metrics, targets, and indicators) are superior to messy human judgment. I also think there's a justified fear of the cell in the bottom right. The transition from a largely compliance-oriented to a more empowerment-oriented managerial environment is *difficult*, and not without risk.

Shifting toward Route E management can mean changing policies, performance metrics, and relationships between bureaucrats, their managers, and citizens. This requires time, complexity, and effort. Frequently, the biggest hurdle is the risk and *likelihood* of bad actions by employees in the short term. While motivated Binas and Samirs are likely to respond positively to Route E reforms, unmotivated Peters may take advantage of loosened controls to slack off or engage in corruption and malfeasance.

This is perhaps a good place to reintroduce politics to our story. I am often asked to speak to some version of the question, "How can agencies learn from failure?" This is a good question. But before we ask it, agencies *first* need to "learn from success"—that is, understand that success might not look the way we expect. Often, reforms that boost performance can also be fodder for negative headlines.

If implementing a Route E reform causes 98 out of 100 employees to perform their jobs 20 percent better, but the performance of two employees drops by 20 percent, that would be a massive net gain in performance. Politically, however, this huge improvement can be overshadowed if those two employees had, say, engaged in theft that compliance-oriented management could have prevented. Accountability for a public agency is not just about performance. It also involves the perceptions of the public and public authorizers, including legislators. Few organizations could respond to the headline "Agency relaxes rules, allows theft!" with anything *other* than the tightening of control. Political actors hence often demand compliance-oriented management, even when that isn't the best choice of an agency. Part III discusses politics and accountability systems more deeply.

Soviet premier Vladimir Lenin reportedly used to say, "Trust is good, but control is better." It is possible this was exactly right—for *Lenin*. As inaugural head of the Soviet Union, he created a bureaucratic culture characterized by distrust and the need to provide politically palatable, rather than objectively accurate, information to superiors.[59] In such an environment, where mission motivation will undoubtedly be low, control may well be better. But in many circumstances, Lenin has it exactly wrong. Trust and empowerment can lead to far better results than can attempting to force compliance.

Claims to Be Tested in Part II

There are a lot of moving parts in this argument. So let me conclude Part I by articulating seven falsifiable hypotheses that have been raised so far and that will be explored in Part II:

(1) *More management for empowerment is associated with greater mission motivation. [A correlation]*
Organizations utilizing empowerment-oriented management will have more mission-motivated employees. This is because:

(2) *Management practice alters individual motivation. [A treatment effect]*
Empowerment-oriented management will increase the mission motivation of employees.

(3) *Management practice affects employees' exit and entry. [A selection effect]*
More empowerment-oriented management will increasingly attract and retain the mission-motivated.

(4) *Peers and organizational norms can influence mission motivation.*
No employee is an island. Mission motivation can be kindled or snuffed out by interactions with colleagues as well as the norms and culture of an agency.

These four hypotheses describe how management affects the mission motivation of employees. But when will empowerment-oriented management lead to improved performance? Route E reforms are likely to translate into better outcomes when . . .

(5) *. . . Mission-motivated or motivateable employees are or can be present.*
Empowerment-oriented management will benefit workplaces that employ or can recruit mission-motivated employees.

(6) *. . . Monitoring is more difficult.*
When monitoring is challenging, the mission motivation of employees matters even more for performance. Empowerment-oriented management practices can enhance and support that mission motivation.

(7) *. . . Mission motivation has not previously been considered in an agency's managerial approach.*
Agencies that have not previously considered the mission motivation of their employees have likely underinvested in empowerment-oriented management.

Exploring These Claims: My Empirics and Those of Others

The next section, Part II, explores these hypotheses. It draws on the work of many other scholars as well as research I have conducted with others in Bangladesh, Ghana, Liberia, Thailand, and the United States. Part II also draws on my analysis of existing data, including a database compiling all publicly available civil service surveys, comprising over 4 million individual and 2,000 agency observations. The Technical Appendix provides more detail on the original empirical projects.

The next chapter, Chapter 3, will begin Part II with an exploration of management practice and the motivation of current employees (Hypotheses 1 and 2). Management practices don't just respond to employee motivation; they *change* employee motivation.

Profile: Florence N. Kuteesa

*Mission-Oriented Leadership in the Ugandan Ministry of
Finance, Planning and Economic Development
(Budget Director)*

"They don't only motivate you, but you have to motivate them."

Florence is clearly excited to reflect on the achievements of her former organization. She jumps right in with her reasons. "I must say, among all other key factors, I think motivation is very important . . . motivation goes with confidence. Motivation goes with discipline. Motivation goes with integrity. Responsibility. Accepting to be accountable to whatever you do."

Florence, now in her sixties, joined the civil service very early in her career. She remembers that time in detail. "We [were] coming from the devastating war in 1986 and the government was all dilapidated. Most of the work was being done by NGOs." In addition to challenging circumstances and unconventional working hours, salaries were very low. She recalls that "many of my colleagues who joined the civil service resigned and secured better jobs, lucrative jobs."

What might sound like a difficult place to start was, for Florence, "an opportunity to deal with the most important critical tool in development, in rehabilitation, in renovation: the budget." She explains, "the public funds were being allocated to priorities, development needs of the people who were displaced, people who didn't have food. We didn't have soap. And so, to me, it was a blessing." The work allowed Florence to contribute to curing the ills faced by her community: "I wanted to be part of that reform. I wanted to be instrumental." It fulfilled her desire to serve the public, to be "impacting on people's lives."

Florence's commitment to her organization's mission, coupled with her fidelity to detail and impact, has earned her a reputation for being a straight shooter, someone who could never be influenced by unprincipled pressures. "I would not be manipulated; everyone knew that."

Florence smiles, "I am what I am because of my mom. My mom is a mid-wife. She instilled all these values ... which motivated me." Among those values were meticulous organization and perfectionism, which Florence ultimately ap-plied to her work in the ministry. "You would wash the clothes—we don't have washing machines here, we can't afford them—you put them outside the house to dry. ... If she found just a nappy or a collar not well washed, every item would go down in the water to be re-washed. That is why I focus on the details." She worked such long hours, she says, that her sister would joke that she had found a secret husband. "I would say my husband is Mr. Budget."

Florence's motivation to serve the mission of her organization was reinforced by a work environment characterized by alignment, support, and trust from management at every level. She recalls the shared dream of better budget man-agement as she and her staff established a new Budget Policy department. "We all had common issues of concern and we all had the same vision to streamline them." She felt support from her team and her immediate political and technical leadership; they all enjoyed the political guidance of President Yoweri Museveni. "At that time, His Excellency demonstrated commitment to reforms, and he did everything possible to support whatever could be done to achieve what he desired: macro-economic stability, infrastructure, universal primary education, and all kids going to school."

Sometimes peers and supervisors would argue, "That cannot be done. You cannot change [what] the law says, the law spells out this." Florence stepped up to resist these views. "We can gradually change the practice, and then the prac-tice becomes a policy, and then later feeds into the law."

Florence once noticed that the annual expenditures on a water program did not seem to result in access to safe drinking water for communities. "And then you'd get a different report on the bore holes being constructed from a min-ister, you get a different figure on access from the Permanent Secretary, you get a different figure from the technical head of the department of water, rural water. But this is not right! So, we discussed the issue with one of the donors. We requested funding for a public expenditure tracking study in the rural water." After a brief pause, Florence's face breaks into a smile. "It was done and was re-vealing!" Florence doesn't seem bothered that it "was not well received by all of the policymakers"; for Florence, what matters is what was right, not what someone in power wants to see happen.

Later, Florence was promoted to Director of Budget in the ministry. As a manager, Florence sought to empower her team and cultivate competence and independent thinking. She led her staff to think deeply about measures that would ensure the budget serves the needs of the public. She knew her team well and played to their strengths.

"I would constitute a working team to make sure a facilitator is there, a resourceful person is there, someone to record the discussion. You must be able to motivate them. They don't only motivate you, but you have to motivate them." Florence's interest in the people on her teams helped foster an environment that was not only mission-motivating but also delivered the reform objective.

Unfortunately, political commitment to the reform agenda changed, shifting in a "demoralizing" direction. Florence felt "we are not serving anymore. We initiated reforms, they were the best in the Sub-Saharan Africa. Now, I think we are retracting operations. I was not interested in backsliding." Florence felt that in the face of declining clarity and consistency in policy, "whatever you had put in place doesn't matter anymore. Then you start wondering what you are doing."

During this period, Florence remembers completing and presenting draft budgets, only to have the Cabinet ask for new initiatives to be added, regardless of alignment with national priorities and availability of funding. Sometimes supplementary budget requests made during the implementation of the budget even exceeded the total original budget. "Every day, the spending agencies would send us new requests for additional funding, beyond what Parliament had approved. It was disheartening to receive those requests without a hope for additional revenue from Uganda Revenue Authority. We were handling emergencies on a daily basis without resources." When the requests came from "the top," the budget department's ability to push back was limited.

In the past, the government would "make sure that all the key departments are available during the annual budget discussions, with a clear intention to build consensus on priorities and funding." The "sense of collaboration and shared purpose" that had been so critical to Florence's work was no longer to found; "the 'we' had reduced."

Florence's twenty-year career in public service was fueled by her exceptional dedication, discipline, and fierce commitment to doing what is best for the future of her country and an empowering work environment. As the mission point of her organization shifted and the work environment changed accordingly, Florence ultimately decided she could no longer have the impact she sought in her post. She left the ministry.

Florence's mission hasn't changed—she still serves the public, but not as an employee of the state. Florence continues to work with an NGO focused on women's economic empowerment and works for international organizations like the IMF and World Bank, helping other countries improve their public financial management. A public sector where people like Florence aren't supported in serving the public is one that will be less likely to retain them.

PART II

DIAGNOSIS

Evidence on How and When
Empowerment-Oriented Management Works

How You're Managed Changes
What You Want to Do

The Impact of Managing for Empowerment on
Current Bureaucrats

> As soon as a teacher is newly recruited, he says, "I can do anything";
> [teachers] enter the system with lots of energy and determination, with
> dreams of overhauling everything. However, after two–three months,
> the environment, the system, the people—all break that attitude and
> they feel jaded.
> —Interview with head of a Delhi school, Aiyar et al.,
> *Rewriting the Grammar of the Education System*[1]

> The chief lesson I have learned in a long life is that the one way you can
> make a man trustworthy is to trust him; and the surest way to make him
> untrustworthy is to distrust him and show your distrust.
> —Henry Stimson, US President Truman's Secretary of War,
> in his resignation letter to Truman[2]

Management affects people's motivation at work. I initially believed this claim
to be so intuitive as to need little empirical support. Everyone who's ever had a
job—or more precisely, a boss—would agree with that statement.

However, I've come to observe that many people act as though motivation
is an unalterable fact of a given individual. This chapter will build on a rich vein
of scholars who have established that claim to be false. One's mission motivation can change over time, especially in response to organizational practices.[3]
As Christensen et al. succinctly put it in a comprehensive review of the literature on public service motivation (a subset of mission motivation, as I define
it), "Employee public service motivation is changeable by both intended and
unintended organizational and management practices."[4]

A Route E managerial reform that allows autonomy, cultivates competence,
and creates connection to peers and purpose can and does increase bureaucrats'

Mission Driven Bureaucrats. Dan Honig, Oxford University Press. © Oxford University Press 2024.
DOI: 10.1093/oso/9780197641194.003.0003

mission motivation. This chapter will take you from rural Thailand, to Detroit, USA, to Dhaka, Bangladesh, exploring the relationship between empowering management and performance. Before that let's start in Liberia, where I had the privilege to work for the Minister of Finance from 2007 to 2009.[5]

Bina, Samir, and Peter in the Liberian Ministry of Finance

The previous chapter introduced three stylized type of employees—Bina, Samir, and Peter. Bina is endlessly mission-motivated, regardless of circumstances. Peter is never mission-motivated. Samir is everyone between them. Samirs can change; empowerment-oriented environments might allow Samirs to be just as motivated as Binas. But under compliance-oriented conditions, they might end up like Peters.

While I have observed examples of Bina, Peter, and Samir in many countries, this "compositional" issue struck me most during my time working in Liberia. Liberia's former president, Charles Taylor, was in jail in The Hague for his role in Liberia's long civil war. Ellen Johnson Sirleaf (a future Nobel Peace laureate) had recently come to power through a free and fair election.

The future appeared bright. But there were reasons for concern regarding Liberia's bureaucrats. The Accra Peace Agreement that ended the civil war had given temporary control of different ministries to warring factions in a transitional government.[6] The agreement sought to induce all parties to put down arms by allowing them to govern—and in reality, loot—the state. The plan worked, but not without substantial implications for state agencies. The Ministry of Finance that Sirleaf and her finance minister (and my boss) Antoinette Sayeh inherited after this transitional period was staffed by many individuals who had helped to defraud the state either during the transitional period or during the preceding Taylor era. In some cases, they had surely been appointed by warring factions for that explicit purpose.[7] Civil service protections precluded the easy dismissal of these individuals, as they had been appointed by a legally serving government.

The Liberian Ministry of Finance had every reason to be full of Peters. Indeed, I can imagine almost no set of circumstances in which we would anticipate finding more. There absolutely were a fair number of individuals who had no interest in the work or who were grossly underqualified.[8] But surprisingly, there were also some Binas—individuals who genuinely seemed to be trying to do good work.

There were also quite a lot of Samirs—many more than I ever would have imagined on first observing a great many seemingly apathetic, inactive ministry employees. I slowly learned that the most important question I could ask was, "What do you think we should do?" Many bureaucrats responded as if this was the first time they'd ever been asked the question, not to mention trusted and empowered to implement their answers. Over and over again, long-serving bureaucrats and teams began working harder as they saw the impact of their labors, saw that what they did at work mattered.

One of the many things I learned in Liberia was that it is easy to confuse a bureaucrat who is "demotivated" for someone who is "unmotivated." It's easy to mistake a lack of effort for a lack of interest in doing good work. I learned that expecting nothing of someone is a self-fulfilling prophecy. If we expect nothing of someone, people will often meet our low expectations.

If there were that many Samirs in the post-Taylor Liberian Ministry of Finance, then Samirs can likely be found just about anywhere. It's worth thinking hard about how to motivate these Samirs to work at their best. As was the case in Liberia, this is particularly true when the tools you have to induce compliance are weak, and the performance of employees is difficult to monitor.

Not everyone that I encountered in Liberia was a Samir. But assuming that they were a Samir and treating them with trust was the best way I had to find out if indeed a given individual's motivation and actions could shift. The evidence explored in the rest of this chapter can be understood as my effort to figure out whether my experience in Liberia was typical or exceptional. My belief is that my experience in Liberia was a bit of both—typical in that we do indeed live in a world with many Samirs; exceptional in that most organizations manage their employees as if they are not Samirs, but rather unmotivateable Peters.

Having realized that management for empowerment was so rare, I set out to look for environments where it was present to examine its effects. I found one such environment in Thailand, under surprising circumstances.

Forced Management for Empowerment: Evidence from Thai Districts

I lived in Thailand for a few years in my twenties, and speak passable Thai. A few years ago, I returned to Thailand for six months to answer a puzzle that had been bothering me. How could Thailand, having experienced twenty coups or coup attempts in the past eighty years, and eleven constitutions in the past fifty years, simultaneously be proclaimed one of the world's "great development success stories?"[9]

Conventional wisdom would dictate that the country's political chaos would take a toll on the performance of its public sector. After all, changes in government, from leadership to policy, have substantial switching costs.[10] Much like a sports team that suffers when its managers constantly change, good performance requires some stability of direction. But Thailand continues to record substantial GDP growth and impressive reductions in poverty, increases in life expectancy, and performance on other standard development indicators.[11] How has the state kept its leadership turmoil from derailing performance for its citizens?

To answer this question, I sought to understand the delivery of Thai government services at the district level, carrying out surveys and interviews of frontline staff and district heads.[12] Thai districts are roughly the size of US or UK counties—containing on average around 100,000 people. They are managed largely from the national capital, with various Bangkok-based officers appointed to the district to implement their ministries' policies. An agricultural officer from the Ministry of Agriculture is responsible for agricultural policy; an education officer from the Ministry of Education is similarly in charge of any educational policies; and so forth. Each district is nominally led by a Head of District appointed by the Ministry of the Interior, who is the "father" of the "district family," as one interviewee put it.[13] Many of these roles have few prospects for promotion or rotation, since there are only a small number of jobs in Bangkok at the next level of the hierarchy.[14] As a result, a given "district family" often remains largely intact for quite a while. I refer to the Bangkok-appointed officials from the various ministries collectively as "vertical bureaucrats," since their chain of command flows up to central ministry leadership.

You might expect these vertical bureaucrats to have become jaded, apathetic, or disillusioned by years of political turmoil. Surprisingly, nothing could be further from the case. The vertical bureaucrats who we surveyed reported remarkably high levels of job satisfaction and mission motivation. Comparing these bureaucrats to the Global Survey of Public Servants (GSPS), the world's largest collection of surveys of civil servant motivation, the Thai district bureaucrats surveyed are among the most mission-motivated, satisfied bureaucrats *in the entire world*.[15]

In interviews these Mission Driven Bureaucrats often described a great sense of purpose, expertise, and competence in their jobs. When asked what attracted them to the work, the most common answer was the official mission of Thai local government: *Bambat Tuk Bumrung Sook*. This motto, displayed in many government offices and quoted in my experience by a great many Thai citizens, means "alleviating suffering and nurturing wellbeing."

Having read Part I of this book, you might imagine that one reason Thai bureaucrats remained so mission-motivated was that they were given a large degree of autonomy. This was not formally the case. The Thai state has an extremely centralized and hierarchical structure. Most authority is retained by the national government rather than delegated to local administrators. Even village heads at the time reported to, and were on the payroll of, the national government.

The strict Bangkok-centered hierarchy offered district heads very few traditional tools to manage their employees, including limited ability to hand out sanctions or rewards. Promotions and transfers were instead managed by the Bangkok-based ministries. The supposed "head" of each district was often painfully unable to instruct other vertical bureaucrats—the district's "limbs"—to move.

To make matters worse, the orders that did trickle down the hierarchy were often inappropriate. District bureaucrats reported frequently receiving instructions that were "unfit and unrealistic," with policy "made and assigned by those in the [Bangkok headquarters] ivory tower," to quote one of our interviews. Over 75 percent of respondents regularly experienced tension between the orders they received and what they believed were the best interests of citizens in their district.[16] A full 40 percent thought that this tension was extreme enough for them to explicitly refuse or alter orders from higher-ups in their ministry.[17]

What, then, was the key to the Thai bureaucracy's success? Our research suggests that the disconnect between Bangkok and local districts was the Thai bureaucracy's saving grace. The huge distance between Bangkok and most districts made it difficult for Bangkok ministries to monitor the districts' activities. District heads were left largely on their own. The circumstances *forced* them to get creative—to find new ways to manage their employees and take ownership of their district's public service delivery.

Unable to induce their employees to comply, district heads chose instead "to inspire and motivate people in [their] district," as one district head put it.[18] Another district head saw his job as offering support and advice to his officials, who were then free to seek and follow it as they saw fit. Another district leader described his primary managerial tool as the demonstration of "care" to his subordinates and "appreciation of their work." Still another described his managerial strategy as "instilling a sense of ownership and pride" in vertical bureaucrats, "cultivating and inspiring" bureaucrats to live up to the mission statement of Thai local government.[19]

In turn, employees generally felt very supported by their district heads.[20] Common interview themes included the value of their district head's mentorship and its salutary effects on the motivation of young staff. Interestingly, even where there was no formal requirement to report to their district head, a number of district officials did so regularly. One district official noted that her district head's managerial approach—acting not like a "boss" but like the "coordinator of a team"—had improved her attitude toward work and increased her propensity to collaborate with colleagues. One public health officer confided in his district head and sought professional advice when faced with challenges, a process he found helped him do his job better. An education officer described his district head as a "captain" responsible both for the "crew" (vertical bureaucrats) and "passengers" (citizens). Another vertical bureaucrat in the same district described how her district head created a "sense of place" that made everyone feel at home.

Thai districts represent unique workplaces where the absence of effective compliance-oriented tools forced managers to engage in empowerment-oriented management. Where they did so, their districts often became thriving, high-performing workplaces of harmony and trust between bureaucrats and managers.

Importantly, this empowerment-oriented style wasn't necessarily successful for *every* employee. We found that some bureaucrats did indeed prove to be Peters, doing very little work in the absence of top-down control. While this highlights the risks inherent in empowerment-oriented management, those bureaucrats were certainly the exception.

Overall, the decision of district leaders to invest in empowerment-oriented management yielded a workforce of bureaucrats who were competent, autonomous, and deeply mission-motivated. Districts left on their own to generate good performance were shielded from elite political turmoil. The apparent weakness of the centralized Thai state in fact was instead one of its hidden strengths.

How Managing for Empowerment
Changes Motivation

Management for empowerment does not just take advantage of existing mission motivation in bureaucrats. It also creates more motivation. Evidence from a variety of sources, both experimental and observational, has shown that empowerment-oriented management increases mission motivation.[21] It does so by appealing to the very psychological foundations of motivation within psychology's Self-Determination Theory (SDT)—the fulfillment of human needs for autonomy, competence, and relatedness.

These three tenets of SDT appear to be key factors in cultivating mission motivation. A study of Danish teachers, for example, found that management that promotes autonomy, competence, and relatedness among employees also increases their mission motivation.[22] Gailmard and Patty similarly find that autonomy is itself a motivator, one likely to increase public servants' investment in cultivating competence, because they will then see returns to that investment. Employees will be motivated to learn how to do better at their jobs when they know they will use the skills acquired.[23] By cultivating expertise, organizations can allow employees to see themselves as trusted professionals. Findings from a variety of settings suggest that a greater sense of professionalism also makes employees more likely to hold each other and themselves accountable according to professional norms.[24] Managing for empowerment can also have long-term health benefits. A follow-up to the famous Whitehall study of UK civil servants found that having greater "decision latitude" at work—more control over skill use, time allocations, and organizational decisions—was associated with a lower long-term risk of coronary heart disease.[25]

As Chapter 2 introduced, this book rebrands SDT's relatedness as *connection*—the connection of bureaucrats to other people through their work, including their colleagues and citizens. One important channel through which management practice influences motivation is by making work feel more impactful. This might mean allowing public servants to directly interact with their beneficiaries, or framing tasks to highlight the impact of their efforts upon citizen welfare.[26] Drawing connections between employees' work and their public value will foster Samir's mission-driven motivation and reinforce Bina's existing motivation.[27] Management practice influences whether employees can make a difference, and whether they feel they are doing so.

Anir Chowdhury, who leads the Government of Bangladesh's Aspire to Innovate (a2i) program, similarly identified autonomy, competence, and impact (and thus connection to purpose) as key pillars in the government's efforts to cultivate mission motivation. Describing a peer-to-peer teacher training program in Bangladesh involving more than 400,000 teachers in a TedX talk, he noted: "Teachers have taken control of their own fate and are training each other. What would trigger such innovation?"[28] He found that the training program worked through three key mechanisms. First, the program promoted a sense of connection to each other, to citizens, and to the impact of their work. Second, the program fostered a sense of autonomy by reducing rules and red tape for teachers, ensuring that "the letter of the law [became] less important than the spirit of the law." Finally, it equipped teachers with a sense of competence in performing their jobs.[29]

Direct management can and does foster an individual employee's mission motivation. But individual changes in motivation are most sustainable when also supported by a broader transformation of systems and practices to support one's motivation. This fits the lived experience of those who work to kindle motivation. STiR (Schools and Teachers Innovating for Results) is a nongovernmental organization that works with over 200,000 teachers in over 100 districts in India and Uganda, with a goal to "change behaviors and attitudes by reigniting intrinsic motivation."[30] STiR's efforts incorporate other gears across the machine of the educational system, including outreach with school leaders, district officials, and even state and national officials.[31] STiR aims to induce not only individual shifts in mission motivation, but also broader system transformations that sustain mission motivation.

As STiR's founder Sharath Jeevan put it: "We've got to change relationships at the core.... We can create the desire of people to want to change and create at these different levels, and create the strong role modeling and relationships that help the whole system move in a different direction."[32] Chapter 5 will return to broader teams and systems and their role in sustaining mission motivation.

The Demotivating Effects of Too Little Empowerment: Evidence from Detroit

I wish I could say that management always enters the motivational equation as a positive force. Sadly, the quote from the Delhi school head that opens this chapter highlights that this is not the case. Bad management can cause employees to feel powerless, seeing their work as meaningless to society. This "policy alienation" reduces their motivation, effort, and effectiveness.[33] Bureaucrats denied autonomy are generally less motivated to implement policies.[34] Meta-analysis of twenty-five studies across half a dozen countries finds that greater "red tape"—administrative processes and procedures that public servants must follow—is associated with lower levels of mission motivation.[35]

The idea that too much compliance can reduce mission motivation and performance in the existing workforce is echoed in research by other scholars. A study of community health workers in India found that employees are held back by a system where they are "managed with suspicion and distrust."[36] The authors argue that workers would be more effective if they did not need to seek permission for everything they did and were empowered to believe that their efforts were improving the health of citizens.[37]

This demotivation-by-compliance is what Lena Boraggina-Ballard, Joanne Sobeck, and I found in our study of social workers employed as specialists by Children's Protective Services (CPS) in my hometown of Detroit, Michigan.[38] CPS specialists investigate whether the home in which a child resides is dangerous to their health and safety, uncovering evidence of abuse and/or neglect. If evidence is found, they determine the severity of the risk and decide whether the child should remain in that home or enter state care.[39]

Detroit CPS specialists contend with some of the most extreme compliance-oriented management that I have ever observed. All visits to homes or interactions with families must be carefully documented and uploaded into a state tracking system.[40] Mountains of paperwork and a tangible fear of falling afoul of the rules typify many specialists' workdays. Chief among these rules is the need to be "in compliance," as caseworkers themselves put it, with state caseload and response time laws—to have no more than the state-mandated limit of cases in their care at any one time, but also to respond to new reports of potentially vulnerable children as quickly as possible.[41]

Mandating a limit on caseloads per worker or a maximum response time for any new report of potentially endangered children seems reasonable. I could imagine voting for such regulations were I, as a citizen or legislator, given such an opportunity. But the easiest way to clear a case is to put children into foster care. In combination with chronic understaffing, these well-intentioned rules create an environment in which specialists feel forced to place children under state care as quickly as possible. State care is no panacea. As one synthesis of the literature on US foster care puts it, children in state care have "poorer school performance; higher rates of school dropout, public assistance, homelessness, arrest, and chemical dependency; lower marriage rates; and poorer mental and physical health."[42]

As one Detroit CPS specialist put it, "You [have to] break policies to see [positive] change. . . . You don't want to remove children from their families prematurely."[43] Another said, "When I have new cases, I'm out of compliance. But instead of [my managers] saying 'thank you, we'll help you work to be in compliance,' I get a blast [of criticism] and [am asked] what I am going to do to get in compliance."[44] This is quite literally managing for compliance.

Imagine that Samir decides to join CPS as a specialist because he cares about helping vulnerable children. After starting his job, however, he finds that all his actions are controlled by tight regulations. He also suspects that many of his actions are not actually benefiting children's welfare, which lowers his feelings of competence and connection. Samir will become more and more demotivated.

Our study found that a great many Detroit CPS specialists are like Samir.[45] They joined CPS because they wanted to "help families," "make a difference," or "let kids know they have somebody who cares about them."[46] But at CPS, they find they often cannot accomplish these goals.[47] Feelings of burnout are common.[48] As one relatively new specialist remarked, "I feel sad for colleagues who are jaded. I am aware that they don't wake up and want to be subpar. It's sad when you see workers have no hope."[49]

Compliance-oriented managerial practices have snuffed out Detroit CPS's greatest asset—the mission motivation of its employees. Working in CPS is already an incredibly difficult job, one that asks poorly paid state employees to witness trauma and make judgments that are likely to change the lives of children forever. But management is not putting these employees in the best position to succeed. Much the opposite—workers seeking to do good work frequently feel as though they need to fight the system to actually benefit the children in their community.

Managing for Empowerment's Impact on Mission Motivation: Cross-Country Data

Neither Thai districts nor Detroit CPS are typical managerial environments. I looked at these cases precisely because their extreme conditions allow us to study the links between management practice and motivation with a clarity that most settings lack. Thai districts highlight the motivational power of empowerment-oriented management in a setting where it's the only tool available. Detroit CPS also sets itself apart—both in the high initial mission motivation of its employees, and in its demotivating compliance-oriented environment.

Since these cases have been exceptional, you might question whether this connection between mission motivation and management for compliance is found in other workplaces, too. There are certainly plenty of examples suggesting it is far from infrequent. For example in Punjab, Pakistan, Majid and Ali find that teachers are much like Detroit CPS specialists, with "monitoring and disciplinary regimes result in teachers experiencing states of fear as pressure mounts to meet unreasonable performance targets."[50] They add that "reform program deliverables are achieved on the backs of teachers living in a constant state of fear and anxiety."[51]

That said, there are literally millions of public servants; however many instances we find, it will be hard from this type of data to understand if management and motivation do indeed move together systematically. To address this I gathered all existing nationally representative civil servant surveys that included questions on motivation and performance. I assembled what is, to my knowledge, the largest existing database of public servant perceptions of management practice and motivation. In the aggregate, the database comprises observations from over 4 million individuals at 2,000 government agencies across five countries.[52]

I performed a series of formal regression analyses exploring the relationship between motivation and indicators of empowerment-oriented management. These indicators measured the extent to which management practice promoted autonomy and creativity, as well as the quality of managerial supervision and feedback. The results were clear: empowerment-oriented management practices are strongly correlated with higher levels of mission motivation. A shift in each of the empowerment-oriented management indicators of one unit was associated with 20–40 percent of a unit's improvement in employee mission motivation.[53]

While interesting, this relationship does not necessarily mean that management practice *changes* motivation within individuals. It could be the case, for example, that some agencies are just managed better overall, and thus attract and retain more mission-motivated individuals. Employee selection and retention is certainly influenced by its management practice, as Chapter 4 will explore.[54]

To identify how management can alter the motivations of the *same* group of employees in an agency, I looked at shifts in a single agency's motivation over time.[55] As only a very small percentage of total staff enter or leave most agencies in a given year, within-agency comparisons suggest that results are driven by individuals shifting their motivation in response to changes in management practices. I utilized the same four indicators of empowerment-oriented management practices, adding one more: psychological safety, or the extent to which one feels free to express thoughts and opinions in the workplace.[56]

Once again, increases in empowerment-oriented management practices were associated with increases in the reported motivation of that agency's employees. This suggests that when management shifts toward empowerment, the *same* employees increase in mission motivation.[57] If, for example, management is 50 percent more successful in promoting autonomy on these measures, they can expect to have a workforce whose mission motivation is 20 percent higher as a result.[58]

Thailand and Detroit were not, after all, exceptions; nor was my experience in Liberia. More managing for empowerment does indeed foster mission motivation, and less managing for empowerment tends to snuff out bureaucrats' motivational fire.

Lessons from Bangladesh: Managing Employees Who Don't Want to Be There

Let's now turn our attention to another study—this time from Bangladesh, where Tim Besley, Adnan Khan, Ferdous Sardar, and I came across a "second choice" government agency. I'll call this agency the Bangladeshi Public Service Agency (BPSA), allowing it to remain anonymous in line with an agreement we made with the agency.[59] I term it a "second choice" agency because it is composed almost entirely of individuals who would rather be employed elsewhere.[60] BPSA's staff are recruited from the small group of individuals who have passed the notoriously tough Bangladesh Civil Service (BCS) exam, with pass rates in the range of 2.5 percent.[61] However, government jobs in Bangladesh are even scarcer, with as few as 1 in 200 applicants (0.5%) actually being offered full civil service "cadre" positions.[62] The BPSA hires from those who pass the BCS test but were not recruited to cadre posts.

Imagine again our changeable Samir, now an aspiring Bangladeshi civil servant.[63] He has spent many years hoping and preparing for a treasured job in the civil service. Perhaps this is because he is inherently mission-motivated, eager to relieve the struggles of citizens that he witnesses firsthand. Perhaps he simply seeks a secure, well-compensated, and high-status position. Whatever his motivation, he receives notice that he has accomplished what many have dreamed of—he has passed the terror that is the BCS exam.

Samir is, understandably, elated. But then come months of waiting, and eventually, he realizes that he will not be getting the cadre post for which he's worked so hard. As he considers his options, he receives an offer to join BPSA. BPSA offers a secure and stable government position. However, it also offers less prestige, less compensation, and fewer career accomplishments in the future than Samir had hoped for. While it is by no means his heart's desire, Samir takes the offer.

Our Samir is, by construction, mission-motivateable, and might well respond to empowerment-oriented management. But what are the chances that this is a workplace where management for empowerment is a good idea? When Samir joins, his colleagues will probably include lots of unmotivated Peters, given that this agency is the first choice of very few. We might expect that employees at BPSA will capitalize on any loosening of workplace rules to enrich themselves, or at the very least, slack off. Any performance-enhancement strategy at BPSA should probably take a compliance-oriented approach—alignment with the mission through monitoring, target-setting, and sanctions.

If you—like me, at the outset—agreed with the logic of the prior paragraph, I'm glad to be in good company. But it turns out that we are dead wrong. In an anonymized survey of nearly 500 district and sub-district (*upazila*) staff, our research found that mission-motivation scores at BPSA were quite high on a comparative basis. In fact, BPSA's mission motivation was higher than the national average in every survey included in the Global Survey of Public Servants (GSPS).[64] One of our survey questions asked the respondents to choose three factors that led them to join BPSA. Over three-quarters chose "serving the country" as one of their top three factors, compared to just 8 percent who chose "income and benefits."

However, 55 percent of these employees also reported that if they were to choose again, they would not join BPSA, in part because management systems keep them from being able to deliver the outcomes for citizens they seek.[65] What employees most desired was more individual authority, freeing them from the burdens of compliance-oriented approvals and bureaucratic processes. Though such compliance-oriented tools might have prevented unmotivated Peters from slacking or engaging in corruption, they also massively slowed down work processes. In fact, it was those with the *greatest* mission motivation who were most desirous of greater authority.[66]

These diagnostics suggest that managing for empowerment would actually strengthen, not stifle, the BPSA's performance. If the agency were to act on my wrong first instinct that compliance-oriented management is the right choice, they might well undermine mission motivation and performance. Even in a "second choice" agency whose staff would *all prefer to be somewhere else*, these diagnostics suggest that managing for empowerment may well unlock performance gains.

Management Changes Private Sector Motivation, Too

The benefits of Route E are better recognized in the private than the public sector, as Chapter 1 suggested. A great deal of research has demonstrated that letting private sector employees make more autonomous decisions increases workplace productivity, even if the outcome would have been the same had managers made their choices for them.[67] Even where employees choose what employers *would have* chosen—for example, the configuration of their office, or their preferred method of reporting—simply giving employees agency improves performance.[68]

Failing to feel a connection to impact is demotivating in the private sector, too. David Graeber's memorably titled *Bullshit Jobs* suggests that around 40 percent of people in the private sector feel their jobs make no difference whatsoever. Those holding bullshit jobs apparently find this deeply demotivating and a cause of great unhappiness, wishing for something productive to do even if their current jobs demand little or no effort.[69] Managing for empowerment would almost certainly benefit these employees and would likely translate into better agency performance.

Route E reforms in the private sector often work by creating a sense of connection to the broader social purpose of the work. Adam Grant's experiments demonstrate that mission motivation increases when phone agents soliciting donations feel connected to the scholarship students who benefit from a share of the funds raised.[70] Work on "job crafting" suggests that even hospital janitors see improved job satisfaction and performance if they view the labor as "highly skilled."[71] When janitors are encouraged to focus on what constitutes *more* work for the same pay—"learn[ing] as much as possible about the patients whose rooms they cleaned, down to which cleaning chemicals were likely to irritate them less"—they in fact feel more satisfied and mission-motivated at work.[72]

Route E reforms can revitalize corporate performance even in settings heavily entrenched in compliance-oriented management. Let me illustrate this using one of the corporate titans of my hometown, General Motors (GM).[73]

GM is a nationally renowned automotive manufacturing company. However, in 1982, GM's Fremont Assembly Plant closed in part because its employees were, in the words of *their own union representative*, "the worst workforce in the automobile industry in the United States."[74] Fremont was fraught with absenteeism, while employees who did show up spent their time smoking, drinking, and otherwise *not* working. The work that did get done was substandard, with frequent defects.

In 1984, the plant reopened as NUMMI, the first joint venture between Toyota and GM. Eighty-five percent of the workers hired by NUMMI came from the GM-Fremont workforce, a concession to the United Auto Workers union that represented the plant.[75] Even former GM-Fremont workers who failed a blood test for illegal drug use were still able to join NUMMI.[76]

The essential new ingredient at the reopened NUMMI plant was Toyota's management system, which sought "to build an atmosphere of trust and common purpose."[77] A key feature was the ability of workers to take initiative—to report problems, suggest improvements, and even stop the production line if need be.[78]

What were the results of these managerial changes? By the end of 1986, NUMMI's productivity was higher than that of any other GM facility and more than twice that of its predecessor, GM-Fremont.[79] As John Shook, an industrial anthropologist hired by Toyota to work at NUMMI, put it:

> The absenteeism that had regularly reached 20% or more? It immediately fell to a steady 2%. The quality that had been GM's worst? In just one year, it became GM's best. All with the exact same workers, including the old troublemakers. The only thing that changed was the production and management system—and, somehow, the culture.[80]

The identities of the workers had not changed, but their behavior certainly had. Even with essentially the same workforce, NUMMI was able to induce skyrocketing performance improvements by managing for empowerment. Fremont Assembly, previously the "worst workforce in the automobile industry," now flourished under its new management.

If GM can transform its productivity by managing for empowerment, why *not* mission-motivated public sector workers? Empowerment-oriented management can be a powerful tool for catalyzing employee motivation and performance in the public and private sector alike. Indeed, it ought to be all the easier to do in the public sector, given that public service work almost always has a social purpose. Those attracted to the public sector are often also those motivated by that purpose, as the next chapter will discuss.

The Underutilized Potential of Empowerment-Oriented Management

Many public agencies are rife with compliance-oriented practices. In Delhi, Yamini Aiyar and coauthors describe compliance-oriented management and demotivated bureaucrats as the current "grammar" of the education system. They describe the system as "built around an assessment, training, and administrative system that coheres around the goals of rote learning and maximizing examination results."[81] This results in "a culture where teachers and administrators have come to believe that they have very little agency and autonomy."[82] Thirty-six percent of employee work time is spent simply complying with administrative reporting requirements. The remainder of their time at work is spent trying to implement a great many orders and instructions, constraining what teachers can do and limiting the time they have to do it.[83]

Delhi schools are far from the exception. Similar workplaces are evident across the world. Hilary Cottam finds that in one UK city, 74 percent of social workers' time is spent on administrative processes such as recording and reporting data for monitoring systems.[84] When the system focuses on compliance, public servants will comply. But is it any wonder that they will be demotivated as a result, often to the detriment of citizens? Aiyar and coauthors see promise in empowerment-oriented reforms that liberate and support teachers.[85] There is good reason, based on this chapter's evidence, to believe they are right.

The more managers offer employees respect, agency, and the opportunity to perform meaningful work, the more employees will be mission-motivated. Allowing autonomy, cultivating competence, and creating connection to peers and purpose change what employees want to do.

Organizations often choose to increase management for compliance in their quest to improve performance; that choice has a clear impact on their employees' behavior. Compliance-oriented tools can absolutely be useful, but they are not the only ones available. Managing for empowerment is a powerful managerial approach that is too often overlooked.

The profile that follows this chapter will introduce you to a real-life manager for empowerment: Uma Mahadevan, an additional chief secretary in the Indian Administrative Service. In addition to reinforcing her team's mission motivation, Uma's leadership approach cultivates competence and autonomy in her team.

The next chapter, Chapter 4, will then shift focus from the employees who are already present to those who are attracted to or repelled from the workplace. Empowerment-oriented management can and does help attract and retain the mission-motivated.

Profile: Uma Mahadevan

Managing for Empowerment in the Indian Administrative Service (Additional Chief Secretary)

"They have the right to love their work as much as I love my work."

"I'm a curious person, as it is. I want to know everything about everything." Uma's voice fills the room when she speaks. She laughs frequently when story-telling, and with Uma, every conversation is a story.

When asked about what drew her to the civil service, Uma speaks of the generations that came before her—to their achievements, but also their hardships. She draws inspiration from family members who sought justice for their country as freedom fighters. Uma "wanted to fight against injustice" with the same commitment her uncle had dedicated to the country. She was also attracted to the civil service because she cares deeply about reducing social inequalities. Her grandparents were born into families that lacked financial resources, unable to access education due to the absence of public support.

Uma had the benefit of greater resources and strong support from her parents. She was struck by the stories of injustice that seemed to surround her. The woman who cleaned her family's house would sometimes arrive with bruises from an abusive relationship that went unchecked. Women in other parts of her family were denied education or control over their futures because of their gender. "I felt that if the government can change that, then I should be a part of that government and I should work there."

When Uma looked around at the urgent social inequities of her generation, she thought, "This has got to be changed and I want to be part of something that can help change this." She "want[ed] to enter public service to actually serve. I mean to do something and to improve people's lives." To say that Uma is motivated to do this work is an understatement. "Ultimately, the only thing that really is exciting about this job is that *you get to work*. It's enormously exciting."

Over the course of her career, Uma has worked in the sectors of land administration, literacy, poverty alleviation, health, atomic energy, agriculture, women's empowerment, nutrition, rural development, and democratic decentralization. In each role, she's kept central the interests of the communities she serves. She was still quite junior when she began taking a principled and creative approach to her roles. "I started appropriating developmental functions to myself. I started saying that if I'm doing a regulatory job, like clearing ten or twenty huts that are in an encroachment, then I will move them *only* if I find the right place where I can move them and build replacement houses for them and ensure that there's water and electricity and so on."

Uma is not just a Mission Driven Bureaucrat in her own right; she also manages in a supportive way, attracting and kindling the mission motivation of others. As part of a campaign that she launched to fight malnutrition in the state of Karnataka, Uma displayed "MRIs of the brains of a stunted child at the age of two and three months, and a well-nourished child." She believes that "it's very important as a leader to make everybody part of the big picture," which is why she showed the pictures of the MRIs not only to the highest-level leadership in the state, but also to all her field-level staff. "We showed the same thing [to everyone on the team]."

In Karnataka, Uma also oversaw a major initiative to support early childhood education, including providing meals to children, educators, and families. She had 125,000 frontline staff members working directly in their communities, and the initiative required everyone to go above and beyond their official work requirements. Uma motivated employees not with financial reward, but by explaining the mission and convincing people of its effectiveness at improving welfare. "I communicated like hell. I mean, I communicated, we all communicated, all of us and we said that every single person must do this because it's the right thing to do." Her motivation and supportive approach "made everybody the owner of a big story, [so] they feel that this is worth achieving and that's what we did."

After she explained the mission to her team and convinced them of its value for the public, Uma saw her staff "carry it forward." When temporary residents who often did not fulfill the program's criteria were in need, employees didn't hesitate to serve them. In fact, staff "didn't feel that they had to ask [Uma or other managers] for special permissions to cover everybody because we said that the scheme is for everybody." These bureaucrats felt empowered to take the initiative to fulfill the program's mission on their own accord.

Uma's management style does not rely on strict hierarchy. She closely consults her staff during all the project she undertakes. "Even while developing the program, it's not that we imposed something saying that this is our wisdom, and we know more than you. We said, how do you think we can do this?"

Passion is the main ingredient to Uma's success as a manager and bureaucrat. The excitement of doing work that matters has paved the way for many great accomplishments. Nevertheless, her individual success is only one piece of the puzzle. She firmly believes that "There's no *I* in government; it's all about getting the entire system to work." As a leader, she knows that "if you show that you're enjoying your work, it kind of becomes a little infectious."

Uma's advice for others in similar environments? Catalyzing the motivation of other bureaucrats is core to her leadership approach. She volunteers that not all bureaucrats have the same level of mission motivation—she believes about 25 percent are already mission-motivated (Binas). Another 50 percent, she estimates, can change with the right leadership and management (Samirs). For Uma, these mission-motivateable Samirs "are the ones who are exciting because that's where I can show and challenge myself [as a leader]."

Uma thinks the mission motivation of employees can change—but she also expresses unprompted that more ought to be done to recruit mission-motivated Binas and motivateable Samirs. She believes that "selection has to get to the heart of what motivates people to get into this." Doing well on an assessment test is not the same as having the mission motivation to do well when serving in the Indian Administrative Service.

Uma acknowledges that the work of government can be "a lot of minutiae and a lot of small talk and boring meetings." But the impact that it can have, to Uma at least, "is just so awesome." For Uma, "it's been the job of a lifetime."

When I spoke to Uma, it had been two and a half years since she had led child education initiatives in Karnataka. She had visited the department the previous week to see if the program was still going strong and felt that it had "carried on because everybody feels that it's their own, and they have the right to. They have the right to love their work as much as I love my work." Having witnessed Uma's passion and approach to leadership, it's easy to imagine Uma kindling the mission motivation and performance of those fortunate enough to serve with her.

Attracting (and Keeping) the Mission-Motivated

> If in your own judgment you cannot be an honest lawyer, resolve to be honest without being a lawyer. Choose some other occupation.
>
> —Abraham Lincoln[1]
>
> Let the Beauty of What You Love Be What You Do
>
> —Rumi[2]

The previous chapter established that empowerment-oriented management can improve mission motivation, just as coaching can improve a sports team's motivation. But just as a sports team benefits from drafting talented players, it is useful for an agency to start off with employees who are already mission-motivated.

This chapter examines how management influences not just the behavior of employees but also *who* those employees are—who comes to the agency and stays there. It investigates Hypothesis 3 articulated in Chapter 2: management practices affect employees' exit and entry. But let's first take a look at who already is in the workforce of the public sector, and what we might know about their mission motivation.

Bureaucrats Often Work for Reasons Other than Maximizing Income

Do public service agencies currently employ mission-driven individuals? There is surely no universal answer to this question.[3] A common stereotype of bureaucrats is that they're lazy, uncaring, and greedy. Is that true?

I attempted to find this out, working with a research assistant to compile every existing study that reports some form of mission motivation that we could

Mission Driven Bureaucrats. Dan Honig, Oxford University Press. © Oxford University Press 2024.
DOI: 10.1093/oso/9780197641194.003.0004

identify.[4] We used this sample to compare the mission motivation of public and private sector workers.

We find that public sector employees have on average slightly higher levels of mission motivation than does the general public in existing studies.[5] This shouldn't surprise us—after all, bureaucrats are individuals who chose jobs that explicitly seek to serve the public. These results are consistent with other studies that suggest that mission-motivated employees are more likely to be found in the public sector than the private sector.[6]

I often hear that bureaucrats are "overpaid." From a normative perspective, this is a matter of judgment, tied up in questions of the social value of an occupation. But from a market perspective, the claim that bureaucrats receive higher incomes than they would in the private sector is often false. American public school teachers, for example, are paid about 20 percent less than other workers with similar experience and characteristics.[7]

Drawing from the Worldwide Bureaucracy Indicators (WBI), which assembles data from over 132 countries, Baig and coauthors found that while there indeed is a public sector wage premium for "clerks" and "elementary occupations," there is also a public sector wage *penalty* for "technicians," "professionals," and "senior officials."[8] On average, mid- and high-level bureaucrats receive *less* compensation in the public sector than what a person with the same qualifications could earn on the private market. This is true for street-level bureaucrats like teachers and nurses, as well as the vast majority of the mid-level bureaucrats most readily disparaged in public imagination. *Some* qualified people might well take public sector jobs with the express purpose of working very little for good money. But this simply isn't true for most public sector workers.

Why would people choose a job that doesn't maximize their potential income? The most straightforward answer is in my view often correct. Most bureaucrats find their jobs meaningful—they *care*. The evidence suggests that most bureaucrats are indeed mission-motivated, such that they would be willing to accept lower salaries to forward their mission.

Many scholars and practitioners I have discussed this with have the intuition that this may be true in their home country, but isn't the case for other countries—particularly countries in the developing world. The argument for this claim usually begins with the argument that employees appointed in a non-meritocratic manner are not likely to be mission-driven. This pattern might be more frequently seen in poorly governed states, which are disproportionately those with lower per capita income. As one group of leading public management scholars put it, "in developing countries with institutionalized corruption and weak rule of law ... 'unprincipled' principals use managerial discretion over hiring, firing, and pay to favor 'unprincipled' bureaucratic agents, who engage in corruption."[9]

The next section will investigate whether a distinction between developed and developing nations truly exists in the data, exploring if members of the Organisation for Economic Co-operation and Development (OECD)—that is, the world's richest countries—are systematically different from the rest.[10] Are Mission Driven Bureaucrats less likely to be found in poorer countries than richer ones?

Mission Driven Bureaucrats Are as or More Common in Developing Countries

You could listen to rhetoric about some developing nations and conclude that their governments are filled with corrupt politicians and bureaucrats who only seek self-enrichment. While I do not dispute that "unprincipled" appointment may be more frequent in the developing world, we have good reasons to believe that it is still, thankfully, very rare. Let's look again at the aforementioned sample I compiled of every study reporting some form of mission motivation. Bureaucrats in non-OECD countries are not less mission-motivated than those in rich OECD countries in this sample.[11] If anything, those in non-OECD countries appear to be slightly more motivated to serve the public than their counterparts in rich countries.

You might be worried that my sample contains too varied a group of surveys, putting its consistency and representativeness into question. Perhaps the survey questions were simply understood differently in certain countries.[12] A better test might to compare bureaucrats and non-bureaucrats in the same country, responding to the same survey. Since we already know that bureaucrats are generally more mission-motivated than non-bureaucrats, we could find out whether this "gap" is larger in OECD countries than in the rest of the world.

To do this, I looked at the 2014 wave of the International Social Survey Programme, or ISSP. This survey asked citizens in thirty-four countries questions about their motivation and employment status, for instance, "To what extent do you think it is important to help people in your country who are worse off than yourself?"[13] In a fairly extensive exploration of these data, which can be viewed in detail in the Technical Appendix, I find that the gap in mission motivation between bureaucrats and non-bureaucrats is not affected by the income level of the country.[14] Bureaucrats are similarly more mission-motivated than non-bureaucrats in countries of varying incomes and levels of development.

There is no support for the conventional wisdom that mission-motivated Binas and motivateable Samirs are more likely to be found in richer countries than poorer ones. This in turn suggests that managing for empowerment is worth consideration in every country.[15] Country music superstar Luke Bryan has a lovely tune entitled "Most People Are Good." That seems to be true for bureaucrats everywhere.

Getting Good People through the Door: Selection In

Let's now turn to the question of how to recruit Mission Driven Bureaucrats. Of all public sector problems, this is one of the easier ones to solve. Mission-motivated young people appear to already be attracted to the public sector, even in many settings where we might expect this not to be the case.

Indonesia and Russia are two countries with established histories of corrupt behavior. On the Corruption Perception Index, the leading global standard of country-level corruption, Indonesia scores 100th of 180 countries. Russia ranks even worse, coming 137th in 2022.[16] Even in these countries, careful empirical work suggests that mission-motivated young people are more attracted to the public sector than those who are less mission-motivated.[17] Consistent with the last chapter, what happens after you're hired matters too. Young recruits increase in mission motivation with time spent on the job,[18] particularly when they witness how their efforts support their organization's mission.[19]

Thinking carefully about recruitment can lead to an even better crop of recruits. Reputation is one important factor; agencies with a reputation for competence and supportive work environments can attract higher-skilled, more mission-motivated applications.[20] Reforms that put power into the hands of employees also appear to attract mission-motivated bureaucrats to a workplace.[21] Advertising can also help; organizations can and have recruited more mission-motivated individuals when they explicitly advertise the ability to serve others and cultivate competence.[22]

Recruitments efforts often highlight how deeply Mission Driven Bureaucrats desire to make a difference. Sarah Thompson, who coauthored this book's profiles, used to work in recruiting for the Broad Residency, an "opportunity for outstanding management professionals [from fields like finance or law] to apply their skills and knowledge to meet the challenges faced by [US] urban public school systems."[23] The Broad Residency offers corporate professionals the opportunity to serve in school district middle management. Sarah was often in the position of asking highly paid professionals if they would be interested in working longer hours at a substantially more stressful job, only to make far less money than they currently did. The supposed "opportunity" would also probably be held in far less esteem than their current jobs.

Some applicants reacted to Sarah's offer in the way that standard economic theory would predict—asking, "Would anyone actually apply for this?"[24] Others, however, saw the same grim proposal as a gift. Some felt ready to use their considerable talents to serve their community, rationalizing that they could still be paid to do work that had meaning to them. Multiple people described receiving her unsolicited email as "divine intervention."[25]

Sarah's experience illustrates that Mission Driven Bureaucrats are all around us. Some may be "hiding" in the private sector, including at fairly advanced career stages. If offered the opportunity to make a meaningful impact, many will choose a job in the public sector over one that pays better or confers greater social status. Agencies just need to advertise the welfare-enhancing nature of public sector work.[26]

I don't mean to suggest that it's a good thing that bureaucrats earn less than they would in the private sector.[27] Low wages can be interpreted by civil servants as a demotivating lack of respect.[28] Additionally, civil servants cannot feed their families on what sociologists call "psychic income"—the non-monetary satisfaction that accompanies a job—alone. Low salaries can encourage civil servants to resort to bribery and other forms of corruption.[29] When civil servants make less than they need to feed their families, many feel they have no choice but to extract additional money from other sources. When I worked in Liberia in 2007, many civil servants made around 50 USD a month, or less than the international "2 dollars a day" poverty line. This could not sustain an individual, much less a family.

Occasionally, I encounter the view that paying bureaucrats more would cause the public service to attract less mission-motivated people. The argument is that the truly mission-motivated would be happy to serve a good cause regardless of their salary. What little evidence we have of what occurs when salaries rise actually points in the other direction. Findings from Mexico suggest that greater financial compensation does not crowd out but rather attracts the competent and mission-motivated to the public sector.[30] Research in Zambia suggests that this is particularly useful if paired with hiring processes that select both on technical skill and mission motivation.[31] To see if this held in my own data, I combined the data presented earlier from the ISSP with data from the World Bank Bureaucracy Lab on wage premiums in the public sector. Higher public sector wage premiums—that is, a larger gap between public sector and private sector wages—are associated with a slight increase in the extent to which public servants are more motivated than private sector workers.[32] It's true that mission-motivated people aren't attracted to the public sector solely for the pay; however, higher wages don't preclude, but if anything encourage, mission-driven people to join the public sector.

Paying bureaucrats better is one way to recruit mission-motivated applicants, but it is not the only one. Another way is to specifically recruit for mission-motivated people through fast-stream civil service programs. The next section will take you to Ghana and Liberia, where these fast-stream programs have been powerful tools to recruit a mission-motivated workforce.

Attracting the Best: Ghana and Liberia
Fast-Stream Civil Service Programs

Some countries undoubtedly have a government with a tradition of failure, rather than excellence. You might think it's difficult for these countries to recruit highly skilled, mission-motivated individuals to their public sector. Reputation (bad), pay (low), and the perceived ability to make a difference (small) may all deter the mission-motivated. As then-Liberian president and Nobel Peace Laureate Ellen Johnson Sirleaf put it just after the country emerged from civil war, "on account of the mediocre performance of the Civil Service in recent times, our people have lost confidence in the Government to meet their needs."[33] This presented a great challenge—a need to "transform the Civil Service from an ineffective and inefficient entity to a competent, professional, and *motivated* Service that is an effective instrument of sustainable human development."[34]

One element of President Johnson Sirleaf's strategy was the President's Young Professionals Program (PYPP), which has been active in Liberia since 2009.[35] PYPP aims to recruit some of Liberia's best and brightest young citizens to the civil service, in the spirit of the Presidential Management Fellowship in the United States or the Civil Service Fast Stream in the United Kingdom. The two-year PYPP fellowship provides fellows with a community of peers and direct mentorship from program staff and experienced civil servants. In Ghana, a similar program began in 2019 under the auspices of PYPP's umbrella organization, titled the Emerging Public Leaders (EPL) program. I partnered with EPL and PYPP to help understand the impacts of their programs in Ghana and Liberia on the civil service.[36]

While I hoped these programs were making a positive impact, I was uncertain this would be the case. One concern I had was that the fast-stream fellows— who, given the rigorous selection processes, surely would have many other job prospects—might quickly choose to leave. The work environment they faced would certainly be challenging and, in my experience, heavily compliance-oriented. I worried this would diminish their feelings of autonomy and competence, reducing their mission motivation. I was also afraid that introducing a young "elite" fellow might disrupt existing team chemistry and cohesion, negatively impacting team performance.

The studies in Liberia and Ghana shared many similarities, though they had slight differences. In both countries, we gathered data on fellows, their supervisors and colleagues, as well as individuals who had applied to EPL/PYPP but fallen just below the cutoff of their selection processes.[37] In Liberia, our survey focused on both current fellows and alumni, additionally seeking out non-fellow civil servants who were comparable in age and background to the fellows. In Ghana, the same group of EPL fellows, supervisors, and non-fellows were surveyed at two separate times, allowing us to observe within-person changes in their mission motivation.[38] Both the Liberia and Ghana surveys asked respondents a varied set of questions about their experience in the civil service, including the length of time they planned to remain employed there, their job satisfaction, as well as supervisors' perceptions of the performance and impact of fast-stream fellows as compared with non-fellows.

The results from Liberia indicated that alumni fellows who were more mission-motivated desired longer careers in the civil service.[39] This suggests that Liberia's public service did not repel the mission-motivated. However, there was also suggestive evidence that the mission motivation of fellows was reduced by exposure to the civil service.[40] This may be because only 36 percent of fellows believed Liberians viewed bureaucrats with a high level of respect, as compared to 51 percent of non-fellows.[41]

In Ghana, joining the civil service did not seem to demotivate the fellows surveyed. The mission motivation of EPL fellows rose slightly as they spent more time in the public service.[42] There was also no evidence that becoming a fellow led individuals to desire a shorter career in the civil service. For some fellows, the placement appeared to increase the length of their desired public sector careers. As fellows became more satisfied with their job placement, their mission motivation also increased.[43]

The impact of these fast-stream fellows on the broader public service is difficult to quantify. That said, 75 percent of their supervisors in Liberia considered them to be higher-performing than their coworkers. Eighty-five percent considered their fellow a leader within their team, and 100 percent believed that the fellows and the program were positive influences on organizational culture.[44] Similar results were found in Ghana, with 74 percent of supervisors considering fellows' performance superior to their coworkers and 82 percent of supervisors agreeing that fellows strengthened public service delivery.[45]

The results from Liberia and Ghana ultimately suggest that the civil service *can* be improved, even in difficult circumstances. Fast-stream programs alter the composition of civil servants, bringing in employees who are both talented and passionate about their jobs. These fellows do not only perform well individually, but also positively influence their peers. The EPL and PYPP programs have not solved all the problems of their civil services, but they appear to have generated marked performance improvements. Recruiting mission-motivated and highly skilled individuals to the government may be a powerful way to transform a workforce.

Exit and Retention: More Hard Lessons from Detroit Child Protective Services

I feared that I would witness the exit of Mission Driven Bureaucrats in Liberia and Ghana. Thankfully, I did not—but I did see this happen when I became involved with my hometown of Detroit's Child Protective Services (CPS).

I was back home and went to visit a friend I hadn't seen in years. She had pursued a master's degree in Social Work with the explicit purpose of helping the city's vulnerable children. She had won a very competitive scholarship to do just that. But, I was surprised to hear, she had recently left her job at CPS. When asked why, she described an extremely compliance-oriented workplace, resulting in a day-to-day experience in which she did not feel she was actually helping children.

In collaboration with Lena Boraggina-Ballard and Joanne Sobeck, I decided to study this phenomenon more systematically. We interviewed and surveyed graduates of the highly competitive scholarship program, asking questions about motivation, career trajectory, and experiences during their employment at CPS.[46] Tragically, our results indicated that my friend's story was a typical case among scholarship awardees. The rigorous screening mechanism did an excellent job; awardees were extremely devoted to child welfare. However, faced with a job that did not allow them to make a positive impact on children—that diminished their feelings of autonomy, competence, and connectedness—they left.

Our interviews found that the overwhelming reason employees wished to leave Detroit CPS was the heavily compliance-oriented management. One employee attributed her desire to leave to "the compliance blast," the overwhelming amount of rules and reporting associated with every action.[47] She summarized the view of many when she declared she was going to leave so she "could be more impactful in a different role."[48] A highly mission-motivated ex-employee commented, "There is no amount of money you could pay me to go back to CPS."[49] Indeed, in surveys we conducted of awardees examining their current employment status and their motivation, those who were more mission-motivated were significantly more likely to have left CPS.[50] In other words, those who cared the most were the first to leave, because they felt unable to serve their mission.

The difficult workplace that Detroit CPS has created affects all its workers. From October 2017 to April 2022, 222 specialists departed Detroit CPS, even though the agency only employed 145 specialists in total.[51] That's a little over 1.5

departures for every full-time position in less than five years. Comparing these figures to those reported by the US Bureau of Labor Statistics, this turnover rate is 70 percent higher than the national average. For every worker lost by a typical government agency, Detroit CPS loses closer to two.[52] This difference is driven by the massively higher rate of voluntary departures at Detroit CPS—making up 95 percent of employee exits, compared to about 50 percent in the US government as a whole.[53] Very few complete their careers at Detroit CPS; only 3 of the 222 departures in the data were retirements.

It strikes me as a really, really good idea to have the people who are looking after my hometown's vulnerable children be those who care the most about those kids. Those who are willing, indeed eager, to accept lower pay than they would otherwise receive. Those who are willing, indeed eager, to face incredibly stressful and difficult tasks. Those who are willing, indeed eager, to do a job that I think is incredibly valuable, but that I am personally neither strong enough nor skilled enough to take on. It turns out people like this, amazingly, *actually exist*. They're willing to make lots of sacrifices—but they aren't willing to make those sacrifices and *not actually be able to help kids*. I don't blame them. And while I'm sad for those Mission Driven Bureaucrats, I'm sadder still for the children of Detroit.

Whether Mission-Motivated Binas Stay or Leave Depends on Whether They're Empowered

Detroit's mission-driven CPS bureaucrats are typical of their kind. Those who feel powerless at their jobs are, perhaps unsurprisingly, those most likely to exit their agency.[54] Chapter 3 introduced my econometric analysis of over 4 million individual observations of bureaucrats over five countries, gathered from nationally representative civil service surveys.[55] Those data shows that the more mission-motivated are also more likely to wish to leave organizations that lack empowerment-oriented management.[56] The more mission-motivated a bureaucrat is, the faster a disempowering, control-oriented environment will prompt their exit.

This reflects what other scholars have called a "dark side" to mission motivation. Those with the greatest desire to serve the public are most demoralized when management practice or other factors prevent them from doing so.[57] As Esteve and Schuster put it, "highly pro-socially motivated employees who do not perceive a societal impact of their work" are "more likely to burn out."[58]

This can have serious consequences for agencies. When Australia's development agency, AusAid, lost its autonomy and was absorbed into the Ministry of Foreign Affairs, demoralized staff felt unable to engage in work they found meaningful.[59] The result was a mass exodus. As one influential review put it, "1000 years of expertise left shortly after integration, and another 1000 years has departed since."[60]

The devotion of Mission Driven Bureaucrats is also an opportunity. The same data that show that lower levels of managing for empowerment is associated with a greater desire to quit for more mission-motivated employees also suggests that cultivating mission motivation is an excellent employee retention strategy. Mission-motivated people are more influenced by managerial practices when deciding whether to remain at their jobs in either direction; higher levels of managing for empowerment are associated with a *greater* desire to remain in the job for the more mission-motivated.[61] The mission-motivated will flee workplaces that do not empower them, and are more likely to remain at workplaces that do empower.

This general pattern is confirmed by other research. Reminding public servants about the meaningful purpose of their jobs decreases their interest in leaving the public service.[62] Turnover in US municipalities can be reduced by removing "over-controlling rules [that] can stifle autonomy and creativity, may be more likely to be viewed as red tape, and can signal managerial distrust towards employees."[63] In Honduras, decentralized municipalities—those in which local officials can act with autonomy, cultivate connection to purpose, and cultivate competence—are better able to retain mission-motivated staff.[64] In Brazil, giving teachers greater autonomy reduces teacher turnover by over 20 percent.[65] Thinking hard about the management practices that will attract or repel mission-motivated Binas is an important component of any performance improvement strategy.

Management Is an Important Piece of the Recruitment and Retention of Mission-Driven Bureaucrats

I once proposed an empowerment-oriented managerial reform to a senior official in a large public agency whom I'll call "Steve." Steve was responsible for a team of hundreds. He had been promoted up the ranks of an agency that had been, in his estimation, poorly managed in the past. This led to the exit of his most skilled, mission-motivated staff. In response to my pitch, Steve said, "You know, when I got here, the people who worked here. . . . I would have trusted them to make the right judgments, they cared about doing the right things. Now, though, I don't think so. These people? No way. They don't have the ability to think for themselves, and even if they did, I wouldn't trust them. If we were able to bring in the right people, maybe then I'd be willing to give this kind of thing a try."[66]

Let's pretend for a second that Steve is correct. Maybe Steve's agency really is a rare case whose staff are largely unmotivateable Peters, unlikely to behave well if empowerment-oriented management practices were employed. I think Steve is *still* thinking about this backward. He's confusing cause and effect.

By failing to trust and empower his staff, Steve is alienating and discouraging them further. He's making existing employees even *less likely* to be trustworthy and dedicated employees. Steve is also increasing the chances that currently employed mission-motivated Binas and motivateable Samirs will leave, while also likely ensuring that in the next hiring round fewer Samirs and Binas will apply. Steve is trapping his organization in a downward, demotivating, demoralizing cycle. *But this can change.*

Chapter 1 opened with a description of Judith Tendler's work in Ceará, Brazil, describing exceptional performance. A few years ago, I had the opportunity to discuss this research with Sara Freedheim (now Newman), one of her coauthors. Sara Newman went on to become a captain in the US Public Health Service Commissioned Corps, "an elite team of more than 6,000 well-trained, highly qualified public health professionals dedicated to delivering the nation's public health promotion and disease prevention programs, advancing public health science" who "respond to public health crises and national emergencies."[67] I had the great pleasure to meet Captain Newman in 2019, when she led public health for the US National Parks Service.[68] We discussed then-President Trump's view that the bureaucracy was the enemy and, as Trump's then-chief advisor Steve Bannon put it, that a primary goal of the president was "deconstruction of the administrative state."[69] Captain Newman had seen how this rhetoric from President Trump and his team had "created fear" in the agency. This wasn't just fear for current employees, but also future ones. For Captain Newman, the public service is animated by a "higher calling and this duty to serve, this feeling of wanting to do something for your country." She has observed that Trump's rhetoric was dissuading some mission-motivated applicants.

I worried, too, that the public service was no longer the obvious place for those wishing to have an impact. The week before, I'd found myself on a delayed flight in San Francisco and had started chatting with my neighbor. It turned out that were both coming from Stanford. I'd been at a conference, while he was attending a visiting students' weekend for admitted first-years.[70] I congratulated him and said it seemed like a wonderful place to spend a few years. He was undecided, even though it was just a few weeks before the fall semester started. From a long list of prestigious schools that had admitted him, he was deciding between Stanford and MIT. He had full scholarships from both and was unsure where he was headed. I asked what was going to determine his final decision. He told me that he "wanted to do the most meaningful work possible to help people in his life, and get the skills to do that."[71]

My neighbor had the markings of a future Mission Driven Bureaucrat; I was, as you might imagined, thrilled to dig deeper into his future plans. With some prompting he revealed that his admission probably had something to do with a vaccine-tracking software he'd developed for a clinic where he had volunteered during high school. The clinic, and others in his home state, had started using his invention. It was saving lives. This impact had excited, motivated, and shaped him.

I expected to hear that this young man was going to study public policy, possibly in some combination with technology. Perhaps healthcare supply chain management? I was wrong. He was focused strictly on software development. His goal was to graduate, work for a big tech firm, and help develop an app that could solve public problems. Why not a career trajectory with a public sector component, I wondered? "Oh," he said. "I want to have a *real* impact on the world." Captain Newman had seen echoes of this. She had witnessed bureaucrats and prospective applicants grow "dismayed or their motivation kind of wanes" when denied the opportunity to engage in productive work.

The young man debating between Stanford and MIT has the motivation that Steve, the agency manager who didn't trust the people who currently worked for him, desired in his employees. But he is precisely the sort of person who will *never* join an agency managed like Steve's. From MIT to Monrovia, Liberia, it appears that attracting and recruiting mission-motivated Binas and Samirs requires changing management practices *first*. Managing for the employees you want, rather than the employees you think you have, will change the composition of your workforce.

This chapter has argued that management matters to who comes, who stays, and who goes. The best people to perform the difficult jobs of public service are those who care the most. If we want them to join the public sector and stay there, we have to empower them to do the jobs they came to do. We have to allow Mission Driven Bureaucrats to feel that their work matters. They won't be working alone, of course; no bureaucrat is an island. The next chapter will examine the role of broader teams and organizational systems in shaping motivation.

Profile: Tathiana Chaves de Souza

*Mission Alignment and Connection to Citizens in the
Brazilian Chico Mendes Institute for Biodiversity
Conservation (Forest Ranger)*

"What direction I should point my energy . . . if I want to contribute to
a fairer world?"

Tathiana Chaves de Souza is an environmental analyst—a "Forest Ranger"—
for Brazil's environmental administration, the Chico Mendes Institute for
Biodiversity Conservation. A biologist by training, she also has a master's degree
in Environmental Engineering and works both in biodiversity conservation and
"participative environmental management."

As discussed in the last chapter, many bureaucrats enter the civil service because they care about doing useful things for their society. Tathiana is a case in
point. As she described it, "I felt in my heart that I was seeking to serve a greater
purpose. I would like to dedicate my life energy to a noble cause."

Public service has allowed Tathiana to realize her desire to follow a "path
to improve people's quality of life; for environmental balance, associated with
people's wellbeing and dignity, and thus, at the same time, ensure the promotion of nature conservation with social justice." When she thinks about how her
passion fits into a greater purpose, she thinks of "the rational use of natural resources, with respect to different lifestyles, getting to know different cultures,
different traditions, and to see ourselves as a part of the whole."

Her story starts in the central western part of the state of Pará, in the Brazilian
Amazon at an ecological station called Terra do Meio. She was attracted to this
agency because its mission point was aligned with her "dream to dedicate [her-
self] to biodiversity conservation and to work with nature protection." From the
start, her relationship with her work was almost spiritual. "I tried to make myself

at the service of something bigger, something that I consider beautiful, noble, and just."

But Tathiana was faced with a tense and difficult reality in Terra do Meio. The government had created a protected area in the name of biodiversity conservation without the engagement and support of the vulnerable people living in the region—traditional populations and family farmers. Any public consultation was short-lived, and demands for change by the marginalized local communities living in the protected areas were not met. As a result, there was "huge resistance to the recognition of the Conservation Unit" from the local community. Many farmers say they were "violently coerced to leave" from land they had lived on for years. The actions and approach of the state thus caused "trauma in the small family farmers."

Public land clearance, which was targeted at large public landholders who were responsible for large deforestation but also impacted small family farmers, was not the only issue. Attempting to crack down on now-illegal uses of the protected land, the government destroyed bridges and highways that represented the only access points for people living in the area. "One father came to me to tell me that his recently born baby caught malaria and he wasn't able to take the baby to the hospital" because of the blocked roads, Tathiana remembers.

Even without the failures of the previous government, the conditions of Tathiana's role would never have been easy. "It was a lawless land and there was a lot of mineral extraction . . . a lot of deforestation . . . it was a dangerous place to be." Tathiana went around the area with police protection until she had gained the trust and respect of its residents. The government had put up park signs around the ecological station to demarcate the boundaries of the protected area that had not been agreed upon by the people living in the region. Tathiana remembers, "six months later you'll find that there are gunshot marks on the signs." Beyond "fighting illegal actions, we were also dealing with land regularization by trying to identify the legitimate occupants of public lands."

The role also came with great personal sacrifice—it meant Tathiana had less time to visit her son, who lived with his father in a different region. "It was a very high cost for me to be away from my child. I needed to make that time count, I needed to make it important, so it was worth being away from my kid." What's more, Tathiana spent most of her time alone. "I was the only servant deployed at the second largest federal conservation unit in the country of Brazil. It has 3 million hectares. One servant deployed to manage all of this space."

Tathiana's mission motivation sustained her as she worked closely with local people (*ribeirinhos*, who are riverside residents and family farmers), their representatives and key partners (especially NGOs, educational, and research institutions), and committed staff at all levels of the Institute and the Federal Public Ministry of Altamira. Tathiana was determined to "create a pact with those [communities] involved" and suggested hiring local inhabitants to recover protected areas that were degraded, generating income and involving them directly in conservation services. She also wanted them to be part of research projects that tested new methodologies aimed at better land use, and she invited locals to join the management council of the park. Tathiana hired "three planes to go fetch those councilors of the Conservation Unit inside the park, from those conflicted areas, to bring them to our meeting twice a year."

Despite the challenging work environment, the loneliness, and personal sacrifices, Tathiana was excited by the prospect of enacting her agency's mission. She felt "very honored to serve my country" and saw the job as an opportunity to rectify the "omission and slow pace of the public power" and to protect nature while "caring for human rights and dignity and the dignity people deserve." The central conservation challenge of Terra do Meio had historically been framed as local people working against the conservation of this rich, natural place. But Tathiana thought differently. "Maybe they are working against conservation because there is no investment in the farmers for transitory or permanent solutions." It was her chance to promote "a more legitimate dialogue, to build consensus and create alternative pathways within the public power" itself, and to place citizens and nature at the heart of the conservation work.

Tathiana also kept the government coordinators constantly updated on "what I was doing, what feedback I was getting from the families, and even what impact we were having on the environment." In the beginning, meetings between the government and local representatives were very hostile, but "in the end, we had the Chico de Mendes Institute, the police, the firefighters, the researchers and the farmers, the family farmers and everybody holding hands together in a circle and local people were opening the meeting." Building trusting relationships with both the community members who live in Terra do Meio and her colleagues at the Chico Mendes Institute ensured shared ownership of an ecologically friendly management and joint decision-making. It wasn't just the farmers who benefited from this close collaboration; the environment did, too. "There was a relationship between the reduction of the impact of deforestation along the time when we built this dialogue and when we held mutual commitments, mutual agreements." Mission motivation and broader community collaboration often go together, as we'll discuss later on.

Unfortunately, with the successive changes in government, in guidelines, and in the board of directors, "the political will changed, so everything that I had been building very carefully . . . all of that was abandoned, filed." The new land agreements for the use and temporary occupation of land that Tathiana and the local community had worked on with so much dedication could not be finalized. The agreement with the *ribeirinhos* was the only one signed several years later. The lack of closure of the agreement that Tathiana had built with the family farmers caused the local community to lose faith in the government and in her as a manager.

Like many mission-driven individuals, Tathiana believed she was "tireless." However, when faced with constant setbacks and a job that no longer allowed her to have the positive impact she desired, she eventually needed to take a break from the work that she loved. Thwarted in her desire to protect nature and the local community, and lacking the control to influence the government's politics, she decided "I really needed a change of landscape and I left with a heavy heart."

Tathiana *is* a civil servant who wants to continue "seeing solutions to challenging and complex problems," but to do the work that she believes matters, she needs to work at an agency with a mission point that aligns with her values. The conditions that caused Tathiana to burn out are likely to also demotivate other Mission Driven Bureaucrats, as we saw in the last chapter.

After five years of service in Terra do Meio, Tathiana moved to Brasília to work in research and biodiversity monitoring. She felt she could have a different kind of impact in her new role. Her exit from the field was not caused by a "lack of commitment to something bigger than myself"; rather, it was an attempt to keep herself in a "virtuous spiral" when the work itself was sustaining of her motivation. She hopes that the government context will eventually change and she will once again be able to bring "happiness and enthusiasm and light-heartedness to find solutions" in this work.

Systems All the Way Down

Peers, Norms, and the Default Ways of Getting Things Done

> When systems or organizations don't work the way you think they should, it is generally not because the people in them are stupid or evil. It is because they are operating according to structures and incentives that aren't obvious from the outside.
> —Jen Pahlka, *Recoding America*[1]

> Thinking about organizations gets you to think about the right order of things. Corruption is embedded in a system of relations. It is a consequence rather than a cause.
> —Oriana Bandiera, Sir Anthony Atkinson Chair in Economics, London School of Economics[2]

What motivates you at work? Perhaps you feel deeply connected to your organization's goals. Perhaps you truly enjoy carrying out your tasks. Maybe you're anxious to impress your boss. But if you're one of those people who feels excited and inspired to show up to work even on the dreariest of Mondays, I'd wager your answer has at least something to do with the people with whom you work.

This book has described management's influence on individuals. But teams and agencies of bureaucrats are collectives with their own norms, values, and cultures. Your peers at work can inspire or exhaust you. Your office's culture can empower or suffocate you.

This chapter is devoted to what management can do to shape their team's culture, including influencing relationships between peers. The actions of coworkers are in large part the product of broader organizational systems and culture. We'll also explore the importance of norms for sustaining mission motivation, as well as management's role in crafting, and when necessary, changing them.

Mission Driven Bureaucrats. Dan Honig, Oxford University Press. © Oxford University Press 2024.
DOI: 10.1093/oso/9780197641194.003.0005

Motivation Is a Team—and System—Game

Peer networks matter greatly to an employee's motivation, forming an important source of connection for Mission Driven Bureaucrats. At their best, peers can encourage a sense of focus, camaraderie, and teamwork to achieve a common purpose.

The power of peers as a motivational force is supported by the original research referred to in the last two chapters. Chapter 3's high-performing Thai bureaucrats talked explicitly and repeatedly about tight-knit "teams" and "families" of vertical bureaucrats, which emerged despite these bureaucrats' reporting to different Bangkok-based ministries. Chapter 3 also documented how a peer-to-peer training program facilitated mission motivation among teachers in Bangladesh. Similarly, for Chapter 4's fast-stream civil servants in Ghana, more positive feeling toward peers was associated with increases in mission motivation over time.[3] In contrast, many ex-employees of Detroit Child Protective Services cited the burnout they observed in their peers as an important factor in their decision to exit.

Research from a range of settings illustrates the power of peer networks. John DiIulio argues that peers are critical to sustaining organizational culture and professional pride among US prison guards. Marc Esteve and coauthors find that highly mission-motivated individuals in the Netherlands "act even more prosocially when the other members of the group show prosocial behavior as well."[4] Military esprit de corps is similarly sustained by peer communities.[5] An excellent way to motivate Samirs, it appears, is to surround them with Binas. Many wise managers already know this to be true and act intentionally to cultivate peer communities.

Leveraging the large-N dataset with 4 million individual observations first introduced in Chapter 3, I find that perceptions of the performance of one's coworkers is a strong predictor of one's job satisfaction and mission motivation.[6] Employees' positive perception of their peers are more strongly associated with greater mission motivation than their perception of their managers. On an agency level as positive perceptions of peers rises, so too does mission motivation.

Empowerment through Peer Learning and Accountability

We have already seen how the good performance of coworkers can inspire an employee to apply greater effort in their own work. Employees can also learn from one another's mistakes or challenges to improve their own skills, cultivating a sense of competence. These processes stimulate the collective growth of public sector units, developing their capacities as a team to deliver services to citizens. For instance, surrounding low-performing teachers with more effective colleagues can lead to marked improvements in their performance.[7]

Many medical systems initiate peer discussions, a simple tool to tap the benefits of peer learning and accountability. Doctors collectively discuss patients who have had poor outcomes. This not only improves the judgment of the doctor directly involved in a given case but also engages an entire team of medical staff in a collective learning process that benefits all their future work.

The US city of Seattle tried a similar model for health inspectors responsible for identifying health and safety violations in restaurants.[8] In a randomized controlled trial, some of Seattle's health inspectors were assigned to discuss each other's findings as part of the formal inspection process. It turns out that there are a great many number of judgment calls to be made in health inspections. Discussing these decisions with peers led to more confident results, increasing the number of violations found and reducing variability across inspectors.[9] Better enforcement of health codes in turn increased citizens' health. As Ho puts it, "peer review as a governance institution can work to improve the accuracy and consistency of administering the law . . . there is little reason for the myriad of agencies with decentralized decision-making *not* to explore, pilot, and test a peer review model."[10] Citizens were made healthier by formalizing ways for peers to learn from each other. Peer networks can increase mission motivation by cultivating competence and connection to peers and purpose.

Discussing one's decisions with a peer, a trusted fellow professional, is also a way of being held to account for one's actions.[11] I've often suggested to policymakers that they should stop thinking of "accountability" only as "accounting" with metrics and targets. Accountability can be a broader process of employees "giving account," justifying their actions and how they contributed performance.[12] I've found that when I succeed even slightly in promoting this perspective, it suddenly seems almost obvious that peer networks are critical tools for building accountability. Peer review systems are excellent ways for employees to foster shared values of excellence.

This pattern is not confined by any means to the public sector. As Claudine Gartenberg and coauthors put it in a study of corporate purpose in the private sector, "high-purpose" (mission-driven) organizations are places where high levels of camaraderie sustain a sense of purpose.[13] Mission-motivating peer networks are arguably all the more important when the purpose of one's work is to promote the welfare of citizens. This is true even when multiple firms are involved—with good performance in collaborative projects in part a function of strong relationships of trust and horizontal accountability among coworkers, implementers, and other stakeholders.[14] It seems that like motivation, accountability is also a team game. Peer accountability networks can be drivers of excellent performance.

Peer networks help ensure employees remain committed to their team's mission. As one group of prominent scholars puts it, "bureaucratic professionalization is a contagious—and thus self-reinforcing—process inside government."[15] John Brehm and Scott Gates conducted studies in over three dozen US agencies, finding that "attitudes about professionalism tend to come more from fellow subordinates than from supervisors on the job."[16] This influences both the effort and performance of employees. As they put it, "we have strong evidence of the effects of fellow subordinates upon a bureaucrat's performance. Solidary preferences were consistently strong determinants of the reasons why a subordinate would work."[17]

These positive peer influences need not be confined to a single workplace. Communities of practice bring together networks of people doing similar work to share their experiences.[18] Work with the UK National Health Service suggests that members exchange "tools" and share tacit knowledge from their work.[19] They "think together" in the way often associated with a supportive team working relationship.[20] Communities of practice cultivate a joint sense of professionalism and purpose. They sustain mission motivation and improve performance.[21]

When people work hard and well, they do so partly because of their commitment to a team—their workplace or their professional community—that they feel a responsibility to honor. This helps reinforce their commitment to their mission point. People will act in service of their organization's mission because their broader community also does so.

Culture and Norms as Drivers of Mission Motivation and Performance

Norms are the shared values and standards of behavior that define a team's identity. Norms are powerful. They shape the actions of present employees, who embody the values expected of a member of their team. They also influence the behavior of future employees, who are socialized to conform to those norms. The norms of a team can significantly influence its performance. This has been foundational knowledge in the private sector management literature for decades.[22]

Norms of empowerment that allow autonomy, cultivate competence, and create connection to peers and purpose can help teams unlock mission motivation and improve performance. In a study of the marked differences in primary education within and across Indian states, Akshay Mangla concludes that norms are often the key differentiator between high-performing and low-performing agencies. High-performing agencies tend to pride "deliberative norms" that privilege discussion, debate, and mutual engagement among bureaucrats and with citizens.[23] Mangla contrasts this with legalistic norms that focus on compliance and the execution of rules, which disempowers both bureaucrats and citizens.[24]

Deliberative norms matter because they "influence the collective understandings and behaviors of officials. Given resource constraints and multiple policy rules, norms allow bureaucrats to interpret policy problems in a practical sense and determine what it means to solve them."[25] These norms strengthen peer accountability, boosting performance.[26] Mangla finds that deliberative norms are especially useful when tasks are difficult to codify, specify ahead of time, and monitor effectively. This echoes Bernardo Zacka's work in a US social support agency, where caseworkers often struggle to fulfill the needs of clients with the complex rules that govern the work. Zacka finds that these competing needs are best managed when workers collaborate actively with their peers, discussing tensions and receiving not just technical, but also emotional, support.[27]

Norms can also influence how bureaucrats interact with citizens. Mangla highlights how norms of deliberation affect the performance of Indian schools by "shaping the ordinary interactions between frontline officials and citizens. As citizens gain exposure to the local state, their experiences condition future expectations and the collective monitoring of schools, impacting the quality of services."[28] Deliberative norms, and empowering cultures more broadly, alter bureaucrats' understandings of their jobs. They encourage bureaucrats to see their job as working "for" and "with" citizens, not just delivering "to" them or complying with formal rules and regulations. This in turn improves the quality of services.

Compliance-Oriented Cultures: A Central Challenge for Public Sector Managers

Undesirable norms can derail a team's performance. One of the most pernicious effects of a compliance-oriented culture is what Mark Smith, the head of public service reform for the English council of Gateshead near Newcastle, calls "defaulting to no, resorting to yes."[29] A system steeped in compliance is one in which individuals will often internalize that there is only one type of "risk" worth worrying about—the risk of doing something that is later judged to have been outside the rules.

Compliance-oriented systems often have a norm of risk aversion that very clearly precludes actions that are in fact permitted and would likely enhance performance, or increase value for money. I have a great many times observed bureaucrats interpret procurement or operational rules even more restrictively than the letter of the rule—refusing to engage in clearly permissible actions because of a fear of even approaching the boundary of what is allowed. In this way, compliance-oriented systems can become even *more* compliance-oriented, autonomy-constraining, and disempowering than legislators or senior officials intend.

This risk aversion often filters through the broader compliance-oriented organization. An HR officer is likely to take a conservative view about what hiring processes must be followed (e.g., whether motivation can be considered when bringing on new staff). A manager is likely to take a conservative view on what she needs to report to her bosses regarding her team's performance, focusing on what can easily be quantified and verified. This manager in turn is going to demand that her team meet target after target so she'll have data to report, even when this takes their attention away from other important tasks.

When governments "contract out" or hire external firms to provide services, this compliance-oriented culture is often perpetuated.[30] Where compliance-oriented cultures dominate, contractors are likely to take cues from their government clients and focus on complying with their contract rather than fulfilling the intended mission as and when there is tension between the contract and the mission.

In *Recoding America*, Jennifer Pahlka describes how this phenomenon unfolded in US government during her time as deputy chief technology officer under President Obama.[31] As she put it in an interview with the *New York Times*'s Ezra Klein, "the culture has definitely evolved to highlight any deviance from process and make it very, very risky."[32]

Pahlka describes a guidance document that required software built for the US government to be interoperable (able to talk to other platforms).[33] The original document listed one strategy as an example: using Enterprise Service Buses (ESB), which help software components communicate and share data. Technologically, ESBs turned out to be a slow and cumbersome way of achieving interoperability. Indeed, there was no requirement to use them. But because they appeared as an example in one federal guidance document, they became a requirement in others, and when the government went to ask private providers to build software, many agencies required that the private providers add ESBs. This made software slow and unusable—something literally no one had intended, least of all the policymakers who had first asked for software interoperability.[34] Pahlka describes that environment as one in which "culture eats policy"—much less flexibility existed in practice than was intended by policymakers.[35]

Both contractors delivering services and the bureaucrats supervising them frequently have little autonomy. As Klein put it when describing Pahlka's work, "the people delivering often don't have any power. They don't have power to interpret the language they're given. They don't have power to say no to the lawyers. There's nobody empowered over a process to [ensure that process is] flexible."[36] In Pahlka's account, this resulted in precisely what I would predict: the exit of the mission-motivated, who left in frustration because they felt unable to help citizens.[37]

Compliance-oriented management is often embedded in deeper compliance-oriented norms. There are indeed unmotivated Peters in the world, people who will "work just hard enough to not get fired," to quote the fictional Peter Gibbons from *Office Space* after whom I named the archetype. But some people will truly *own* the rules. They will come to think that complying with the rules is the same as doing their best possible work and serving their organization's mission.

I feel saddest about the state of the bureaucracy when I meet a bureaucrat who seems to *really* care—to act earnestly even in the absence of oversight—appear engaged in enforcing tedious processes rather than fulfilling their mission point. They remind me of airport security employees who insist that because only 3 ounces of a liquid can be allowed through security, you must throw out your nearly empty 4 ounce bottle.

How do we resolve this problem? I think the answer lies in reinforcing missions and empowering employees that want to serve those missions. We have to move away from processes and toward outcomes. Luckily, this is possible. Once one starts to look for it, there are examples all around. In a common Hollywood plot, a team starts out demotivated and dysfunctional. But by building peer accountability and cultivating motivation, the team changes both individually and collectively, accomplishing more than they could have dreamed.[38] Coaching is essential in catalyzing this change.

An excellent example comes from TV's *Ted Lasso*. The show revolves around an American coach leading a fictional UK premiere league football team, AFC Richmond.[39] Ted improves his team's performance not by knowing anything about football, but rather by changing team norms and building strong links between players. In Season 3, Ted abruptly changes his team's tactics mid-season, adopting an improvisational, player-empowering system known as "Total Football." Many think this is sure to fail, but a journalist who is following the team has a flash of insight. "You haven't switched tactics in a week," the journalist tells Ted. "You've done it in three seasons."[40] The journalist elaborates that this three-season transformation occurred "by slowly but surely building a club-wide culture of trust and support through thousands of imperceptible moments, all leading to their inevitable conclusion."[41]

Management can be that coach who transforms their agency's norms. They will be most successful when they do so with intention and purpose. Managers can facilitate peer networks and create an environment in which new ways of working—new cultures—will take root. These reforms need not necessarily (and certainly not exclusively) focus on reducing compliance but can instead aim to increase empowerment-oriented management. As Part I of this book discussed, management for empowerment can often be increased without changing formal compliance procedures in any way.

One example of this comes from STiR, the program introduced in Chapter 3 that aims to kindle teachers' intrinsic motivation in Uganda, India, and Indonesia. STiR operates in part by bringing teachers, school leaders, district officials, and others together in a single forum to discuss performance, management, and motivation. This is not a one-off event. Meetings occur on a regular basis in an effort to change actors' collective understandings of what their work in education is truly about. Their journey starts by shifting workplace norms and culture—and ends by immensely improving performance.[42]

Changing Culture by Centering Citizens: Empowering Bureaucrats Can Empower Citizens, Too

When bureaucrats are confronted by compliance-oriented norms, they often act in ways that undermine rather than enhance citizens' welfare. One striking example in Pahlka's book comes from the US Department of Veterans Affairs. An IT system meant to facilitate veterans' applications for benefits was not working. Veterans faced error messages and were unable to complete their applications over and over again.[43] Pahlka's team was sent in to solve the problem.

Under the compliance-oriented norms of US government procurement, however, there *was* no problem—the software delivered by the contractor was in accordance with their technical requirements. Pahlka's team was "literally told there was no work to be done because the requirements in the contract had all been fulfilled and all the boxes had been checked."[44] Anyone who cares about government performance would surely disagree; veterans still could not actually file applications for benefits. This had real-world consequences. At the time, eighteen veterans were committing suicide a day, many while still waiting for benefits like mental health treatment.[45]

What changed? Two of Pahlka's colleagues recorded a video of a veteran named Dominic encountering errors and being unable to complete his application over and over again.[46] They showed that video to senior agency leaders.

All of a sudden, compliance with the terms of their contract was no longer the central concern of the agency. Bureaucrats received the autonomy they needed to actually fix the problem. A new and improved application was rapidly rolled out, with a central focus on user experience.[47] Veterans were able to file for the benefits they were due, improving their health and welfare.

Focusing on citizens' needs and shifting away from compliance-oriented norms can be key to solve many public sector problems. You might recall the English council of Gateshead mentioned earlier in this chapter, whose system "defaulted to no."[48] The council frequently struggled to requisition support for their clients quickly.

Mark Smith and his team managed to resolve Gateshead's problems using a distinctly empowerment-oriented approach. Key to their strategy was offering caseworkers autonomy. Caseworkers were issued procurement cards with which to spend small amounts of government money on food, clothing, and temporary electricity for citizens in need.[49] They also used this money to help socially iso-lated citizens engage with the wider world—buying them a bus pass, or coffee, or accompanying them somewhere they needed to go.[50] Gateshead's reforms helped build trust between citizens and caseworkers.[51] This was coupled with a careful learning process to figure out what was actually helping citizens, and how this support could be made more impactful.[52] Smith described their strategies as "lib-erated methods of engagement and support between caseworkers and citizens."[53]

Gateshead's reforms improved welfare outcomes for citizens, including by greatly reducing evictions. Caseworkers spent more money engaging with clients upstream, but this reduced the usage of emergency healthcare, ensuring net savings for the local government, not to mention cultivating a happier and healthier community.[54] The strong relationships forged between autonomous caseworkers and citizens were central to the reforms' success. As Smith put it, "Even when we get things wrong, the humanity of it helps."[55] Those relationships acted almost like antibodies, resisting unhelpful compliance-oriented norms and enabling bureaucrats to promote their citizens' welfare.

Mangla's study of Indian schools, introduced earlier in this chapter, provides another example of the benefits of strengthening citizen-bureaucrat relationships. Mangla describes how deliberative norms that privilege discussion, debate, and mutual engagement enabled active participation by bureaucrats in Mother Teacher Associations. These community fora were not just for gathering citizen input, but for making consequential decisions.[56] Moving away from compliance often involves shifting real power toward frontline operators and citizens— allowing them autonomy. Mangla notes that this effect is not limited to schools. He documents how a women's empowerment program, Mahila Samkhya, created structures that encouraged the emergence of deliberative norms, shifting the state toward more genuine and fulsome engagement with citizens over time.[57] This shift was in part initiated by mission-motivated "local fieldworkers committed to reform, [who] promoted girls' education by mobilizing marginalized citizens and mediating local conflicts."[58] Mission Driven Bureaucrats often want, and will seek out, this citizen engagement.

Management practice toward bureaucrats can translate into bureaucrats' engagement with citizens. When management treats bureaucrats as individuals who must be made to comply, this encourages those bureaucrats to treat citizens similarly. If bureaucrats are assessed based on their delivery of easily monitored metrics (e.g., number of clients seen), they will focus on those numbers. Treating bureaucrats as rich and complex beings who ought to be empowered enables them to treat citizens with the same respect and dignity.

Bureaucratic Empowerment Can Improve Citizen Relations Even When the Work Involves Conflict

My office at University College London sits in the London borough of Camden. Like Detroit and most cities around the world, Camden has to confront issues related to child protection. But Camden takes a very different approach to safeguarding vulnerable children than does my hometown of Detroit, where we saw Child Protective Services specialists labor under a heavily compliance-oriented system.

Camden is focused on bringing citizens and bureaucrats together to make collective decisions under long-term partnerships.[59] An important part is the borough's use of Family Group Conferences (FGCs), in which social workers and families meet to discuss the difficult and contentious topic of child welfare concerns in their households.[60] Research on the FGC model describes it in part as a response to social workers who "may be disempowered by system regulations and oppressive structures," and the realization that "there are negative consequences for caseworkers—and the clients they serve—when the agencies and organizations for which they work promote only formal legal, administrative, and expert-dominated solutions to problems of child maltreatment."[61]

FGCs leave much to the empowered judgment of the social worker. They require management that allows autonomy, cultivates competence, and particularly creates connection. Indeed, the core focus of FGCs is the long-term relationships of trust and empowerment between social workers and families.[62] In these meetings, "professionals play the role of information giver, community organizer, lender of their expertise, and resource provider based on family identified needs, contradicting decades of practices and beliefs."[63] Changing the standard practices of a compliance-oriented system is a slow process, requiring time and reinforcement. Nevertheless, it is one that social workers and families both find empowering, and that sustains mission motivation.[64]

FGCs, coupled with other empowering managerial changes, appear to have made a remarkable impact.[65] Since their rollout in 2014, the rate of children pulled from homes in Camden has fallen by more than 40 percent, and children in foster care by nearly 50 percent.[66]

While it is possible that other factors might have caused these improved outcomes, Camden's empowerment-oriented approach is surely an important driver.[67] This is evidenced in part by Camden parents' lived experience with child services, compared to the experiences we observed in Detroit. Before FGC intervention, one parent whose children were removed from her care remarked, "I was stood in court and told I could not parent adequately."[68] With FGC, she has come to question that assessment—"Was it that I couldn't parent adequately, or was that I just needed a little bit of time??"[69] FGC has helped her build relationships with child services over the long term. As she described, "my support network [now] is primarily social workers—which is shocking."[70] I suspect Detroit Child Protective Services workers would share that shock—and dream of a system that celebrates relationships between social workers and parents.

Even in a Compliance-Oriented System, Managing for Empowerment Can Improve Things

Changing a compliance-oriented culture does not have to happen at the agency level. Managers can also work within the system to change their teams' norms at a smaller scale. Erin McDonnell's *Patchwork Leviathan*, for example, identifies "pockets of bureaucratic effectiveness in developing states."[71] Her work draws on a variety of evidence from different contexts including banking regulators in Brazil, courts in Ghana, agricultural development agencies in Kenya, food and drug regulators in Nigeria, and commodity standards monitors in China. These are all high-performing units and agencies, situated within systems whose overall performance left much to be desired. McDonnell terms these "pockets of excellence."[72] But how do these pockets emerge and persist?

McDonnell highlights the importance of management practice that empowers its members to take collective ownership and internalize a commitment to the organization's goals. As she puts it, "If you let a small group of officials make important, consequential decisions about how a house will be built, they will defend it for a lifetime."[73] The same can be said for staff who are able to define how a mission point is served.

As McDonnell demonstrates, managers do so in part by cultivating new empowerment-oriented norms.[74] They engage in what McDonnell calls "boundary marking"—making clear that their team is different, and managed differently too, from others in the agency.[75] These managers also work to protect their team from compliance-oriented pressures that might otherwise undermine performance.[76]

Developing and reinforcing a clear mission point is another way that managers can build a mission-motivated culture and a strong team identity. As Paul Zak put it, "people are substantially more motivated by their organization's transcendent purpose (how it improves lives) than by its transactional purpose."[77] Managers can be proactive in reinforcing this narrative among employees, "devising mechanisms that relentlessly communicate the organization's mission in ways that not only clearly articulate what the [team] hopes to accomplish, but also how the [team] hopes to accomplish it and why such accomplishments benefit the community it services."[78] As a group of leading public management scholars put it, managers can "model behaviors that reinforce that vision, and help employees build confidence and pride in the organization goals and activities."[79]

Managers can create thriving, mission-driven teams even within broader institutional environments that would otherwise be demotivating. This is exactly what I found in the Thai districts introduced in Chapter 3. Burdened by political turmoil from the top and an extremely centralized government structure, it would have been easy for Thai bureaucrats to grow disillusioned at the state of their bureaucracy. However, their managers instead built cohesive and mission-motivated teams at the district level—by acting, in the words of one bureaucrat, not like "boss[es]" but like "coordinator[s] of a team." In turn, employees demonstrated remarkably high levels of mission motivation and job satisfaction,[80] sustaining Thailand's impressive development progress.[81] Mission-driven teams can become beacons of excellent performance within institutionally challenging environments.[82]

This is good news for managers and team leaders, especially those operating within heavily compliance-laden governments. Institutional change can be extremely difficult; a manager may have little say over the actions of her superiors. The influence of team culture and team-level norms means that managers can focus their energy on building the team that *they* lead, however small, into a haven for Mission Driven Bureaucrats. Proliferating norms of empowerment can be an excellent way for managers to reliably boost their team's motivation and performance.

Reforming Mission Points by Shifting Norms

Norms don't always serve the public interest—and importantly, neither do the mission points that these teams serve. Mission points are the objective of a team or agency, as understood by those who work there. In this book, we've seen plenty of bureaucracies pursuing missions that I suspect most readers will think are good. However, mission points are not always good, and in such cases, neither is the pursuit of them.

There is an important but tricky distinction to make between the problems of corruption and the possession of a sinister mission point. Some agencies may serve a wonderful and noble mission point, such as educating children, but be plagued by actors who siphon funds for their own personal gain. Other agencies may boast devoted and highly mission-driven employees but serve a mission point that is itself problematic. Such agencies face a larger challenge than simply reducing corrupt acts by individual actors. Rather, the agency's mission point itself requires reform.

Citizens may reasonably disagree about what serves their long-term welfare, or whose welfare deserves precedence—the rich or poor, current or future generations. We can also disagree about whether politicians seeking changes have a legitimate basis for shifting agencies' missions.[83] Bureaucrats or agencies may be involved in this contestation. Finance ministry officials may oppose an expansionary fiscal policy that privileges full employment over debt minimization. Trade promotion officials may not wish to consider the environmental sustainability of investments in determining whether an inward investment is worthy of government support. Border patrol officials may resist changes to migrant and refugee enforcement policies. Police officers may be discriminatory against some citizens and resist attempts to alter their behavior.

Shifting an agency's mission point is no easy task. As noted in Chapter 2, mission points are self-reinforcing and relatively stable, and people apply for jobs at organizations whose mission point they believe in. Once hired, entrants are socialized to believe in this mission point and observe the norms of the organization. Those who reject the mission point are more likely to exit, further reinforcing the status quo. Empowerment-oriented managerial strategies encourage bureaucrats to forward their mission points, even where those mission points are morally repugnant.

To take one of history's most extreme examples, the German bureaucracy during the Nazi era appears to have had quite a bit of empowerment-oriented management.[84] This was "effective" in the narrow sense of helping agencies fulfill their terrible goals. Route E was effective in this context in large part because a careful and intentional political process had purged the bureaucracy of Weimar-era appointees who would have resisted the Nazis' mission point.[85] The Nazi government worked very hard to replace these dismissed bureaucrats with loyal—I might even say mission-motivated—members of the Nazi party.[86] The more Mission Driven Bureaucrats are devoted to an existing mission point and empowered to support it, the more potential changes will be resisted. The bureaucracy thus often acts as a counterweight against change. Mission-driven "ownership" of the status quo can make it very difficult to intentionally alter a mission point—but not impossible.

As we will see in the next profile, Judy Parfitt was tasked with reforming an agency populated by employees who were hired during the Apartheid era in South Africa. She needed to reform its mission point to serve all the citizens of South Africa. It may seem unlikely that Judy would be able to reform the agency's culture and practices without starting with a fresh slate of new staff. However, Judy and her unit successfully reformed the agency's norms and boosted its performance by changing employees' understanding of their work, by cultivating competence, and by creating a new team identity.

Attempts to shift mission points can occur through either Route C or Route E, just as with managerial reforms. A compliance-oriented Route C reform could involve the external, top-down imposition of a new mission point. This would likely be accompanied by monitoring regimes to ensure that employees comply with the new mission. In contrast, an empowerment-oriented Route E reform could involve recruiting new staff aligned with the new mission point and a process of encouragement, suggestion, and consensus-building with existing staff. This is the approach that Judy and her colleagues largely took in South Africa. As with managerial reforms more broadly, the best reform of an agency's mission point depends on the nature of its employees and the monitorability of the behaviors that one seeks to change.

Let's take a closer look at one sector where agencies have mission points that many believe are in need of reform: US police forces. While keeping citizens safe might certainly be a noble mission point, many Americans believe their police forces systematically discriminate against non-White members of the community. Mass protests and broad social movements have articulated the need for reform; I vehemently agree.[87]

In their work on bureaucracy, Brehm and Gates highlight the importance of peer networks and norms in sustaining the deeply troubling status quo for US policing. As they put it, "when the preferences of fellow subordinates were consistent with the preferences of the public, then subordinates can be a positive influence. When the preferences of subordinates run counter to the public, and when those subordinates are in a state of great uncertainty, then the role of fellow subordinates can lead to such disastrous breaches of civic authority as police brutality."[88] Peer learning can "teach" the wrong things—employees can be influenced to model both the desirable and undesirable behaviors of their colleagues. The norms that typify an organization's culture influence whether an individual will participate in malfeasance.

Given the deep-seated nature of the problem, police reforms have often attempted to shift conduct through monitoring and compliance. The logic is clear and understandable: the problem is the officers' behavior, so let's force them to change that behavior. Route C reform strategies range from civilian review boards, to new reporting requirements, to body cameras. Laudable though the goal may be, these Route C reforms have precious little to show for all their time and effort.

Despite being adopted by over 80 percent of large American police departments, body cameras appear to have had little to no effect on officer behavior on average.[89] The prospect of civilian accountability for their behavior in arrests may lead police officers to pursue criminals less vigorously, enabling criminal activity. After all, officers cannot be held accountable for an arrest they fail to make. In Los Angeles, these review boards have done just that, resulting in fewer criminal arrests.[90]

I believe that there is a strong argument for pursuing Route E strategies to shift US police department mission points. Rather than relying on "good but not great" monitoring, managers could focus on changing the norms of behavior that typify US police departments. This could involve recruiting and retaining those who truly believe in the reformed "mission point" of a fair and just police force. This could also involve socializing these norms more broadly across policy forces

My Georgetown colleague Andrea Headley has published a series of papers that explore the impact of hiring more representative police officers in the United States.[91] In one she and a coauthor assess the benefits of hiring Black officers in the overwhelming White police department of New Orleans, whose residents are also mostly Black, on officer conduct.[92] Recruiting officers aligned with the desired mission point is important, these papers find. However, it appears that this strategy works only when officers are also given sufficient autonomy and empowering managerial support; "in the absence of substantial discretion, Black officers may conform to traditional police culture and norms that have been known to favor White civilians."[93] There is no disputing that officers' use of their autonomy and discretion in discriminatory ways is part of the problem. Nevertheless, this autonomy is also part of the solution, empowering reformist officers to make a real impact.

Interestingly, when reform-minded officers have been hired and empowered, civilian review boards *do* seem to help encourage equitable behavior by police officers.[94] This suggests that a compliance-oriented accountability tool, like civilian review boards, can complement the empowerment of reformers inside the system. Compliance-based oversight can be part of the solution—but only a part. These strategies need to work together in what Jonathan Fox has termed a "sandwich strategy," one in which mission-motivated bureaucrats, engaged citizens, and accountability of bureaucrats directly to citizens collectively produce cultural change and improved performance.[95]

If compliance-oriented management could get us the police departments that citizens deserve, I would be all for it. But in policing, as in Indian primary education, Detroit Child Protective Services, Thai district governance, and well beyond, it appears that compliance cannot take us to the destination we seek. We need to change the behavior of bureaucrats when they are unobserved and unobservable, not just when they can be actively monitored. Achieving the change we seek likely requires an empowerment-oriented approach.

Conclusion: It's Systems All the Way Down

This chapter has focused on how peers and organizational norms can affect the motivation and performance of employees. Fortunately, peer relations and norms can also be changed, including through the interventions of supervisors. Of course, it's rarely possible for a team leader, middle manager, or agency leader to transform their agency on their own. Mission motivation depends on many things. Agency reputation, salaries, career concerns, and a myriad other factors influence the extent to which employees will be mission-motivated. These vary between and within agencies, teams, and tasks.

A long tradition in political science makes clear that agencies often face political limits regarding what managerial reforms are possible in the real world. Not all technically optimal solutions are politically feasible. Agencies are sometimes intentionally under-resourced or managed in compliance-oriented ways because of legislatures, executives, and other stakeholders who are opposed to seek to undermine the agency's work.[96]

Nevertheless, it is rarely the case that a manager or a peer can do *nothing* to help her team become more mission-motivated. Some reforms indeed lie outside the boundary of what is politically possible. But *loads* of positive things can be done within those limits—including changing management practices to build peer networks, improve culture, and shift norms to support Mission Driven Bureaucrats. In my experience, very few agencies are anywhere near the limits of what is politically possible.

The bureaucracy may seem like a giant, complex, and constantly shifting machine. Thinking of the bureaucracy in these terms can make institutional change sound practically impossible, especially for a single reformer. But the big system of the government is composed of little ones. At those smaller system levels, there's almost always good work to be done in improving team-level performance. As Judy explains in the profile that follows, changing an agency's norms requires thinking about how to change not just observable behaviors, but the attitudes and mindsets of employees. It is about the heads and hearts, not just the observable hands, of bureaucrats.

While I've touched on the performance benefits of managing for empowerment throughout, the last few chapters have primarily focused on how more empowerment-oriented reforms can improve the mission motivation of bureaucrats. Chapter 6 explores when and how managing for empowerment will translate into improved performance—and ultimately, better lives for the citizens and residents public agencies serve.

Profile: Judy Parfitt

*Shifting Mission Points and Cultivating Mission Motivation in
the South African Revenue Service (HR Director)*

"How you will benefit, how the organization will benefit, how the
country will benefit?"

In 1998, Judy Parfitt took a role in the South African Revenue Service (SARS).
Judy arrived when formal Apartheid in South Africa had recently ended. With
a new government under Nelson Mandela and a new mission for this public
agency, the scale of change that was needed was "radically ambitious." Judy
joined as the director of human resources just as the agency was starting to plan
these large-scale reforms.

Judy was initially hesitant to leave the private sector but was persuaded by
the new leadership that there was meaningful work to be done. The new SARS
commissioner, Pravin Gordhan, was "really accomplished at mobilizing and
galvanizing people." In convincing Judy to join, Gordhan passionately explained
"the critical role that SARS could play in creating a better life for all, because to
the extent that revenue administration improved—and there was a lot that could
be improved—that would swell state coffers and social spending would increase,
which could help to redress some of the many wrongs of the Apartheid era," Judy
recounts.

When Judy accepted SARS's job offer, she was attracted by the idea of
reforming the tax agency to motivate employees to serve "a higher purpose" of
a new South Africa. Her choice illustrates that Mission Driven Bureaucrats are
attracted to workplaces that share their values and goal of serving the public.
Judy chose the agency as much as SARS chose her.

Judy entered an incredibly challenging environment. She vividly remembers
"walking into my office on the first day of work and wondering what I'd let myself in for." The atmosphere was stuffy and oppressive, the culture hierarchical.

On her first day, she recalls, "my secretary came in, and the first question she asked me was *'What tea set would you like? When you become a senior manager, you get to choose your own tea set.'*" Judy was also greeted by not one, but two coat stands—"[my secretary] said it was because I was on a particular level that I was entitled to two."

Most of SARS's 13,000 employees had been hired under the Apartheid regime. While serving in that government, they were rewarded for loyalty, not competence, in administering the country's tax system and customs service. There was little mission-driven action. People "progressed through the ranks just by staying [at SARS]." Employees were incentivized based on total revenue raised—service, enforcement, and quality-related measures were neglected. The agency was also failing to meet revenue targets, and salaries and promotions were typically unrelated to performance. These practices were negatively impacting the department's ability to execute its mandate and serve the South African public.

Judy worked with Commissioner Gordhan to "radically restructure the organization." They called the transformation program Siyakha, a Zulu word meaning "we are building"; their mission statement was "Build SARS, build the nation."

All HR policies were revised. Competency assessments and a new focus on diversity became part of recruitment and selection processes. The number of job levels was dramatically reduced, new remuneration policies and practices were introduced, and a new HR IT system was implemented.

Achieving shifts in management practice and norms requires thinking about how to change not just observable behaviors, but the understandings of the staff, as discussed in the previous chapter. The new leadership at SARS had to convince employees that their purpose was to serve *all* South African citizens.

A drastic change in mindset was also required in the customs arm of the agency. It needed to move away from a focus on busting international sanctions imposed because of international opposition to Apartheid, and toward a focus on implementing trade agreements. As the organization's mission point shifted, leadership shifted to manage for empowerment.

A key initial step in the transformation program was the reconstitution of the executive team, followed by a requiring that most managers reapply for their jobs. A "jobs for votes" norm had applied previously, resulting in managers and staff that were aligned with the old Apartheid-era government. Now SARS managers were required to successfully complete competency assessments of leadership attributes. The introduction of these assessments significantly increased the diversity of managers appointed by the agency. Long-serving managers who demonstrated the competencies required and embraced SARS's transformation goals were rewarded with value-adding roles in the new structure.

Since winning over staff to the new vision was a critical step in SARS's reform process, its new leadership organized coffee chats with small groups of employees. The goal was to help dissenters understand and embrace the new mission and norms and leave behind the organization's old practices.

Judy remembers, "it felt important to persuade long-serving White Afrikaans-speaking employees who had considerable institutional knowledge that they still had a place in the sun in the new SARS—if they signed up to our goals and ambitions." Those goals were made clear and uncompromising. Having a well-defined mission and team identity can facilitate mission motivation. After clarifying SARS's goals, the message to employees was clear: "get on board or be left behind."

These changes were paired with other reforms, including more competitive salaries. SARS also ended automatic promotion based on years of service, made the organization less hierarchical, and introduced a "leadership competency framework"—rewarding merit and ability, not simply seniority. Throughout the reform process, Judy's unit carefully collaborated with the two trade unions recognized by SARS. After reaching an agreement that guaranteed employment security in exchange for employee flexibility in relation to what work they did, and where, when, and how they did it, the leadership of both the agency and the trade unions did a roadshow explaining the reforms. As Judy put it, "if we get this right, this is how you will benefit, this is how SARS will benefit, and this is how the country will benefit—everyone will benefit" from these reforms.

An empowering management approach that created connection to impact and cultivated competence improved the mission motivation of existing staff. In large-scale change, Judy explains, "typically you have a band of disciples and evangelists and a small number of radical dissenters or saboteurs. Many people are largely undecided, and this is where the focus needs to be—on winning them over." There was no need for major layoffs, despite the massive changes in the organization's mission and management approach.

Early successes helped to win over initially undecided employees. At SARS, eventually, "the majority of the employees started to believe in and identify with this purpose of creating a better life for all." The management team at SARS also capitalized on the "sheer momentum of the change and the success" that it found early, to help this middle group lean toward the new mission. Even in this possibly unlikely setting (given the Apartheid history of personnel), most of the staff turned out to be mission-motivateable Samirs.

These achievements were reinforced by external praise. President Mandela came to congratulate the staff. He praised their work and "what their good efforts [would] do for nation-building in South Africa." Their work meant that "extra schools and clinics could be built, roads could be paved, and other social services previously withheld from the majority of the population could be provided." This became an important source of pride and reinforced staff mission motivation.

SARS was able to move from a procedure-oriented work culture to a culture of empowerment where mission-driven behavior became the norm. SARS's mission point was changed, as were broader norms, by managerial reforms. The results were impressive: SARS exceeded its revenue targets for the first time in anyone's memory. Four years after she joined an agency that had been embedded in the Apartheid government and plagued by poor performance, Judy marveled at her employees and co-workers—they were, on the whole, "so competent, so committed, and so effective."

Pathways from Managing for Empowerment and Managing for Compliance to Results

> [Compliance-oriented] Theory X offers management an easy rationalization for ineffective organizational performance: It is due to the nature of the human resources with which we must work. [Empowerment-oriented] Theory Y, on the other hand, places the problems squarely in the lap of management. If employees are lazy, indifferent, unwilling to take responsibility, intransigent, uncreative, uncooperative, Theory Y implies that the causes lie in management's methods of organization and control.
>
> —Douglas McGregor, *The Human Side of Enterprise*[1]

> I am of the opinion that no matter how much money you spend, how beautiful your schools are or how good your courses are, unless you show your teachers respect and involve them in decision-making, no work on education is possible. The teacher is not a delivery person. Teachers are institutions that convey the knowledge of one generation to another, point out the faults of the previous system to the next generation and develop new knowledge.
>
> —Sisodia 2019, as quoted in Aiyar et al., *Rewriting the Grammar of the Education System*[2]

The last three chapters have focused on how management practices—the actions of managers, organizational leaders, peers, and other actors in the system—can nurture Mission Driven Bureaucrats. Management for empowerment can increase mission motivation, attract mission-motivated employees, and build mission-oriented teams. Empowerment-oriented management is also likely to lead to a better workplace experience for public servants. I suspect many readers will think this is lovely, but not as important as what the public sector produces for citizens. This chapter examines when and where empowering managerial reforms are likely to improve performance.

Mission Driven Bureaucrats. Dan Honig, Oxford University Press. © Oxford University Press 2024.
DOI: 10.1093/oso/9780197641194.003.0006

This chapter ultimately asks what combination of managerial strategies maximize performance for a given agency. We'll examine high-performing agencies that thrive at relatively empowerment-oriented (E) or compliance-oriented (C) managerial approaches, but also agencies that fail to deliver on their promises to the public. We then will consider attempts to improve performance, comparing Route E and Route C reforms in the rare instances where they have been trialed simultaneously. Finally, we look to a range of strategies that suggest that incorporating Route E need not entail abandoning existing compliance-oriented management.

High-Performing Agencies and Empowerment-Oriented Management

It is remarkable how frequently (academically) famous examples of high-performing public agencies are typified by Mission Driven Bureaucrats and empowerment-oriented management. Multiple generations of students have now had the pleasure of reading Herbert Kaufmann's classic account of US forest rangers.[3] In Kaufmann's account, what forest rangers do cannot be observed. Rangers are managed for empowerment, with a great deal of autonomy and a culture of commitment to organizational norms and the agency's mission point. Jon DiIulio argues that *esprit de corps* and mission motivation are essential to good performance in US prisons.[4] Similarly, Charles Goodsell finds that the highest-performing US public agencies empower mission-motivated individuals to autonomously exercise judgment in service of their mission, coupled with a broader culture that supports and reinforces that mission.[5] Goodsell's examples of high-performing agencies include a number of US federal agencies (such as the National Weather Service), but also state (e.g., the Virginia State Police) and local (e.g., Mecklenburg County, North Carolina's Department of Social Services) cases.[6] Dan Carpenter attributes the US Food and Drug Administration's excellent performance to the manner in which the agency's reputation for excellence allows organizational autonomy, in turn enabling empowerment-oriented managerial practices.[7] Collectively, these are a lot of agencies, doing a lot of different kinds of things. They are also all examples of organizations possessing strongly empowerment-oriented management practices.

The examples above are all in the United States, as the study of public agency performance has historically (and in my view, unfortunately) focused on the United States and other developed countries.[8] But to the limited extent that scholars have cast attention to the developing world, they have found that there, too, exceptionally good performance is often accompanied by empowerment-oriented management. As this book's introduction described, Judith Tendler's

Good Government in the Tropics found pockets of exceptionally high-performing agencies even in one of Brazil's historically least well governed states, Ceará. She attributed this performance in large part to empowerment of what this book has called Mission Driven Bureaucrats.[9]

Tendler was the rare scholar to highlight good public performance in the developing world, but she is not the only one. Merilee Grindle examined evidence from twenty-nine agencies responsible for elements of macroeconomic management, agricultural extension services, and maternal and child health in Bolivia, Central African Republic, Ghana, Morocco, Sri Lanka, and Tanzania.[10] She found that the most successful agencies were those that offered employees the autonomy to make consequential decisions and feel a strong "sense of mission."[11]

These examples are just that—examples, which collectively demonstrate that managing for empowerment *can* work well in many cases. Whether a Route E reform is a good idea is a separate question. Route E might be helpful for high performers, but not for those with more modest performance. Tennis great Roger Federer had an unusual training strategy in his playing days, steeped much less in metrics and performance tests than most elite tennis players. He relied instead on the wise eye of his longtime fitness coach, Pierre Paganini.[12] This does not mean that such a strategy would work for me—a man who has never picked up a racket. Just because something works for top performers does not mean it's generally appropriate or advisable. How, then, can we know that Route E is worth our investment? The rest of this chapter will look at evidence that seeks to help us figure that out.

The Monitoring Challenge at the Heart of Compliance-Oriented Reforms

Just as I will never become Roger Federer on the tennis court, most organizations will never be among the world's top performers. The question we ought ask of Route E (empowerment-oriented) reforms is not whether they will generate superlative performance, but rather whether they are more likely to improve performance than the alternative of Route C (compliance-oriented) reforms.

Route C reforms can and do yield performance improvements. Often, they do so not by catalyzing the performance of exceptional outliers, but by raising the "bottom"—creating a floor for the worst-performing. There are massive gains to be had from reforming the lowest-performing schools.[13] A small minority of teachers globally (but a significant number in some countries) simply lack the competence or knowledge to do the job.[14] In these cases, Route C strategies like providing teachers scripted lessons can be effective at improving students' test scores.[15]

Compliance-oriented strategies will induce a change in those actions by employees that are monitored—but no more. This is true even for perhaps the most seemingly autonomy-compatible of Route C reforms: introducing pay-for-performance schemes. Pay-for-performance schemes reward employees according to their fulfillment of some measurable target or goal.[16] By focusing on outcomes, pay-for-performance offers employees some autonomy in their work processes. When the measures used to assess employees' performance are excellent and well monitored, these schemes can improve performance. However, this is not often the case.

As Chapter 2 suggested, monitoring in practice is frequently "good but not great"—in large part as there are often no excellent holistic measures that capture the range of things we wish a given employee to accomplish. Teachers who seek to improve only measurable indicators of their students' performance, like their test scores, have a tendency to neglect other important parts of students' education, such as emotional development or life skills.[17] Teachers may also be incentivized to teach to the test in ways that do not improve students' actual knowledge, even as they improve test scores.[18] Pay-for-performance may even lead to teachers "discouraging low-achieving students from enrolling or taking tests."[19]

In a review of over 200 impact evaluations, Ganimian and Murnane find significant evidence of these various distortions. Improvements in the aspects of performance that are monitored and tied to payment (e.g., test scores) need to be considered in light of what Ganimian and Murnane call "dysfunctional responses."[20] Dysfunctional responses are not limited to the education sector, of course. In one illustrative example, an attempt to monitor and incentivize better behavior from public health workers in Karnataka, India, shifted corruption from the limited range of tasks that could be monitored to those which could not.[21]

Even for the indicators that are well monitored, performance improvements are often thwarted by the difficulties of implementation. A randomized controlled trial in Rajasthan, India, with the evocative title "Band Aid on a Corpse," found that monitoring healthcare workers' performance and rewarding them with financial incentives failed entirely. It was simply impossible to monitor employees well enough to ensure the reform positively influenced their behavior.[22] Rivaling "Band Aid on a Corpse" for clever titling of compliance-oriented failure, "Command and Can't Control" examines a compliance-oriented digitalization program in Punjab, Pakistan, intended to enable the "centralized management of frontline staff." Though the program compiled over 3 million observations of employee behavior, the data failed to translate into actual performance improvements.[23]

These failures of pay-for-performance are typical. In a comprehensive review of civil service reforms in Africa, Martin Williams found that only 1 of 32 initiatives to introduce performance-linked incentives actually distributed any incentive. That's right—31 of 32 pay-for-performance schemes *did not end up rewarding good performance*. The one scheme that did distribute incentives was also incompletely implemented and only lasted a few years.[24] Unsurprisingly, none of these efforts showed any performance benefits.

Perhaps most tragically, Daron Acemoglu and coauthors describe what they call "The Perils of High-Powered Incentives" in the Colombian military during its conflict with armed guerrillas in the mid-2000s. Colombian army personnel were rewarded with financial incentives for killing guerrillas. Their eagerness to earn these rewards also led them to misrepresent innocent civilians as combatants, resulting in over 1,000 unnecessary and tragic civilian casualties.[25] These examples illustrate that despite the performance gains that can be derived from preventing the worst performance, Route C reforms can sometimes have worrying unintended consequences. Managers planning to institute such reforms should be cautious of these hazards, implementing Route C reforms only where they are appropriate for the context.

Empowerment-Oriented Reforms Often Appear to Work Better, Particularly When Monitoring Is Imperfect

Both Route E and Route C reforms can improve performance. Both can fail. This section seeks to compare the two, examining which approach may work better in a variety of contexts. We will first explore the effects of the same managerial approach across different agencies. We then look at instances where Route C and Route E reforms were initiated in the same context, investigating which worked better and why.

Let's first look at examples in which the same managerial approach was utilized across different contexts. Imran Rasul and Dan Rogger conducted a study of 4,700 Nigerian public infrastructure projects in which they examined whether the likelihood of project completion differed under different managerial approaches. The Nigerian public sector is certainly not an exemplar of clean, transparent governance; Nigeria is tied for 150th of 180 countries on Transparency International's 2022 Corruption Perception Index.[26] One might expect that in such a context, managerial approaches that offer discretion would enable fraud, delaying project completion.

The opposite was true. The authors found that projects managed under controlling managerial approaches were *less* likely to be completed. As the authors put it, "increasing bureaucrats' autonomy is positively associated with completion rates, yet practices related to incentives/monitoring of bureaucrats are negatively associated with completion rates."[27] Even in a system where there were well-founded concerns about the potential misuse of discretion, greater empowering managerial practices were associated with better performance. This finding was later echoed by Rasul and Rogger's joint work in Ghana with Martin Williams, first mentioned in Chapter 2. Examining the performance of forty-five Ghanaian agencies across over 3,000 tasks, they find that "the provision of incentives or monitoring to bureaucrats [was] negatively correlated with the likelihood of task completion," while "monitoring practices providing bureaucrats [with] more autonomy and discretion [were] positively correlated with task completion."[28]

Why was this the case? What characteristics did the Nigerian and Ghanian agencies share that made them suit empowerment-oriented management? Monitorability plays an important role in the answer. As Chapter 2 theorized, agencies performing tasks that are less easily monitored tend to benefit from empowerment-oriented practices. This is precisely what the authors find in both Ghana and Nigeria. More compliance-oriented management was even more strongly associated with lower performance when a project was more difficult to monitor.[29] As the authors put it, "organizations could benefit from providing their staff with greater autonomy and discretion, especially for types of tasks that are ill-suited to predefined monitoring and incentive regimes."[30] Management for compliance appears to be even more deleterious to performance when tasks are difficult to monitor.

Drawing on my sample of over 4 million observations of bureaucrats one final time suggests one reason why management for empowerment is even more beneficial when tasks are hard to monitor. In workplaces where it is difficult to verify the outcomes of employee work, management for empowerment is even more strongly associated with an employee's mission motivation.[31] I think this is because employees working on things that are harder to verify may themselves struggle more to see the positive impacts of their work on the lives of others. In these settings, managers can play a larger role to motivate employees by helping reinforce their work's valuable purpose.

In addition, where it is harder to verify performance, it is all the more likely that misguided compliance-oriented practices will persist. Precisely because it is difficult to measure performance, organizations can all the more easily end up with compliance-oriented practices without realizing they are undermining performance by doing so.

I have seen this pattern in my prior research. In prior work, I found that foreign aid agencies that offer field staff greater discretion often perform better than those engaged in tight monitoring.[32] This is especially true when tasks are difficult to monitor and environments are unpredictable. In those environments, compliance-oriented targets and practices particularly conflict with what fieldworkers believe will actually forward the goals of their aid projects—goals which many of these individuals have joined their organizations to pursue.[33]

The studies above are purely observational. They examined whether greater empowerment or compliance was associated with better performance in a particular context. What would be better would be to explore instances where both compliance and empowerment reforms have been attempted in the same place, to allow us to more tightly focus on which managerial reforms in fact better improve performance. We only have a few of these examples, but they too suggest that management for empowerment is worthy of our collective investment and attention.

Muhammad Yasir Khan examined the relationship between mission motivation and performance among community health workers in Balochistan, Pakistan. The workers were tasked with supporting families with infants by visiting their homes and providing advice and support.[34] The study divided these workers into two groups in a randomized controlled trial. The first group was offered Route C "performance-linked financial incentives" for conducting more home visits. The second group was offered no financial rewards. Instead, they were asked to watch a video "describing and emphasizing the mission [of the Department of Health] and then participate in reflection sessions with a facilitator to discuss [that] mission" once a month for three months. The aim of this Route E reform was to connect workers to their peers and reinforce the mission of their work. Usefully, this study examined the intervention's impact on overall child health outcomes, not just the number of home visits conducted.

The study found that the Route E reform was far more effective at improving performance than the Route C reform.[35] Those who were financially incentivized to show up did, indeed, do so—home visits increased by a greater amount for the Route C group. But it turns out that promoting child health requires much more than just showing up. The kindling of mission motivation led workers to devote attention to efforts that also contributed to child health outcomes but were harder to monitor. These workers performed higher-quality health checks and assisted parents to understand practices that prevent disease.[36]

In a second study, Oriana Bandiera and coauthors used a randomized controlled trial to explore different management strategies for procurement officers in Punjab, Pakistan. The procurement officers worked in public agencies across many sectors. The study only examined the procurement processes for generic goods for which quality could be easily compared, such as stationery, furnace oil, and newspapers.[37] One group of procurement officers was given greater autonomy in decision-making and exemption from some reporting and monitoring requirements (a Route E reform). A second group received bonuses if they were able to produce greater value for money (a Route C reform).[38]

This is a context in which Route C management strategies might seem preferable to Route E ones. Since the quality of goods can be easily observed and verified, monitoring is relatively easy. Buying cheaper stationery to save the government money also feels, to me at least, unlikely to attract mission-driven employees. We might also worry that bureaucrats who are part of the Route E reform could take advantage of greater autonomy for self-serving purposes. After all, Pakistan is 140th of 180 countries on Transparency International's 2022 Corruption Perceptions Index.[39]

You can probably guess where this is going. The Route E reform *still* performed better. The Route C incentives did not increase value for money in any detectable way. On the other hand, the Route E approach lowered the prices paid for equivalent items by 9 percent. The authors estimate that the Route E pilot saved the government enough money in a single year to operate five additional schools or add seventy-five hospital beds.[40]

This study took place in a quite easily monitored setting, one which Chapter 2's theory would suggest is best managed with a fairly high degree of management for compliance and low degree of management for empowerment. But prior use of management for empowerment was apparently so low in Punjab's procurement system that Route E reforms still notably improved performance. Route E reforms yielded benefits in this relatively unfertile setting—and likely will in many others—precisely because they have been so underutilized.

More Empowerment, Not Less Compliance

This book has discussed various circumstances where public sector agencies have used too much compliance-oriented management. But many agencies face a broader problem—not of having too much compliance-oriented management, but too little management *at all*. Most agencies can invest in empowering strategies without needing to reduce their compliance-oriented practices. These managerial reforms increase empowerment without reducing compliance, or alternately combine E and C elements. In so doing these reforms on balance shift management practice toward greater empowerment.

An excellent example of a reform strategy that increased empowerment without reducing compliance comes from Ghana, where Michael Azulai and coauthors conducted a randomized controlled trial of a civil service training program. This training program was aimed at mid-level civil servants from a range of government departments.[41] Some trainees undertook a standard training module focused on increasing productivity. Others instead attended a new empowerment-oriented training module focused on changing workplace culture, specifically designed to create a sense of agency within trainees to improve their workplace practices and performance. The results illustrated that those who attended the empowerment-oriented training catalyzed genuine changes in the culture of their teams without reducing compliance-oriented reporting and managerial practices in any way.

Civil servants became more open to new ideas and collaboration, seeing themselves as more able to make a difference in their work.[42] This cultural shift also translated into performance gains. Teams where a member had attended the empowerment-oriented training produced higher-quality work at a more efficient pace, as rated by external assessors.[43] This reform changed nothing about their agency's formal management practice. It nonetheless was a Route E reform with marked impacts because of the ways it changed organizational culture and team cohesion.

Some systems are so steeped in compliance-oriented management that they can respond to little else. In their work on Delhi schools, Yamini Aiyar and coauthors find schools that currently focus on compliance itself rather than student learning or thriving as their de facto goal.[44] Changing this focus requires, in their view, "a granular understanding of the precise ways in which the low-level performance culture and practices shape belief systems and attitudes."[45]

In these kinds of systems, it may be useful to package empowering managerial reforms in compliance-oriented language. This is often the type of language that managers, employees, and political authorities find attractive. One strategy is to redefine what a system's compliance-oriented targets are. For example, quantitative indicators of individual performance can be replaced with targets based on an agency's collective performance at fulfilling their mission. The group-level targets can foster a cultural shift to direct attention toward the organization's mission.

Group-level targets have been successfully employed in a number of settings. In UK hospitals, team-based incentives have had salutary effects where peer monitoring and connections are strong.[46] In the education systems of Brazil, Mexico, and Kenya, system-wide targets created space for the autonomy and empowerment of teachers, while placing focus on the education system's wider mission of supporting student learning.[47] These measures increased the mission motivation of both teachers and principals.[48] Seemingly compliance-oriented targets can play a Route E role in promoting mission among employees.

Route C reforms can also sometimes stimulate Route E changes in work culture, to the surprise even of those initiating those reforms. A prominent recent study examined the randomized rollout of a program called Kiufunza in Tanzania.[49] Kiufunza instituted performance-linked pay for teachers, accompanied by unconditional financial grants to schools.

Kiufunza was relatively successful at achieving its goal. It was an apparent Route C success, incentivizing teachers to increase their effort at work with its pay-for-performance scheme. But where Kiufunza worked best, it seemed to trigger a series of unanticipated Route E changes that directed schoolwide attention toward their ultimate mission of educating children. As the final report from the initiators of the reform put it, Kiufunza created a school environment with a "focuses on learning, solutions, and performance," where "teachers, students, and parents bonded in their joint pursuit of performance."[50]

The reform increased feelings of autonomy, competence, and connectedness among teachers. It promoted "self-image recovery" for teachers who began to identify as "purposeful professionals."[51] The reform was only successful when teachers also received greater "job support" from management.[52] Despite its design as a Route C reform, Kiufunza depended on Route E managerial practices to be impactful and contributed to a thriving empowerment-oriented work culture.

How did this happen? How could a pay-for-performance scheme, with an explicitly Route C theory of change, initiate an empowerment-oriented shift in a system? For answers, we might look beyond the education sector, to a similar phenomenon that occurred when a pay-for-performance scheme was introduced for Malawian health providers.[53] As was the case for Tanzanian schools, this pay-for-performance scheme indeed improved the performance of health providers. Julia Lohmann and coauthors explored the motivational mechanisms underlying this effect in a paper entitled "The Money Can Be a Motivator, to Me a Little, but Mostly [Performance-Based Financing] Just Helps Me to Do Better in My Job."[54] They found that the reform worked primarily by "providing direction and goals to work towards," instilling "a sense of accomplishment" and "feelings of recognition" among employees, and "improving teamwork towards a common goal." These are all distinctly Route E channels, improving performance by increasing employee mission motivation.

Compliance-oriented reforms can drive surprisingly empowering managerial changes in a system, whether or not reformers expect this to happen. This occurs where Route C reforms clarify and reinforce mission points. Clear mission points focus attention, allow autonomy, cultivate competence, and foster connection to peers and purpose. In some circumstances, Route C and Route E may be complementary.

Some of the most effective C-oriented reforms explicitly integrate Route E–oriented features. Take, for example, Performance-Based Financing (PBF) in the health sector. PBF seeks to improve health outcomes in mostly low-income countries. It does so through a Route C carrot-and-stick approach—offering health facilities financial rewards for good health outcomes, as opposed to the status quo of providing funding upfront. Importantly, PBF rewards an entire health facility for good performance, rather than individual employees. These collective rewards serve to reinforce mission points with collective rather than individual targets.

A recent World Bank report entitled "Improving Effective Coverage in Health: Do Financial Incentives Work?" summarized findings from a range of careful studies across many countries including Cameroon, Nigeria, Kyrgyz Republic, Tajikistan, Rwanda, Zambia, and Zimbabwe.[55] The report found that PBF projects often did improve performance compared to the status quo. However, it also found that the compliance-oriented components of PBF—the performance-linked payments—were not the primary drivers of this change. PBF projects worked in large part by increasing "autonomy, decentralization, empowerment-oriented supervision to the frontlines, and community engagement."[56] PBF projects increased mission-driven motivation in some individuals by increasing recognition for good performance and changing the broader work environment to be more empowerment-oriented.[57]

What is true of management is also true of recruitment—a focus on motivation need not mean abandoning incentives. In Nava Ashraf and coauthors' careful examination of healthcare recruitment in Zambia, they found that highlighting extrinsic career benefits led to a less mission-driven applicant pool, but one with higher skills.[58] By then selecting for applicants who were also mission-driven, these incentives help recruit the most competent, mission-motivated staff. In a randomized controlled trial, the authors found that these higher-skilled and mission-motivated community health workers also worked harder, encouraging more women to seek appropriate clinic-based prenatal and antenatal care for themselves and their children. The result was an incredible 25 percent decrease in child malnutrition over a seventeen-month period.[59]

Compliance-oriented and empowerment-oriented management approaches can sometimes be fruitfully combined into a hybrid reform package. This is true even in workplaces where tasks are difficult to monitor, as long as incentives are provided at the appropriate level. The inclusion of Route C components could even assist a reform package to garner political support or donor dollars. That said, the evidence suggests that in the small number of cases where scholars have tried to determine *why* these hybrid strategies work, the Route C elements of hybrid packages are often less important than Route E elements for boosting performance. It might even be possible to bypass them altogether.

Thinking about Systems: Performance Possibility Frontiers and Getting to the Best Possible Performance

We often think of organizational reforms in terms of what economists might call *additive utility*. Each reform is treated as a separate item, with net improvements measured simply by adding up the effects of multiple reforms. A lot of things work this way. Most sports, for instance, determine the winner by adding up

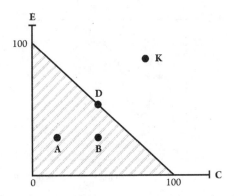

Figure 2.5 Managing for compliance and empowerment are sometimes (but not always) in tension.

a team's scores over the course of a game or match. But I would argue that it's not how reforms work. Reforms can have multiple impacts that radiate through an organization, transforming an entire system. Each reform is just one step in a long, shifting journey toward our end-goal of maximizing performance—a journey that is more than the sum of its parts.

One way I've begun to illustrate this is through something I call a *performance possibility frontier* (PPF) for an organization. Back in Chapter 2, I introduced Figure 2.5, reproduced here, to describe the relationship between empowerment-oriented and compliance-oriented managerial practices. It shows that there can be *some* tension between empowering-oriented and compliance-oriented practices when agencies exist on the frontier, such as at Point D. However, most organizations actually exist below the frontier, at points like A and B, where organizations can invest in either Route E or Route C reforms—or some combination of both.

I suggested that if we were modeling this fully, we would want to add a third dimension to this graph—a z-axis that represented performance. This would allow us to map management practices to performance at all possible combinations of managerial practices. However, in practice, such a graph would be impossible to create, because we have no way of quantifying exactly how an agency's managerial practices translate into performance in every possible combination.

A PPF imagines that we could do the impossible. It imagines that we actually know all the parameters that translate management practice into performance.[60] I have drawn a sample PPF, for a hypothetical agency, in Figure 6.1. For simplicity's sake, Figure 6.1 compresses empowerment and compliance into a single x-axis. This x-axis represents the overall balance of an agency's practices; the ratio of empowerment-oriented to compliance-oriented management. The y-axis is the performance generated from that ratio of managerial approaches if they were implemented to the greatest extent possible in the agency's current environment.

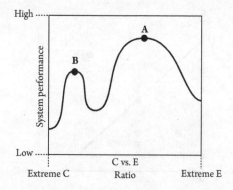

Figure 6.1 Performance Possibility Frontier (PPF) for a hypothetical agency

Figure 6.1, and my drawing of PPFs more generally, reflects that the extremes are almost never the best approach. The complete absence of compliance is unlikely to lead to the best possible performance, and so is management focused solely on compliance. An agency's peak performance is likely to be found somewhere in the middle.

Figure 6.1's PPF features two peaks—one closer to the E-end of the spectrum, and one closer to the C-end. The two peaks are relative or local maxima, reflecting the best performance that can be induced when management strategies lean in either direction. Though the agency in Figure 6.1 certainly experiences its best performance at Point A, under more E-oriented management, it also might experience a smaller peak at Point B, under more C-oriented management. This agency could enjoy relatively good performance under a highly compliance-oriented system. However, it could potentially perform even better if it invested in Route E reforms and moved to Point A.

You might notice that the E peak in Figure 6.1 has a gentler slope than the C peak. I think this is likely to be true for many agencies, because of a key difference between E and C managerial strategies. While C-oriented strategies are focused on employee actions, E-oriented strategies are grounded in culture—on hearts and heads, not just hands. E peaks are more gently sloped in both directions, as Route E reforms cultivate norms and values that are more resilient and need less precise optimization.

Following this book's argument, an agency with a PPF like Figure 6.1—with a higher peak under relatively more empowerment-oriented managerial practices—is probably one performing tasks that are not easily monitored, and whose employees are highly mission-motivated or motivateable. A good example of such an agency might be a social work agency. In contrast, an agency performing tasks with highly observable or verifiable outputs, like a vaccine delivery team, would probably experience the highest peak in its PPF under more compliance-oriented management. Every agency's PPF will be different, with its shape affected by its unique tasks and employees.

Figure 6.1 also suggests that moving from Point B to Point A won't be easy for the hypothetical social work agency it depicts. If the agency at Point B relaxed its C-oriented practices just slightly, sliding toward the E-end of the spectrum, it would actually experience a sharp *performance decline*. This might be because this agency currently has employees who will only respond well to C-oriented practices—a lot of un-mission-motivated Peters and demotivated Samirs, with very few mission-motivated Binas. That composition can and will change over time as management practices shift, but this may take time. Cultivating the mission motivation of existing Samirs may well also take some time.

There are surely agencies that are exceptions to almost everything I've described above. As I said in the beginning of this section, PPFs are not hard facts, but simply thinking tools. I cannot draw accurate PPFs for every agency—in fact, I can't draw them perfectly accurately for *any* agency.

You might rightfully ask, how are PPFs actually helpful? Well, managers can draft PPFs to visualize some of the important questions they'll have to answer when crafting their agency's managerial system. Will their agency perform best under a more empowerment-oriented or compliance-oriented system? How steep or gentle would those E or C peaks be? Each agency's answers—and PPF—will be entirely unique. Chapter 8 will take a closer look at how a manager might begin to investigate these questions and put PPFs to use. PPFs allow us to visualize whether our agency or task is likely to experience its best performance under a more compliance-oriented or empowerment-oriented managerial approach.

A PPF Case Study: Teachers, Cameras, and Performance Improvement via Attendance

To make all a little less abstract, let me give a real-world example of a case I believe fits Figure 6.1's general shape.

One of the most academically well-known examples of a compliance-oriented reform occurred when cameras were used to record the attendance of teachers in schools run by Indian NGOs. Prior to the intervention, these schools struggled with poor teacher attendance, to the detriment of their students' education. The reform tied teachers' salaries to their attendance in the classroom. The intervention was studied in a seminal 2012 paper by the Nobel laureate in economics Esther Duflo and coauthors.[61]

The study was very clear about the intervention's compliance-oriented theory of change—it was entitled "Incentives Work: Getting Teachers to Come to School."[62] Monitoring teachers with cameras did successfully increase their attendance, even leading to modest gains in student learning. But before we consider how to introduce cameras like these elsewhere, we need to ask ourselves whether this Route C strategy ultimately left schools better off.[63]

In 2021, Yamini Aiyar and coauthors provided a counterpoint to Duflo et al.'s compliance success story in a different set of Indian schools.[64] Studying the Delhi school system, they described Indian education as a world of so many top-down rules that teachers feel as though their job is one of compliance, not education. In Aiyar et al.'s account, this is extremely demotivating—contributing to absenteeism, the exit of the most-motivated teachers, and classrooms where far less education happens even when teachers are present. They argue that clearing away such compliance-oriented infrastructure is likely to lead to better school performance. In a pilot attempt, they found signs that school cultures in Delhi can and are slowly shifting toward empowerment, resulting in performance improvements. However, they argue that there is much, much further to go. Transformation will take years, not months.

These opposing results might have been driven by differences in the schools studied. But my guess is that the Route C camera strategy, if implemented, would have improved performance in the schools that Aiyar and coauthors studied too.[65] Compliance-oriented reforms can indeed improve performance.

However, the camera intervention also leaves schools full of teachers who, left to their own devices, *would not otherwise be there*. These are teachers who, I suspect, will not put much effort into all the components of teaching that go beyond physical presence. They might respond to the incentive to appear, but will otherwise do very little. It seems reasonable to surmise that this group of teachers will be less excellent educators than those motivated by the mission of the school system. That means fewer teachers with a commitment to, in the words of the Singapore Ministry of Education's mission statement, provide children "a balanced and well-rounded education, develop them to their full potential, and nurture them into good citizens, conscious of their responsibilities to family, community, and country." If I had to choose between a teacher I thought even had a *chance* of being mission-motivated, and one I knew would show up because there's a camera around, I'd choose the former for my child.

Figure 6.2 illustrates the "cameras in classrooms" reform using a performance-possibility frontier (PPF).[66] Monitoring teachers with cameras might take schools toward the local C maximum at Point B in Figure 6.2's PPF, but this is quite far from the global E maximum. Once teacher attendance has improved, what then? Such a reform is difficult to intensify; teachers cannot show up more than once a day. Beyond attendance, very little of what it means to be an effective educator is tractable to oversight using cameras and tight controls.[67]

One might argue that the camera intervention would still be desirable if it substantially improved learning. The reform Duflo et al. studied did offer gains of 0.17 of a standard deviation—enough to move a student from approximately the 50th to the 57th percentile.[68] This is a notable improvement. However, this reform took place in an education system where, at the time, 25 percent of Grade 4 students could not read a single word, and over 70 percent of Grade 4 students

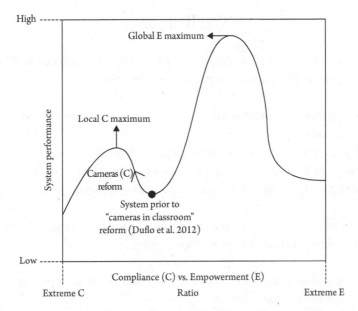

Figure 6.2 Cameras in classrooms on a Performance Possibility Frontier (PPF)

could not read at the level expected for a student in Grade 2.[69] It thus matters quite a bit whether the school system can build upon the intervention's gains. If this intervention is the first step on a long path of reform, it is a substantial one, an exciting start. But if this reform is simply a dead end—if there's nowhere for the system to "go from here"—it is far from sufficient.

I believe this compliance-oriented reform was the wrong choice for teachers in this school system partly because it did not appeal to what actually motivates teachers. In other work, Duflo argues for stricter monitoring and attendance-linked pay because "teacher compensation structure is at the heart of the teacher motivation problem."[70] Duflo is a Nobel laureate whose work I deeply respect, but on this point, I strongly disagree. While teacher compensation certainly matters, evidence from programs focusing on increasing teacher motivation suggests that compensation is not at the heart of the teacher motivation problem. The key to motivating teachers, evidence suggests, is to help them *believe they are making a difference*.[71] Teachers must feel empowered by schools to positively impact children's lives.

Installing cameras in classrooms might be a method of improving educational outcomes that is quick, straightforward, and easily transferred to other settings. Compliance-oriented interventions like these can, at least in theory, spread rapidly across space, limited only by time and money. Empowerment-oriented management interventions, by contrast, will travel across space more slowly even in the best of conditions. They require getting into the details of the specific context to determine what actually motivates bureaucrats, in a way that installing cameras doesn't.

Part II in Sum

Chapter 2 laid out a series of empirical hypotheses to be explored in Part II of the book, which this chapter brings to a close. They were:

(1) *Management for empowerment is associated with mission motivation. [A correlation]*
(2) *Management practice alters individual motivation. [A treatment effect]*
(3) *Management practice affects employees' exit and entry. [A selection effect]*
(4) *Peers and organizational norms can influence mission motivation.*

Empowerment-oriented management reforms (Route E reforms) are more likely to yield performance improvements when . . .

(5) *. . . Mission-motivated or motivateable employees are or can be present.*
(6) *. . . Monitoring is more difficult.*
(7): *. . . Mission motivation has not previously been considered in an agency's managerial approach.*

The last three chapters provided evidence that empowerment-oriented management indeed yields greater mission motivation (Hypothesis 1). This is due to changes in motivation for existing employees (Hypothesis 2) and in the types of people who are likely to seek employment and remain employed at the agency (Hypothesis 3). Individuals are also influenced by their peers and the broader norms within their agency (Hypothesis 4). Hypothesis 5 is largely untested, as Chapter 4 suggests it is difficult to find places where mission-motivated Binas and mission-motivateable Samirs are not or cannot be present. Taken as a whole, the evidence strongly supports considering management for empowerment as means of increasing an organization's mission motivation.

This chapter explored the links between motivation and performance articulated in Hypotheses 6 and 7. There is indeed suggestive evidence that the optimal level of managing for empowerment is higher when monitoring is more difficult (Hypothesis 6). However, in the empirical cases explored, empowerment-oriented Route E reforms have exceeded expectations, proving superior to Route C reforms even in highly monitorable settings. I take this as evidence that Hypothesis 7—the historic under-consideration of mission motivation in management—may often end up being an important feature of the world we find ourselves in. Even in settings which should theoretically suit a compliance-oriented approach, managers may have been using too many, or inefficient, compliance-oriented strategies. Agencies rarely thrive at the very extreme of compliance, and that is where far too many organizations currently reside.

In nursery school, my son learned that combining blue and yellow make green. If compliance was yellow and empowerment was blue, I'd say that most systems would thrive in some shade of green, needing a mix of each. However, most agencies frequently only focus on adding yellow—more, more, and more compliance-oriented Route C. We thus live in a world where the modal managerial problem is that the shade of green is too light; in many settings, we need to figure out how to add more blue.

The final part of our journey together, Part III, starts wrestling with how to do just that. It focuses on prescription—how to actually create more empowerment-oriented managerial practice. The next chapter explores questions about accountability and corruption, exploring the relationships between bureaucrats, politicians, and citizens. Critics of Route E often point out that one component of empowerment, autonomy, may enable actors who do not act in the public's best interest to engage in fraud or corruption.[72] How does that limit Route E's potential to improve performance? Chapter 7 will tackle these questions.

Profile: Labanya Margaret

*Management That Empowers at the South Sudanese National
Bureau of Statistics (Director General)*

"Voice for the voiceless."

Labanya is the answer to a question I had shortly after the first South Sudanese census came out—*"Why is this data so good?"*[1] In my work, I often start by looking at official statistics. When I go to investigate a problem as an academic or in partnership with a government, I usually find that the official statistics are somewhat, but not completely, accurate. This was not the case in South Sudan. The data were *excellent* despite the country's large size and newly independent status. I couldn't imagine how this could have occurred. Then I met Labanya, and it all made perfect sense.

Labanya's curiosity for the quantitative shape and description of her country is seemingly endless. Her voice fills with energy as she asks, "What is the current workforce of South Sudan? How many people are available? What are their grades? Their qualifications?" She adds, "I naturally want to attach evidence to everything I do. . . . I always take numbers of the people I meet."

When she joined the public service, South Sudan was a "baby country," having just secured its independence after decades of civil war with Sudan. Labanya tried to help us understand how this moment felt. "My father fought all his youthful years. We were born when they were fighting the war. We grew up, the war was going on. Now they have called the war to an end and you're seeing yourself being part of . . . a dream—2008 was seeing a dream come true. 2009 was working on that dream and vision."

Labanya immediately accepted when offered the role of director general for the National Bureau of Statistics. It was "a grand opportunity to be part of setting up a statistical system and a statistical institution that would regenerate statistics for the whole country." She joined because she believed the data she collected "will be used by not only the government, but the donors, and the whole world, to set a course for South Sudan."

Even with Labanya's passion and expertise, building up the National Bureau of Statistics in her new nation was no small feat. The first census in 2008 involved 11,000 data collectors. The country had no baseline data—almost all information was being collected for the very first time. It is hard to imagine a more difficult environment for monitoring performance, and thus for managing for compliance. How could Labanya know if her staff had collected accurate data, if there was nothing to compare it to?

There were also plenty of reasons why the data might well prove difficult, if not impossible, to collect. South Sudan had very little infrastructure of any kind. Much of the population had fled the war as refugees and were in the process of returning. As Labanya puts it, "The country literally had no access. The roads were so bad, many of the places were inaccessible . . . the logistical challenges, the return of the people who were out of the country in order for the census to be implemented, and the funding issue" were major hurdles to the work.

Instead of being discouraged by these difficulties, Labanya saw them as exciting challenges that offered connection to peers and purpose and helped her cultivate competence. Labanya was fortunate enough to experience empowerment-oriented management. Her supervisors empowered her to exercise judgment and implement the solutions she thought were most effective. "I had two wonderful bosses. I'll never forget them, and I thank them forever. They looked at me as part of this triangle, a triangle because the three of us had to work and really generate the momentum for the work to get done. They had the force to push you forward. You tumble, they lift you and get you through." Her bosses were supportive peers, as much as they were supervisors.

As director general of the bureau, Labanya worked to create a sense of shared mission and collective commitment. Labanya was "loving and respecting" of her staff. She focused on "understand[ing] the interest of [her] team. Generate and connect with them. Allow them to explain their position to you." She remembers, "whenever we went to the field, I made sure to place [the staff in my mind], to connect the face to the place where I saw him or her."

Like her supervisors, Labanya placed great emphasis on living up to her commitments to staff. "When you say you will pay them, you have to pay them on time. '*We will pay you, and we're going to pay you $10. It's $10, not less*'."

Labanya saw the census as a joint effort between the many members of her team and the population participating in the survey. "The numbers are telling exactly what [the people] are going through: the pain they are suffering, the joy, and their future visions." She reminds us, "the data is not for the Bureau of Statistics. It is the voice of the voiceless. The population is the one *saying* they did not eat. . . . The health data *says* women are dying while delivering." She wanted her staff "to know that whatever we had done was not our effort but the effort of a collective team and also their own, the people from whom we collected this information, so we constantly went back to thank them and to really recognize their contribution."

During our interview, Labanya talked about those early days of independence as halcyon days, a relatively idyllic period despite the challenges that have now come to an end. She explains, "the government realized that our numbers are going to hold them accountable. Numbers expose you. They expose your strengths and your weaknesses. They expose your ability to perform and not to perform." Not everyone in the government wanted to be held to account.

Those with political power began to marginalize statistics. "[Political support] started pulling out of numbers and that's how the Bureau of Statistics started suffering, moving away from being cared for from the cradle of the government to being cared for by the donors." It was difficult for Labanya to witness this decline because she firmly believed that the conditions in her country can and must be improved. To her, the numbers "are living things." While "data can tell the sorrows, data can also give improvement."

Labanya's bureau resisted the immense pressure they sometimes felt to alter or diminish the data. When asked what made her stand her ground and maintain the integrity of the statistics her team collected, Labanya is incredulous—the question nearly doesn't make sense to her. "When you survey someone, you ask *'What's your name? When did you last eat?'* When the person tells you, *'I last ate four days ago,'* Will you say no? Will you change it? You can't! That is exactly what we will record." This is the passion, the sense of importance in her mission, that led the bureau to remarkable success.

Sadly, the lack of support from the government eventually did undermine the bureau. People who cared about the bureau's work had little support to achieve the agency's mission, and funding cuts reduced salaries. This created a vicious cycle. More and more personnel left the bureau. They left with the knowledge, they left with the ability to do most of the work the bureau was doing.

Labanya's hopes for her country start with bureaucrats. "I think South Sudan, as a country, we need to move more on developing human capital. . . . Capacity, training, more focus on the growth of the human than on the other [things]." She adds, "You need to invest in the human capital on the capacity building. You need to invest in their motivation."

Labanya holds tight to her belief in the power of numbers. She remains proud of the ability of data to bring transparency to the realities of her people and wants to "create awareness on the benefit of using the numbers." The potential to improve the lives of the population and to "plan for the next generation," to prepare the future of her country, is an endless source of motivation for Labanya.

Her voice swells as she punctuates each word: *"Numbers. Change. People's. Lives."*

PART III

PRESCRIPTION

Why Empowerment-Oriented Management Is
Underused and How to Change That

Rethinking Accountability
for Mission Driven Bureaucrats

> Bureaucrats who adhere to these [accountability] rules must pay heavy compliance costs. Public-spirited bureaucrats thus confront a trade-off between adhering to accountability rules and maximizing their agency's bureaucratic capacity... the very mechanisms that limit opportunities for government misbehavior can also limit opportunities for building bureaucratic capacity.
> —Jessica Rich, "Outsourcing Bureaucracy to Evade Accountability"[1]

> Freedom can (and does) lead to chaos when we fail to couple it with a strong sense of responsibility. That is why freedom and responsibility go together.
> —Netflix's official culture statement, *Seeking Excellence*[2]

This chapter kicks off Part III of this book, which is about solutions. How can we put management for empowerment into practice? Part III connects the findings of Part II to a broader set of actors, including politicians, the media, and citizens.[3]

Management and politicians reasonably worry that bureaucrats may use additional autonomy to act in their own interests rather than their organization's.[4] Empowerment is more than just autonomy, of course; indeed, there are many ways to empower without changing the level of employee autonomy. But neither is it true that allowing autonomy will inevitably lead to more corruption. This chapter focuses on political control, accountability, and corruption. It explores how accountability regimes can improve performance in ways that reduce corruption while kindling rather than suffocating the motivational fire of Mission Driven Bureaucrats.

Corruption and fraud are obviously bad—but the best way to tackle them may not always be control and oversight. If this seems confusing on its face, you are among the many I've encountered who think of accountability as meaning "reporting upward to one's superiors." This isn't what accountability does, has, or

Mission Driven Bureaucrats. Dan Honig, Oxford University Press. © Oxford University Press 2024.
DOI: 10.1093/oso/9780197641194.003.0007

must always mean. Building better public organizations requires rethinking our dominant approaches to accountability.

Perhaps the first question we should ask is, What kind of problem is corruption? Is it the kind of problem where the only acceptable level is zero? What should we do when preventing corruption is more costly than the corruption itself? Are we more interested in minimizing corruption or maximizing public welfare?

A conversation with my good friend Nealin Parker brought this home for me. Nealin currently runs the US office of the NGO Search for Common Ground. During part of the Obama administration, she served as the chief of staff to Secretary Julián Castro at the US Department of Housing and Urban Development (HUD).[5] Nealin and I were discussing the way oversight of government programs creates inflexibilities that sometimes undermine performance. Nealin said something like, "Yeah, and it also just costs a crazy amount of money—sometimes as much as the program itself." With Nealin's help, I found the numbers.

It turns out that Nealin was wrong in saying the costs were equal—sometimes oversight costs *exceeded* actual program costs. In one case, a 2013 law gave HUD's office of Community Planning and Development (CPD) money (supplemental appropriations) to help communities rebuild from Hurricane Sandy, a 2012 storm that wreaked havoc on America's east coast.[6] The law also provided the exact same amount of money to the Inspector General's office to oversee spending of the HUD funds.[7] HUD needed to spend money to help those affected by the hurricane, pay staff, and pay for internal oversight by CPD.[8]

Adding the costs of oversight incurred by both Inspector General and CPD, more dollars were spent ensuring money wasn't wasted than on actually helping citizens recover from the hurricane. The *majority* of funds were spent overseeing the *minority* of the spending.

To make matters worse, oversight costs more than just money. An Inspector General will ask for a paper trail—documentation demonstrating that money is well spent. This forces government agencies like HUD to ask citizens to produce formal documentation of their eligibility for funds. You know who really doesn't have time for that, and may not have all the formal documents they need? *People who have just survived hurricanes*—particularly, poor people. As Trey Reffett, HUD's senior advisor for disaster recovery, put it to me:

> Punitive oversight leads to a perpetuation of poverty; in a disaster, perfect paperwork is the last thing displaced families are focused on. The poorer the family, the less likely they'll be able to produce the documentation. Time spent responding to the Inspector General is less time spent on grant activities in a world of finite budgets. But maybe even

more importantly, overly cautious program design and implementation results in poor people being left out.[9]

If I sound a little bit emotional about this, that's because I am. HUD staff standing with a resident at their demolished home shouldn't have to force the resident to find a deed or mortgage statement to document that their home has been reduced to rubble. Forcing them to do so demotivates staff, frustrates residents, and hurts the poorest most of all.

Fraud and corruption are surely important problems. But just as surely, compliance-oriented accountability regimes that sometimes cost the public vastly more than the fraud that they prevent—and upset citizens in the process.

If you are thinking, there must be a better approach, you're right—there is. There are more effective and less costly ways to tackle corruption. We just have to look for them. Improving our approaches to accountability requires thinking through what normally is left unsaid when we ask for more accountability—accountability to whom, for what, how?

Rethinking "To Whom": Sometimes the Bureaucrats Care the Most about Delivering on the Mission

Bureaucratic accountability is frequently seen as a relationship between agents and principals. Principals, the leaders at the top of the bureaucratic hierarchy, attempt to limit the bad actions of any corrupt agents at the bottom. The ultimate principals of the bureaucracy are politicians. The "to whom," then, is up the hierarchy, from subordinate to principal.

This upward accountability is useful when principals always want laudable things to happen, while many agents want the wrong ones. But how often is this depiction correct? How often is the principal actually the "knight" and the agent the "knave?"[10] Bo Rothstein suggests that it is frequently incorrect to assume that there is an honest principal overseeing the bureaucracy.[11] If the principal cannot be trusted, giving them greater control over employees will not reduce corruption.[12]

Bureaucrats at the frontlines, whom we often suspect to be perpetrators of bad actions, sometimes turn out to more devoted to their mission than their supervisors. In the last chapter, I discussed a study in Punjab, Pakistan, that found that greater autonomy for frontline procurement officers improved value for money.[13] The benefits of autonomy were higher when those officers had supervisors who had a history of delaying approvals, which is suggestive of awaiting corrupt side payments in return for moving paperwork forward. The authors argue that though frontline personnel might not be perfect people, offering them autonomy can reduce corruption if they are at least more mission-motivated than their supervisors. To reduce corruption, we do not have to put more power in the hands of *perfect* actors, only *better* actors.

The results from Pakistan have parallels in historical economic studies of the US government. In the 1880s, the US government implemented the Pendleton Act, a major civil service reform that limited political patronage. The act turned what previously had been appointed posts into competitively recruited civil service positions, with clear hiring criteria and meritocratic assessment processes. The conventional wisdom is that the Pendleton Act improved things by enabling better-qualified people to enter the bureaucracy. But a recent study suggests that in the US Post Office the benefits came from the *existing* mission-motivated workers being more protected from political meddling.[14] Just like in Pakistan, the agents were not the problem—their principals were.

Elections can exacerbate this principal problem. The pressure to secure electoral support can lead politicians to resort to bribery. Studying political-bureaucratic tensions in Ghana, Sarah Brierley found that "political control of bureaucrats can increase corruption when politicians need money to fund election campaigns."[15]

Corruption by political principals may also come in the form of patronage. In countries across the world, politicians may use their power to appoint co-partisans to permanent positions in the bureaucracy, irrespective of their talent or mission motivation.[16] Unprincipled principals—politicians who seek personal gains from public office—may use their power to appoint unprincipled agents, or bureaucrats who support and facilitate their malfeasance.[17] For instance, in Argentina, Valentin Figueroa found that impending national elections cause high-level bureaucrats to collect more in bribes, likely at the request of politicians who need the funds to campaign.[18]

Corruption is not the only reason we ought to worry about political control of the bureaucracy. A substantial thread of US public management scholarship, largely inspired by Gary Miller and Andrew Whitford's work, argues that politicians frequently interfere too much in the work of the civil service.[19] By limiting bureaucrats' autonomy, these political interventions can undermine bureaucrats' ability to cultivate competence or expertise.[20]

One way to mitigate the effects of corrupt principals is to invest in mission-motivated agents. Mission Driven Bureaucrats can serve as an important check on politicians who might wish to subvert the delivery of their organizations' mission. For example, Chapter 3 introduced us to highly mission-motivated bureaucrats in Thai districts, who buffered the services they delivered from political turmoil at their top. Similarly, Mission Driven Bureaucrats in Brazil appear to have been more likely to resist unprincipled principals during the Temer presidency in the period 2016–2018 after the impeachment of his predecessor Dilma Rousseff on corruption-related charges.[21]

Of course, politicians do not always want the wrong things. Many genuinely want to benefit citizens. Being a politician can be such an unpleasant job that I find it probable that most politicians have at least some mission motivation. Otherwise, why would anyone do it? As a politician, your every move is scrutinized, and you need to spend quite a lot of your time asking people for money. Former UK prime minister Tony Blair recently suggested that he would not want to become a Member of Parliament (MP) today. "There are so many interesting things you could do," Blair remarked. "Why would you become an MP to be abused? It's worse for women. It's frustrating because we have to produce quality people again. It's not that the US and Britain don't have them, but politics has to be structured in a way that encourages them back. It's not really about money in the end. I think it's much more to do with whether people think they are going to join something where they can really make a difference."[22]

Evidence from across the world suggests that the stereotype of the self-serving politician is far from universally true. In Pakistan, for example, a randomized controlled trial by Saad Gulzar and Yasir Khan found that emphasizing the ability of politicians to help the public during candidate recruitment makes it more likely that mission-motivated people will run for office.[23] Once in office, these mission-motivated politicians are also more likely to implement policies that improve citizens' welfare.[24] In another study, Brigitte Seim and coauthors observed that politicians in Malawi may be genuinely interested in maximizing the welfare for their citizens. When given information about which Malawian schools received foreign aid, politicians chose to allocate government revenues to needy schools that did *not* receive aid, forwarding equity even where doing so was not the wisest choice from an electoral perspective.[25]

These are indications that not all politicians are self-serving. The Apolitical Foundation focuses on cultivating something like Mission Driven Politicians. Their mission is built on the realization that it matters who serves as a politician.[26] It is perhaps no coincidence that this foundation grew out of the Apolitical Network, the world's largest learning platform for bureaucrats. Politicians are people, just like bureaucrats. Perhaps not all politicians have the public interest at heart, but neither do all bureaucrats. To improve the bureaucracy, we have to figure out who actually wants what. Only then can we figure out if upward accountability is an answer "to whom" that may possibly benefit performance.

Even if principals do mean well, "for what" and "how" questions should give us pause. Accountability regimes that ensure bureaucrats obey their leaders will only be as effective as those leaders are . . . *and* how good the monitoring tools are. But as we've seen throughout this book, those tools are often far from perfect, and may also demotivate those forced to comply. The next section will explore various approaches to build accountability in the public sector, considering the lessons on monitorability, mission motivation, and performance from Part II of this book.

Rethinking "For What" and "How": Corruption, Compliance-Oriented Accountability, Mission Motivation, and Performance

Robert Klitgaard famously described corruption with the simple formula "Corruption = Monopoly + Discretion – Accountability."[27] Any corrupt act, whether by elites or non-elites, requires the actor to have the power to exercise judgment with impunity.[28] The most common approach to preventing corruption is to strengthen compliance-oriented accountability regimes (Route C). Such regimes seek to reduce employee discretion and tightly monitor their actions. However, even with the best-intentioned principals, Route C accountability regimes may have little real impact on reducing corruption. They can even make matters worse.

We are naturally inclined to believe that corruption is always deleterious to public sector performance. While this is often true, acts that we commonly call corrupt can sometimes even be performance-*enhancing*. In Brazil, Guillermo Toral demonstrates that patronage helps ensure bureaucrats are trusted by political principals and given sufficient autonomy and resources to perform at their best.[29] Yuen Yuen Ang finds that certain types of extralegal payments (access money, in her terms) played an important role in enhancing China's rapid economic development, albeit while generating economic distortions and inequality.[30] Jeff Weaver finds that bribes for promotions in the health sector of an anonymous developing country improve health services, as those with a greatest desire to serve citizens are also most willing to pay.[31]

Do these examples imply that corruption is actually a good thing—that we should simply leave it be? Certainly not. These examples do, however, illustrate that the relationship between corruption and agency performance is highly nuanced. We often speak as though any intervention that reduces corruption is good, without considering whether that intervention actually benefits public sector performance. Instead, agencies should focus on selecting the *right* accountability regimes—that improve performance *and* reduce corruption.

Anti-corruption efforts commonly pursue what Lant Pritchett and I have in other work called an accounting-based accountability approach. This form of accountability answers the "how" question by increasing central oversight, quantification, and verification to count, track, and otherwise monitor employee actions. When successfully implemented, these compliance-oriented tools do reduce petty corruption. A clerk being tightly observed will not solicit or accept a bribe in exchange for expediting a service.

This does not mean that compliance-oriented accountability necessarily increases performance, however. We cannot expect the same tightly observed clerk to feel that they are managed in a way that allows autonomy, cultivates competence, or creates connection. A system that focuses on compliance is one that will reduce mission motivation.

In 2020, three distinguished scholars of anti-corruption efforts published a study of a compliance-oriented attempt to reduce bribery in the Ugandan health sector.[32] They found that the intervention markedly reduced corruption. However, it also had the effect of "undermining morale among frontline health providers and probably also citizens' trust in health services," ultimately hindering healthcare delivery goals.[33] By suffocating the motivational flame of mission-driven employees, this compliance-oriented strategy clearly did not contribute to the best possible healthcare services for Ugandans.

By demotivating employees, compliance-oriented accountability regimes can actually make corruption worse. Compliance-oriented accountability is likely to induce the exit of mission-motivated Binas or Samirs. It leaves agencies with a greater proportion of unmotivated Peters—those most likely to engage in malfeasance. This ultimately increases the likelihood of corrupt acts within an agency. This is another context in which the wisdom of Harvard's Jane Mansbridge, one of the world's leading political philosophers of accountability, seems apt—"sanction-based accountability not only stems from distrust; it creates distrust."[34]

Moreover, as highlighted in this chapter's introduction, compliance-oriented accountability regimes can end up being costlier to agencies than the corruption they are meant to prevent. In Italy, three leading economists studied the costs of accountability regimes in procurement agencies, differentiating between what they called active and passive waste.[35] Active waste refers to money that offers private benefits to individuals, such as income from a bribe. Passive waste encompasses the costs of monitoring and complying with processes devised to reduce active waste. The authors found that over 80 percent of all waste is passive.[36] The massive costs of passive waste are side effects of an attempt to attack the disease of corruption using Route C.[37] The goal of reducing corruption is laudable. But if the side effects of any treatment are creating—as in Italy—four times the problem of the disease itself, then the treatment is being massively overprescribed.[38]

Compliance-oriented accountability mechanisms also can undermine the ability of agencies to develop productive capacity. They prevent corruption by threatening employees with punishment for bad behavior. As I argued in my prior book *Navigation by Judgment,* this may encourage bureaucrats to avoid potential punishment by outsourcing tasks to others, avoiding accountability pressures and limiting their own liability for anything that an auditor might later contest.

This seems to be a broader phenomenon. Jessica Rich finds that Brazilian agencies often outsource tasks to special projects or non-state actors to avoid onerous processes steeped in compliance-oriented accountability.[39] However, outsourcing also prevents bureaucrats from learning valuable skills in the process of implementing projects themselves. This reduces an agency's capacity to deliver other projects and public services, undermining performance in the medium run.[40] As Rich observes in this chapter's first epigraph, "the very mechanisms that limit opportunities for government misbehavior can also limit opportunities for building bureaucratic capacity."[41] The same pressures can also lead employees to generate flawed data. As Tu and Gong put it in a study of oversight efforts in China, bureaucrats may often "[play] it safe or [fabricate] performance information. Sanction-based accountability therefore does not offer a panacea for bureaucratic shirking."[42]

Indeed, some have argued that compliance-oriented accountability will only work if norms of rule following are already widely internalized, with compliance-oriented accountability unlikely to improve things where bad behavior is widespread. As Mushtaq Khan puts it, "External enforcement only works if 90% or 95% of people are already following the rules . . . the vast bulk of rule-following enforcement is actual horizontal peer-to-peer monitoring. If that doesn't work, the enforcement from a vertical enforcer—a third party coming in—is extremely unlikely to work on its own."[43]

In an effort to reduce corruption, compliance-oriented accountability regimes can interfere with the delivery of public services. One of the authors of the aforementioned study in Uganda, Heather Marquette, reflected that this raised the question of what the "actual goal was; was it reducing bribery, or was it improving service delivery and health outcomes? . . . Should we be thinking about anti-corruption interventions as ends in themselves, or as means to other important ends?"[44]

My personal answer to this question is clear: the end is people's welfare. Anti-corruption is one means to that end, but it is far from the only one. Sometimes compliance-oriented accountability will get us to better welfare; but often it will not. Luckily there are alternative answers possible for accountability to whom, for what, and how.

An Alternative Approach: Empowerment-Oriented Accountability

An empowerment-oriented approach to accountability relies on the presence of Mission Driven Bureaucrats. These are the employees who, as this book has argued, will be least likely to engage in corrupt acts and most likely to proliferate norms of integrity within an agency. Jane Mansbridge, the renowned political philosopher of accountability previously quoted in this chapter, envisages something like Mission Driven Bureaucrats as the core of accountability systems. As she puts it, a well-functioning accountability system will "require . . . a selection core and a sanction periphery."[45] Building a selection core involves recruiting people, like Mission Driven Bureaucrats, who embody the right norms of behavior for an agency. This core can then allow compliance-oriented monitoring and sanction regimes to police the periphery. This is consistent with Chapter 6. Few agencies, after all, will have performance possibility frontiers (PPFs) that peak all the way at the extreme E side of the spectrum, implying that an empowerment core may need a compliance periphery to realize the best possible performance.

How can we achieve an empowerment-oriented approach to accountability, which cultivates and relies upon Mission Driven Bureaucrats? I see two possible strategies: shifting the *direction* of relationships of accountability ("to whom"), or changing the *form* of accountability that agencies adopt ("for what" and "how"). Both strategies have the ultimate goal of shifting accountability away from reporting, monitoring, and sanctions, and toward the promotion of mission-driven behavior.

Let's first examine how the direction of accountability relationships can be changed. Accountability does not have involve answering to one's bosses. Chapter 5 already introduced another direction of travel—horizontally to peers. Bureaucrats will act in mission-driven ways because they feel a responsibility to honor a commitment to their peers, holding each other accountable for good behavior. Peer networks can promote norms of shared commitment to an agency's mission.

Citizens are the principals of politicians—the bosses of the political supervisors who in turn supervise bureaucrats.[46] When we give more control to politicians to monitor bureaucrats, we're engaging in what international development folks call the long route of accountability. The route is long because it involves a lot of steps—citizens empower politicians, who then supervise bureaucrats to do better.[47] But there is also a short route—a more direct channel for citizens to engage with those who provide them services.[48]

This short route is often conceived as *also* compliance-oriented—with citizens, rather than managers, doing the monitoring. This can and does work.[49] In perhaps the most famous successful example, Ugandan newspapers published information regarding central government fund transfers to local schools. Previously, very little of these funds were reaching students, presumably pocketed by government officials and intermediaries.[50] But armed with data, parents and communities were able to better monitor how monies were spent, with positive effects on school enrollment and student learning.[51]

Short-route compliance faces some of the same monitorability challenges as long-route compliance. Its focus on quantifiable data can distort performance, as the things that can be monitored are sometimes very different from the things that matter.[52] I believe short-route accountability can and should often be based in empowerment instead of compliance. It should focus on creating a deeper connection between bureaucrats and the citizens whom they serve. By fostering mission motivation, empowerment-oriented accountability to citizens can cultivate Mission Driven Bureaucrats. It can make accountability processes a *positive* experience for both citizens and bureaucrats.

What do I mean, exactly? Recall Chapter 5's discussion of two reform efforts by local councils in the UK, Camden and Gateshead, that sought to build relationships of trust between citizens and caseworkers. Those interventions are also accountability interventions, in that they ask the bureaucrats to be accountable to clients directly. Indeed, a recent report on the Human Learning Systems movement described the approach as having "a laser focus on accountability to the right people—the people we support."[53]

Empowerment-oriented accountability can center the direct relationship between state agents and citizens.[54] In this approach the accountability process *is itself* the thing that empowers bureaucrats and citizens alike. Local politicians often favor this direct citizen accountability. Not only does it increase performance, it leads to more satisfied voters.[55]

This direct accountability to individual citizens can also cultivate competence among bureaucrats. Samir Garg and Suchi Pande provide one such account for community health workers—members of local communities employed by the state—in the Indian state of Chhattisgarh. The authors find that engaging citizens on the ground enables workers to learn directly from beneficiaries about their needs.[56] Empowerment-oriented management can then help create the space for them to act on those needs. In Chhattisgarh, as in other cases, this requires frontline workers and their managers to push back on top-down compliance-oriented accountability regimes imposed by those from further up the hierarchy.[57]

Education is one sector that has often tapped on the strengths of citizen accountability. Melanie Ehren and coauthors find that the most effective school accountability reforms are those which aim to foster intrinsic motivation among teachers.[58] These reforms empower teachers with the autonomy to make judgments that forward their mission of educating children. When staff feel empowered to fulfill their mission, trust and accountability can be cultivated among teachers, other officials in the education system, and community members.[59]

Citizen and peer empowerment-oriented accountability can be wonderful complements to empowerment-oriented management. They nurture autonomous, competent, connected, and mission-motivated bureaucrats who will act in the spirit of the organization's mission, even in the absence of compliance-oriented monitoring.

This has echoes of what some scholars have begun to call "values-based approaches" to anti-corruption that aim to alter system norms.[60] These Route E approaches to improving accountability seek to create an underlying culture of non-corrupt behavior rather than control the observable actions of bureaucrats. If the traditional Route C solution seeks to attack the disease of corruption using the antibiotics of monitoring and control, a values-based Route E approach seeks to cultivate good bacteria that will ultimately outcompete the disease. It is a strategy focused more on norms than actions, on hearts and minds than on hands. This approach has noted particular success in difficult environments, where monitoring is often incomplete.[61]

Data and Rules as Inputs, Not Answers

Few systems will do away with "upward" accountability altogether—from subordinates to superiors, or from agencies to politicians. Nor is this desirable; politicians and superiors should absolutely have insight into what is being done in their and the public's name, in part so they can guide work appropriately. The question is what kinds of upward accountability routines are likely to promote the best possible performance.

Collecting data about employee performance is necessary for monitoring in a compliance-oriented approach. But the problems this chapter has explored do not originate from the data collection per se, but from how these data are then used. Instead of using these data to punish or control employees, they can be used to promote learning and collective solution-finding.[62] Don Moynihan and coauthors demonstrate this in a Danish public hospital, finding that "when managers use data in ways that reinforce the perception of performance management as an externally imposed tool of control, professionals withdraw effort. However, when managers use data in ways that solve organizational problems, professionals engage in goal-based learning."[63]

When performance data are used to supplement learning rather than sanction employees, many of the negative effects of what I previously called "accounting-based accountability" will fade away. There is an alternative—what Pritchett and I term "account-based accountability."[64] This approach views accountability as a broader process of justification, of giving account. It shares many similarities with Charles Sabel and Jonathan Zeitlin's notion of "dynamic accountability," an accountability regime "in which actions are justified" if those actions "advance organizational purpose."[65] If done well, account-based accountability can be empowering. It can foster mission motivation.

There are many excellent existing examples of an account-based approach to accountability. For instance, Chapter 5 described group discussions among doctors to review processes after bad outcomes. These discussions often incorporate both supervisors and subordinates. Indeed, at the center of account-based accountability are dialogues between a superior and a subordinate where the subordinate is given an opportunity to explain *why* they engaged in certain actions.

Data can be inputs into account-based accountability. The key is that they must not be the only input. Employee performance must not only be measured by compliance with rules or success at hitting targets.

Account-based accountability can still successfully identify, discourage, and reduce bad behavior. When an employee is failing to contribute to an organization's mission, they can still be identified and dismissed. Managers will simply have a more holistic vision of their employees' performance. Mission Driven Bureaucrats will be given the space and autonomy to do what they do best—forward their agency's mission. The role of accountability won't be to "check up" on bureaucrats. It will instead be to ask collectively: what is the mission? Are we serving it as well as we can? What can we do to further improve performance?

This need not mean abandoning all rules. I have generally discussed rules with a negative implication—rules as unnecessary red tape, as a weapon used to force individuals to comply. In my experience, this is how rules are often experienced by bureaucrats. However, rules are also coordinating devices—ways of codifying understanding and clarity about what should be done.

Rules in this sense can become what public management scholar Leisha Dehart-Davis calls "green tape."[66] In contrast to red tape rules, green tape rules are designed and implemented with supporting bureaucrats in mind. They might clearly define an organization's goals, or articulate when bureaucrats can exercise discretion and judgment. Green tape rules ultimately seek to provide bureaucrats the right amount of autonomy for the task at hand.[67] As a result, green tape rules are associated with higher job satisfaction and likely mission motivation.[68]

At their best, rules are not something to be enforced on bureaucrats but rather tools to be referred to and utilized to forward their jobs. Like data, they can be extremely useful in helping bureaucrats make better decisions. Take the concept of dynamic accountability that Sabel and Zeitlin introduce, which describes a good action as one that forwards an organization's mission. We could imagine trying to codify that in a rule: "Actions that forward the organization's goals but are prevented by any other rule in this rulebook are acceptable, when accompanied by sufficient justification to superiors."

We see examples of empowering green tape rules in the private sector, but rarely in the public sector. Take Netflix's expense policy, which is five words long: "Act in Netflix's best interest."[69] This is an accountability rule well aligned with Netflix's "Valued Behaviors," which include "You seek what is best for Netflix, not yourself or your team," "you make wise decisions despite ambiguity," and "you use data to inform your intuition and choices."[70] As Netflix puts it in one of this chapter's epigraphs, "Freedom and responsibility go together." I think this is *exactly* right.

For Mission Driven Bureaucrats to thrive, upward accountability to senior bureaucrats and politicians need not go away. It must, however, mean something different from mere compliance with centrally determined objectives and quantitative targets. An empowerment-oriented approach to accountability can reduce corruption while focusing squarely on serving organizational missions and increasing the welfare of citizens.

Toward Better Performance with Less Control: Rethinking Accountability for a Mission-Driven World

When I first started using the phrase "Mission Driven Bureaucrats," I realized that the expression has religious connotations for some people (though not for me). This prompted me to explore the etymology of the word "mission"; and indeed, the word does have religious origins. In its original meaning in the 1590s, a mission referred to religious missionaries being sent abroad—the "act of sending, a dispatching."[71]

Mission Driven Bureaucrats arguably share some similarities with missionaries—not because they possess any particular religious faith, but because they frequently feel a deep sense of purpose in the outcomes they seek to achieve. This realization led me to try to learn something about the managerial practices of those original Jesuit missionaries, sent on long voyages in isolation.[72] Whatever one thinks of their goal, there is something to be learned from the ways the Jesuits managed their vast organization.

Church leaders would surely have preferred to perfectly observe every action by missionaries, but that was impossible. They knew that on landing at a distant shore, it would have been exceedingly easy for a missionary to shirk their responsibilities and do very little. Church leaders thus worked hard to recruit the most mission-motivated to set off on the journey.[73] Leaders understood that the right approach was not to monitor (poorly) and attempt to control the few things they could, but to manage for empowerment.

Any external involvement by church leaders sought to sustain mission motivation, not exact punishment through sanctions. [74] The church promoted peer accountability; missionaries wrote to and received anonymous letters from peers, allowing them to access peer guidance.[75] This helped kindle a feeling of community—of being part of a larger whole despite the great expanses of space and time over which missionaries operated. This sustained missionaries' mission motivation and performance.[76] There was much to admire, I believe, in the Jesuits' approach to management and accountability.

Public agencies generally seek to enhance public welfare. This chapter has argued that our status quo approach focused on compliance isn't always the best approach to help them do so. Compliance-oriented accountability regimes may minimize damage by the worst actors. But even where those attempts are *successful*—and often, they are not—they are accompanied by many hidden costs that threaten performance. By demotivating employees and driving out the mission-motivated, these strategies may make corruption worse. By insisting on formal documentation for every action, these strategies induce bureaucrats to demand the same of citizens. As we saw in the HUD case that opened this chapter, this can undermine trust in the relationship between citizens and the state.

The next Mission Driven Bureaucrat profiled, Preetam Ponnappa, manages to comply with his organization's accountability regime while meeting his own value-based standards for good work. Preetam feels ultimately accountable to the public, not to his supervisors. This makes him far less likely to engage in corruption, and far more likely to serve his mission unsupervised.

Shifting management practices toward empowerment is far from easy. But there is plenty that an agency, individual manager, or bureaucrat can do to help with this shift. The next chapter, Chapter 8, discusses practical Route E reforms a range of actors can do to support Mission Driven Bureaucrats and improve performance.

When it comes to accountability, there are no universal truths, just universal tensions. To get better solutions to accountability, we need to remember to ask better questions and to consider alternatives other than simply attempting to increase compliance-oriented accountability. Different answers to whom, for what, and how will maximize performance in different environments. It is this performance, not anti-corruption per se, that we should be focused on as we design accountability systems.

Profile: Preetam Ponnappa

Mission-Motivated Accountability in Karnataka,
India (Social Auditor)

"A place where my existence mattered."

Preetam grew up in the small village of Coorg. As a child in this beautifully green but isolated town, Preetam always dreamed of what lay beyond the horizon. He reminisces, "we used to come out of the house and look at airplanes flying above thinking, 'What kind of life would have been there on the other side?'"

In an effort to answer that question, Preetam left for Bangalore, India's "silicon valley" after finishing his education. He landed a job at one of Bangalore's best companies and earned a good salary with great employee benefits. He knew that his salary and benefits would become even greater if he stayed, but he longed for more meaningful and fulfilling work. "I have always believed that it's not the money that I want. It's the difference that I want to make somewhere." Preetam moved from job to job for years, always looking for "a place where my existence mattered." When his father became ill, he returned to Coorg. A neighbor who worked for the government referred him for a job opening as a social auditor. Preetam took the position with great hesitancy because he worried that he would not be able to have a positive impact as a bureaucrat.

He has now been working as a social auditor for ten years. His job is to verify the outcomes of government programs that employ citizens to perform public works. He also examines the quality of the work, asking, "Has the beneficiary really benefited out of it? Is it reaching him on time?"

Preetam's job is meant to be focused on compliance—reporting up the hierarchy against targets set from above. Preetam chooses a different path, one very focused on direct accountability to citizens. "I don't booze. I don't smoke. I keep my private life as good as my professional life. When I walk in town, it's not a different person walking out there. I walk my work."

This virtuous behavior allows him to "win the trust" of his fellow citizens who benefit from the government schemes he audits. "What happens is in most of my cases, ... [people] are only listening to me because [of how] I have portrayed myself. Not as a social auditor, not the power that I actually execute at my office level." Preetam works far more than the required hours because he feels accountable to the public. "These beneficiaries, these end users ... are completely dependent on the system. They're hoping that this system will save them, because, for the beneficiary, it's *their life*."

Preetam knows that he could do his work and meet his supervisor's expectations without going above and beyond. Indeed, most of his colleagues do. "At 5:00 o'clock, the bell rings to go home, so that's it" for many of his peers. Preetam stresses, "They're not cheating, they're not being non-ethical." But it does lead to far different ways of working, and results.

If the government hires unemployed workers to build a well, Preetam's superiors simply want to know that the well was built. If the well was built, the employment scheme is understood to be successful, even if it was designed to support unskilled workers and only skilled workers were hired to do the construction. In this case, "the scheme [was] going right [according to my superiors], but the objective [was] not being followed."

As we've discussed, compliance-oriented accountability regimes can undermine performance by reducing the mission motivation of employees. Preetam acknowledges that this dynamic is "very tough actually." He sometimes worries, "maybe [a] bureaucracy which is [operating] in this manner is not actually helping anybody." He admits that he spent the first years in his government job "saying that I can't make a difference." He was "carried away with those stories that people started to say, that you can't make a difference in the system. Your existence hardly brings anything, you know, ... you may not make any kind of an impact anywhere."

Luckily for Preetam's agency, he has decided to meet both his supervisors' requirements and his own standards for good work. "I make sure I give [my supervisors] the exact data ... so they are happy about that on their part, and I keep this value system with these people also alive." Without the compliance-oriented data, Preetam believes, the agency "will remove me and get a person who is working on the data." After initially struggling, Preetam has found a way to combine compliance-oriented and citizen-based accountability. Preetam works to fulfill the spirit, not just the letter, of the program. This leads to an ongoing tension—"There was always a friction. ... I stand on *values* and they stand on the *data*."

Some of Preetam's managers have started to support his value-based approach. They "feel that I'm a better social auditor—they have given me that credit." What would make it easier for other social auditors to behave more like

Preetam does? In his view, management needs to change their perspective on performance. Employee success should not simply mean meeting targets, but ensuring that the true purpose of the government programs has been fulfilled.

Preetam thinks that these changes should be coupled with hiring process changes. "The whole selection process of people who are social auditors needs to be changed." There are, in his view, many people—our Binas and Samirs—who would be attracted by management that focuses on conducting meaningful work and being accountable to citizens. "With a purpose, people can come into this system and make it really better." Preetam's confidence returns to his voice as he imagines this reality. If mission-motivated individuals served as social auditors, "there will be an impact."

Career sacrifices, conflicting values at work, and managerial friction have brought strife to Preetam's journey. Despite the challenges, he remarks, "I'm happy that I'm here. I'm happy because I can actually do something better than what is required of me." His mission motivation has not been suffocated by the compliance-oriented regime of his workplace, and he has chosen to combine the compliance-based approach of his organization with his own mission-driven interpretation of his role. "I've got a job where I'm supposed to be. . . . That's all that matters."

Strategies to Improve Performance

Diagnosing an Organization and Prescribing Route E Reforms

> Those trained only to reheat pre-cooked hamburgers are unlikely to be-
> come master chefs. It is when teachers feel a sense of ownership over
> their classrooms and when students feel a sense of ownership over their
> learning that productive teaching takes place. That is the fundamental
> problem of systems where administrative accountability arrangements
> stifle autonomy, they do not generate and sustain capacity.
> —Andreas Schleicher, director, OECD Directorate of
> Education and Skills[1]

At its core, managing for empowerment is about changing who leads an organization. This doesn't mean replacing all its managers and senior executives. Rather,
it means shifting whose judgment guides the actions taken by an organization.
Under compliance-oriented management, managers and bosses at the top of the
hierarchy are the ones whose judgment matters. Managing for empowerment,
by contrast, shifts power to Mission Driven Bureaucrats throughout the organization. The role of management is less to instruct or control workers than to
support them. When discussing work with a subordinate, an empowerment-
oriented boss might begin the conversation with, "What can I do to help and
support your work?" rather than "Let me hear your performance report." By
allowing autonomy, cultivating competence, and creating connection, managing
for empowerment can sustain and even increase employees' mission motivation
and organizational performance.

This chapter turns to the question of how empowering Route E reforms can
take hold in an organization, focusing primarily on organizational leaders and
managers. But before turning to *how*, the chapter first discusses *whether* to do
so—the diagnostic process of deciding whether Route C or E is more likely to
improve performance.

Mission Driven Bureaucrats. Dan Honig, Oxford University Press. © Oxford University Press 2024.
DOI: 10.1093/oso/9780197641194.003.0008

When a doctor prescribes medicine, she does so by considering not only the nature of the disease, but also the patient—their habits, history, and personality. Our "patient" is an agency trying to achieve an important public purpose. Reform prescriptions should similarly start with an understanding of that agency's organizational nature.[2] Key aspects of that nature include the type of tasks its employees perform, the current state of its management, as well as its unique mix of mission-motivated Binas, changeable Samirs, and un-mission-motivateable Peters.

Diagnosing the Organization's Tasks, and Their Monitorability

The first factor managers should consider is whether the work can be easily and effectively monitored. A compliance-oriented managerial approach may be exactly the right one for an agency with tasks that can be reliably monitored and contracted upon. In Chapter 2 I suggested that compliance-oriented practices are much like a screwdriver—perfect for some tasks (e.g., tightening a screw), useful to have in every toolkit, but terrible for other tasks (e.g., changing a tire). When compliance goes wrong we shouldn't get angry at the screwdriver itself or toss it out of the toolbox. We also shouldn't keep using it for jobs where the screwdriver doesn't help performance. Route C performance improvement strategies can be wonderful managerial tools, but they have to be used in the right conditions.

Many agencies in the public sector don't meet the conditions required for extreme compliance-oriented management to thrive. Recall Labanya, who managed the first South Sudanese census. Labanya couldn't manage her staff through compliance-oriented tools because she couldn't monitor her employees when they were in the field. There were also no data with which she could have verified their results. But some version of this problem has appeared in many profiles. For example, Preetam grew frustrated with monitorable targets that miss the spirit of the mission, while Judy's agency previously focused only on observable rules rather than unobservable performance.

Imperfect "good but not great" monitoring is very common given the complex nature of public sector work. We try to rely primarily on compliance even when it's not the right tool for the job. Where this is true, and it often is, Route E reforms that aim to increase empowerment-oriented management may be more appropriate.

As I suggested in Chapter 2, one way to think about this would be to ponder what would happen to an agency or team if its employees embarked on a "work-to-rule" strike—refusing to do anything not required by formally written rules or contracts and observed by monitoring regimes. If there would be minimal performance loss during such a strike, then a fully top-down, compliance-oriented managerial approach may work well. But if such a strike would yield a marked reduction in performance or require prohibitively expensive or technically impractical types of monitoring to prevent that reduction, then that agency may be a good candidate for Route E reforms.

Diagnosing Bureaucrats' Mission Points and Motivation

The second factor to consider when looking to diagnose an agency's performance is the people who work in the agency. Who populates the system? What are their motivations, constraints, and abilities?

Managerial approaches and employee response are mutually reinforcing.[3] Compliance-oriented management is appropriate for employees who are not mission-motivated and would otherwise shirk. But it also *creates* these employees, both through treatment (demotivating the motivated) as well as through selection (inducing the mission-motivated to exit). Empowerment-oriented management, by contrast, allows autonomy, cultivates competence, and creates connection. This approach in turn creates employees who thrive under an empowerment-oriented management style through treatment (kindling mission motivation) and selection (attracting and retaining the mission-motivated).

In Chapter 2, I introduced three "types" of employees: mission-driven Bina, persistently unmotivated Peter, and Samir, who could become mission-motivated if placed under the right managerial conditions. Of course, these are stylized types; people are far more varied in real life. Nevertheless, these rough groupings help us imagine the impacts that a given set of reforms might have on different employees. Managers can tap on a variety of informal methods to get a sense of the distribution of personnel within their organization, from focus groups to the assessments of middle managers. Perhaps even more important, managers and leaders can learn about individuals' mission points. This includes learning both what individuals see as their personal mission point and what they understand to be their team or organization's mission points. One of the "lightest-touch" Route E reforms is to establish and clarify mission points, creating unity and a sense of collective purpose.

Understanding workers' personal missions also sheds light on whether they are likely to be mission-motivated if empowerment-oriented management is increased. If, as is usually the case in my experience, an agency is mostly populated by motivateable Samirs, then managers' central consideration should be how to increase mission motivation. If an agency has mostly already mission-motivated Binas, the central focus should instead be on empowering them to act in service of the agency's mission point. Of course, a desire to maximize the performance of Binas must be balanced with the potential costs of fewer constraints on unmotivateable Peters. In an agency with a significant number of Peters, managers must ponder whether, when, and how these employees might do damage following Route E reforms, and subsequently how to prevent it without stifling the mission motivation of Binas and Samirs. Managers with a "Peter problem" can, for instance, seek to recruit more Binas and Samirs, consider shifting Peters to tasks or teams where more compliance-oriented management is appropriate, or encourage Peters to exit.

When Judy Parfitt helped reform the South African Revenue Service after Apartheid, as described in her profile, she did two distinct things. First, she helped shift the actual mission point of the agency. Second, she helped shift the agency's managerial approach toward greater empowerment. In so doing she discovered what in my experience many, many reformers do: that their agency, and the world more generally, has far fewer Peters and far more Samirs than they would have imagined. Many of the people who seem like they will never change, actually do. Those who appear to be part of the problem are also surprisingly often part of the solution.

Judy's example highlights how tricky diagnosing motivation can be, even to those who work closely with the bureaucrats whose motivation they seek to understand. Understanding not just *what* people do but *why* they do it is really, really hard. Another approach is *not* to diagnose motivation, but to instead initiate Route E reforms and see who responds, allowing Samirs to reveal themselves. Particularly where the risk of greater fraud or malfeasance in doing so is relatively low, simply assuming the best and piloting Route E reforms can sometimes be the best way forward.

Diagnosing Current Managerial Practice

Characterizing an agency's current managerial approach is a surprisingly challenging task. It might seem obvious that managers would be aware of the tactics they use to manage their employees, but this is often untrue. In my work with public sector organizations, I've found that even if the management approach is "common knowledge" for employees, it isn't always so for their supervisors.[4] Management's perceptions of themselves often differ from the perceptions of the people they supervise.

The easiest way to figure out where an organization's management currently lies is to ask its employees. This can be done quite informally, though ideally not by bosses directly; employees tend not to tell their supervisors if they think management is too controlling. Managers can also employ some of the formal methods mentioned above, such as surveys and focus groups.

If your organization is running staff surveys already, there may be existing questions that speak to management and motivation. But if there isn't one, you can add a simple question that my coauthors and I have employed in the past: "In your opinion, what is the balance in your organization between providing freedom for staff to pursue organizational goals (however they are defined) as they see fit on the one hand, and tightly controlling staff through targets, monitoring, oversight and incentive schemes?" Figure 8.1 represents their answers on a 0–100 scale, where 0 is "complete control of staff action" (full management for compliance) and 100 is "complete freedom for staff" from a survey over 1,300 public sector workers from twenty-eight countries.[5]

We see two notable clusters: one compliance-leaning and one empowerment-leaning.[6] Similar patterns are observed across the twenty-eight countries (see Technical Appendix Figure A.9). More public employees around the world labor under compliance-oriented managerial practices then empowerment-oriented practices. This is consistent with Part II's finding that compliance-oriented

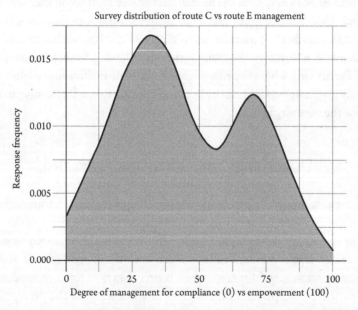

Figure 8.1 Survey distribution of management for empowerment vs. compliance (1,300 bureaucrats across twenty-eight countries)

management is likely overused, given that the nature of most public sector work would suit an empowerment-oriented approach.

Using the data gathered from surveys and interviews—or no formal data at all, just their sense of the organization—agency or team leaders may find it helpful to try to draw a Performance Possibility Frontier (PPF) for their agency. The PPF, as discussed in Chapter 6, imagines that we could accurately map how different management practices translate into performance. A manager, or better yet an entire leadership team, can draw a PPF for their agency, estimating their current position and identifying a reform path toward their global maximum performance.[7]

Figure 8.2 presents a hypothetical PPF for a social work agency delivering job and life counseling to disabled veterans. This is a task that is clearly going to require frontline providers to exercise judgment. For example, social workers might organize counseling sessions differently depending on the client's needs. It is also a task that will be both difficult to monitor and likely to attract mission-motivated Binas and motivateable Samirs. As a result, this agency's higher performance "peak" is likely closer to the empowerment side of the spectrum. However, as discussed in Chapter 6, *some* compliance-oriented technology is still likely useful for the agency to reach its best possible performance.

Having plotted the performance-possibility frontier, how can this hypothetical social work agency use it to chart a reform path? First, it needs to identify current managerial practice. Let's imagine that managers have sent out surveys and conducted multiple focus groups, uncovering that many employees feel stifled by compliance-oriented management. The surveys also suggested that many existing managerial tools aren't being implemented well. For instance, the online system that their agency uses to track the number of clients reviewed per day is prone to malfunction, poorly capturing the quality of employee work. On Figure 8.2, our hypothetical social work agency sits closer to the compliance end

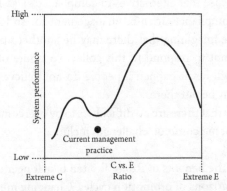

Figure 8.2 Performance Possibility Frontier (PPF) for a hypothetical social work agency

of the spectrum and below the curve, reflecting the inefficiency of its current managerial practices.

This agency has several options for performance improvement. It could improve the implementation of its current practices, which would move it vertically upward toward the frontier—the curve itself. Alternatively, it could invest in either Route C *or* Route E managerial practices and move diagonally upward toward the C-oriented peak or the E-oriented peak. That said, the shape of the frontier, with a higher E-oriented peak, suggests that empowerment-oriented management is a better strategy to lead this agency toward its global maximum.

This brings up the question of "how." How can this agency—or any agency, for that matter—in fact shift toward empowerment-oriented management?

Overcoming Obstacles to Route E Reforms

A lot of the people that I talk to outside of government seem to think it's not obvious that agencies should engage in more management for empowerment. Partly in response to that, a lot of this book has set about developing an evidence base for when and where managing for empowerment is a good idea.

In contrast, a lot of the people that I talk to inside government—frontline workers, managers, organizational leaders, politicians, advisors, committee staff doing oversight—need no convincing whatsoever that their system is far too compliance-oriented. When I start explaining the core arguments of this book to someone in government service, I frequently have the genuinely wonderful experience of people responding in ways that make it clear to me that they feel "seen" by what I am saying.[8] I have heard example after example of yet another new technology for monitoring and compliance, despite that general approach's prior failings.

Quickly, the conversation turns to "So what do we do about it?" There is often surprisingly little sense that alternatives to compliance exist. Many people have been steeped in compliance-oriented management for so long that they genuinely have trouble imagining that there may be another way. The rest of this chapter is an attempt to respond to this collective failure of the imagination. After all, change will never happen if people do not believe it is possible, and better solutions may be out there.

This is not to say that there are no difficulties to be overcome in implementing Route E reforms. Some common challenges include:

- *Time Horizons*: The benefits of Route E often take longer to appear than the standard time horizons of promotion cycles. Changing mindsets and culture is a much longer process than simply changing rules. This may incentivize managers to pursue compliance-oriented Route C reforms, which promise quicker and easier performance results. Furthermore, subordinates have time horizons too and often expect to remain in their posts longer than their managers or leaders. They often worry that what is changed by today's manager will be changed back by tomorrow's. Subordinates therefore frequently suffer "reform fatigue," having seen many false "transformations" come and go. This may lead lower-level bureaucrats to resist change, even when they support the reform's objectives.

- *Career Risks*: Modifying incentives or creating new rules for staff are conventional ways to improve performance, and they are also easier to directly connect to performance outcomes. Taking a different path is inherently risky. Managers considering Route E reforms may be dissuaded by concerns about the impacts of unsuccessful reforms on their careers.
- *The Limits of Individual Power*: Individual managers may lack the authority to enact Route E reforms on their own. As Chapter 5 argued, managers considering Route E are often constrained by compliance-oriented rules or accountability regimes that come from their bosses (and their boss's bosses).
- *Political Pressures*: A leader who wishes to pursue Route E may face political pressures to choose Route C. Some (but not all) forms of empowerment-oriented management increase the risk that unmotivated Peters will engage in greater waste or fraud. Even if a Route E reform improves the performance of 99 bureaucrats, but enables just 1 bureaucrat to commit fraud, this exception may overshadow the successful outcomes in the public eye. Chapter 9 will explore this further.

Many of these problems might sound overwhelming, beyond the ability of any one bureaucrat or organizational leader to change. To some extent, they are—no single individual can eliminate broader structural issues. But there's also a sense in which they aren't. I have never encountered a bureaucrat, wherever their position may be in the hierarchy, who couldn't do *something* to move management for empowerment forward if they wished to. What exactly those things are depends on a person's position and organization. It also depends on what, precisely, is likely to prove empowering for their task, team, or system.

There is no one-size-fits-all way to manage for empowerment. Empowerment-oriented management involves tackling each agency's specific context and crafting solutions that suit its tasks, culture, and workforce. This chapter therefore does not contain "Route E widgets" that are as simply and broadly applicable as many Route C tools. What I can offer instead is a menu of ideas for implementing Route E.

The rest of this chapter presents a set of potential reform ingredients to be customized and adapted as appropriate to a given organization. The ideas that follow are drawn in part from my own empirical research and that of others, but also from experiences and conversations I've had with agency leaders, politicians, and bureaucrats around the world. My hope is that many will find something that seems useful as a starting point for their own organizationally tailored approaches to encouraging more management for empowerment. The menu that follows is divided into three sections: manager-level reforms, peer approaches, and agency-level reforms.

The parentheses after each item highlight the relevant Route E core principles involved: allowing autonomy, cultivating competence, and creating connection to peers and purpose.

Manager-Level Route E Reforms

While empowerment-oriented managerial changes *can* start at the top of an organization, they don't have to. Route C reforms might rely on those at the top of the hierarchy to change formal rules or install new technology, but Route E reforms can be initiated by many different actors across a system. Change can begin with a single manager. Some strategies for individual managers include:

- **Removing or Insulating Your Team from Red Tape** (Allow Autonomy, Create Connection): When an employee appears to lack mission motivation, the first question that managers should ask is whether they are unmotivateable or simply demotivated. If it is the latter, the simplest solution is to remove that which is demotivating them. Often, this comes in the form of red tape. "Red tape" is a term that refers to bureaucratic rules and processes that have a well-documented history of slowing or preventing employees from doing their best work.[9] Savvy managers can collect feedback from their staff about the rules and practices that are most time-consuming, irritating, or frustrating. With this knowledge, they insulate their teams from such requirements. This might involve re-engineering processes, or invoking exceptions to rules where they are undermining performance.

- **Connecting Actions to Results** (Create Connection): Remind employees that what they do *matters*. This often involves connecting them with clients or beneficiaries, allowing them to witness the positive consequences of their actions at work. While this is felt most powerfully through in-person contact,[10] evidence suggests that even small "micro-interventions," such as messages that remind bureaucrats of their impact, can have salutary effects on mission motivation.[11]

- **Encouraging Self-Directed Development** (Allow Autonomy, Cultivate Competence, Create Connection): The simplest way to engage in empowerment-oriented management is quite simple: ask employees what they want to learn, how they want to grow, and what they want to do. Then, support them in doing so. Employees should be empowered to adopt a leading role in their own development, rather than simply following instructions under tight micro-management. If this hasn't been the traditional method of management in an agency, staff may initially be reticent to take up this offer. However, given time and persistence, there is good evidence that organizational culture can and *will* change. The profiles in this book—for instance, of Judy Parfitt and Uma Mahadevan—provide compelling illustration that transformation is possible. Key is to build trust, including by establishing what organizational psychologists call psychological safety. This is the belief that everyone on a team has something to offer and will not be punished for voicing ideas, even if those ideas do not prove actionable.
- **Treating Your Subordinates More Like Equals** (Allow Autonomy, Cultivate Competence, Create Connection): Make the "you" and "them" more of an "us." Managers can lead not just from above their team of employees, but also as a part of it, as the Thai district managers and Joseph's experience at the US State Department both demonstrate. Rather than simply giving out instructions, managers can collectively discuss policy options with their teams. Encouraging a more horizontal relationship between managers and employees will promote psychological safety, encouraging team members to offer their own ideas for performance improvement. This may then activate a virtuous cycle, where employees effectively and self-reliantly strive to fulfill their purpose.
- **Establishing a Clear Mission Point** (Create Connection): As this book's evidence has suggested, a clear and widely understood mission point is pivotal for agency performance. Not only does a well-defined mission point orient the actions of employees, it also attracts and retains Mission Driven Bureaucrats. While this can be done at the agency level, establishing a collective mission point is something that team managers can do as well.[12] This can make employees' work feel meaningful, clarifying their connections to beneficiaries. Clear mission points can foster a sense of unity and kinship between peers and within teams as well.

A shift toward empowerment-oriented management is possible even within organizations where compliance management generally dominates. Even in these environments, the power of a single manager investing in Route E should not be underestimated. Norms of empowerment-oriented management can originate from one reformer and spread outward.

Managers' Role in Strengthening Peer Networks and Creating an Empowering Culture

Managers and systems play important roles in fostering connection between peers, and between citizens and bureaucrats. Sharath Jeevan (the founder of STiR, the motivation in education charity first mentioned in Chapter 3) put it eloquently in saying, "the [peer] horizontal layers are important, but they need support from the [managerial] vertical as well, because you're in a bureaucratic system. It's about giving space. So [how does] the leader above that network— whether that's the principal in the school or the district inspector . . . 'bless' [it] and create that space where teachers feel they can support each other safely?"[13] By creating pathways for peers to connect and inspire each other to serve their mission with competence and passion, managers can impact the performance of their teams.

Managers can also support their teams to make mission-driven behavior the norm. Key to doing so is, as one prominent study of the effect of leadership on mission orientation and motivation put it, "engaging employees' existing values, infusing jobs with meaning, and highlighting and rewarding public service values."[14] Managers can build self-sustaining, mission-driven teams of employees from the ground up.

A few of the many ways that managers can encourage better performance using the power of teams and peers are:

- **Catalyzing Peer Reviews and Discussions** (Cultivate Competence, Create Connection): Bringing a group of peers together for a discussion of their mission can be an excellent way to connect employees to their shared purpose. Peer review systems used by health inspectors in Seattle improved performance and act as a form of peer accountability, as we saw in Chapter 5. Chapter 6 discussed a study of Pakistani health workers, which found that bringing a group of peers together for three discussions of their shared mission improved performance more than did financial incentives.[15] That such a simple intervention could be so effective suggests that this may be a very promising reform indeed. It is also an example of a Route E reform that need not reduce any current compliance-oriented managerial practices.
- **Promoting Professionalism** (Cultivate Competence, Create Connection): Previous chapters have illustrated that the development of professional pride is a wonderful way to foster mission-driven motivation. As Grindle puts it, employees performed better when they "believed that they were behaving according to professional universal standards" of mission-driven behavior.[16] Fostering a sense of professional pride in workers' identity as nurses,

social workers, and so forth can be an important part of sustaining mission motivation.

- **Reinforcing an Empowerment-oriented Team Narrative** (Allow Autonomy, Cultivate Competence, Create Connection): As Chapter 5 described, managers can help shape a strong team identity that centers norms of integrity, honor, and commitment. To do so, they can create, communicate, and reinforce a narrative of their team's positive impact on citizens. Employees who take pride in being a member of their team will act in mission-oriented ways.

Agency-Level Route E Reforms

There is a great deal that those at the top of the organizational hierarchy can do to catalyze Route E reforms. In addition to the reforms above, agency leaders seeking to improve the motivation of their current employees might consider:

- **Setting Up Systems to Listen** (Allow Autonomy, Cultivate Competence, Create Connection): Those closest to the work often have lots of good ideas about how to make it better, but many organizations do not have established systems for providing such practical feedback to agency leadership. One Route E strategy is to set up safe channels for employees to offer their ideas and suggestions. This is essentially a formal, agency-wide version of the team-level strategy suggested earlier. In Ghana, for example, a civil service training module "designed to encourage mid-level civil servants to identify potential work process improvements and put them into action," notably improved project completion rates.[17] Agencies must also nurture a culture where employees feel comfortable to make honest suggestions. As Williams and Yecalo-Tecle put it, "most officials do have meaningful ideas for improving performance. However, the overwhelming constraint to voicing these ideas is [psychological threat-based] hostility by supervisors to new ideas from their subordinates."[18] Empowerment-oriented management benefits from being open and receptive to the feedback of employees.

- **Adding Green Tape** (Allow Autonomy, Cultivate Competence, Create Connection): As we've seen, rules can *empower*, if they're written correctly. Agency leaders can, for example, clearly outline where judgment and autonomy are allowed, or even encouraged. These rules could also establish that accountability must focus on "account," not "accounting." Take, for instance, Netflix's five-word expense policy introduced in the last chapter: "Act in Netflix's best interest."[19] Revise the organizational playbook by adding rules that support, rather than constrain, Mission Driven Bureaucrats.

- **Cultivating Communities of Practice** (Cultivate Competence, Create Connection): As discussed in Chapter 5, communities of practice bring together groups of people who perform similar tasks within different teams or agencies. Agency leaders can organize formal or informal gatherings of people performing similar functions in different units (e.g., procurement, planning, human resources) to help facilitate peer learning and peer accountability as well as foster mission motivation.[20]

- **Building "Better" Bosses** (Allow Autonomy, Cultivate Competence): Organizations can encourage managers to consider their managerial choices more deeply, and potentially invest in empowerment-oriented management. Managerial communities of practice could, for example, gather to discuss methods to implement green tape, implement Route E reforms, or how to implement and respond to subordinate performance reviews of managers themselves.[21]

- **Formally Delegating Authority** (Allow Autonomy, Cultivate Competence, Create Connection): Agency leaders can formally delegate decision-making authority to those lower down the hierarchy, from middle managers to frontline workers. Bureaucrats can be given the opportunity to make independent judgments and witness the consequences of those decisions firsthand. Empirical evidence suggests that autonomous units are likely to develop greater competence, as they know they will be able to use these skills.[22] Many employees might be initially hesitant to make use of these new liberties. But with time, encouragement, and implementation support, employees will grow comfortable exercising discretion. When they do, it is imperative that staff do not fear that any incorrect judgment will result in punishment. Rather, they must be allowed to experience and learn from both successes and failures.

- **Centering Citizen-Bureaucrat Interactions** (Allow Autonomy, Cultivate Competence, Create Connection): As Chapters 5 and 7 have explored, it *is* possible to have citizens and bureaucrats work together, particularly where they already interact directly with each other. Giving bureaucrats more autonomy to help citizens, and making citizens' satisfaction an important part of what bureaucrats aim to promote, can be an excellent Route E reform.

- **Recognizing and Rewarding Mission Motivation** (Create Connection): Creating connection requires employees to believe in the value of their actions at work. Managers can facilitate this by the celebrating the mission-driven actions of employees. For instance, managers can offer awards to employees who have gone above and beyond to forward their agency's mission. Not only will this recognition cultivate mission motivation, it will also incentivize future mission-driven actions.

- **Facilitating Downhill Managerial Trust** (Allow Autonomy, Cultivate Competence, Create Connection): By setting an example of empowerment-oriented management, agency leaders can enable managers lower down the hierarchy to follow suit. If your manager's boss demands "answers" (e.g., reportable metrics) from your manager, every employee in the world knows what will likely happen next—your manager will turn to *you* and demand the same. When leaders manage their subordinates in a compliance-oriented manner, treating them as conduits to implement their orders rather than judgment-makers in their own right, those managers will have no choice but to do the same with *their* subordinates. This perpetuates an unfortunate cycle that traps an agency in management for compliance. Instead, those at the top should take steps to institute norms of empowerment-oriented management. While implementing Route E policy changes is important, they should also simply act in more supportive ways themselves, creating space for their subordinates to do the same. Trust, empowerment, and support can roll downhill.

The ideas listed above are methods for leaders to institute empowerment-oriented management at an agency level, bolstering the mission motivation of current employees. But as Chapter 5 suggested, management can also play a role in selection—attracting and retaining the most mission-motivated Binas. Organizational leaders can set broader human resources policies that "crowd in" Mission Driven Bureaucrats. These might include:

• **Selecting for Both Mission Motivation and Competence** (Cultivate Competence, Create Connection): The simplest way to bring mission-motivated people into an agency is to include motivation in one's selection criteria. Selecting applicants not only based on technical ability but also on mission motivation will ensure that the most talented *and* mission-motivated candidates are hired. There need be no trade-off between technical competence and mission motivation.[23] This may be a particularly viable strategy for agencies that have many more applicants than available positions. Assessing the mission motivation of applicants, for instance through interviews or job trials, is a great way to increase the future motivation of an agency's workforce.

• **Instituting Fast-Stream Entry** (Cultivate Competence, Create Connection): Chapter 5 introduced the work of Emerging Public Leaders and the President's Young Professional Program, which organize fast-stream civil service programs in Ghana and Liberia. Many other countries also employ similar programs, from the United Kingdom's Civil Service Fast Stream program to the Presidential Management Fellows program in the United States. Such programs attract talented and mission-motivated recruits to positions in the civil service. Across the world, introducing mission-driven young recruits can help shift organizational culture and norms. Bringing in more mission-driven Binas may itself increase the mission motivation of Samirs. As one supervisor in Liberia put it, motivated young people "serve as influencers to other colleagues based on [their] good performance."[24]

- **Paying People Better** (Cultivate Competence, Create Connection): Increasing salaries may attract the most competent among the mission-motivated, who likely have the best outside options.[25] Increasing pay can also be seen as a signal of respect and trust, increasing mission motivation.
- **Utilizing Exit Interviews** (Allow Autonomy, Cultivate Competence, Create Connection): Savvy organizations also learn from exits. Why are individuals leaving a given agency? Is it red tape that has them heading for the door? Or is it their inability to accomplish what drew them to the job? Learning from departing employees is an excellent way for leaders to identify how their agency can improve, preventing the exit of other mission-motivated people.

This section has presented a range of potential Route E reforms. We have explored both reforms that increase mission motivation among current employees and that foster a mission-motivated future workforce. Table 8.1 summarizes the full "menu." I suspect that most agencies and managers will find there is something in this list that could be adapted to their organization, improving performance by empowering Mission Driven Bureaucrats.

The Role of Outside Catalysts (e.g., Donors) in Route E Reform

We've now discussed many steps that actors within the public sector can take to institute empowerment-oriented management. But what about the many actors outside the bureaucracy, who often have a significant influence on public sector activities? These might include domestic foundations, foreign aid donors, or civil society organizations.[26]

External organizations almost always *mean* well in their efforts to strengthen the state. But that doesn't mean they always *do* well. External funders tend to be big fans of compliance-oriented managerial solutions, if they focus on management at all. Route C solutions like introducing a new monitoring system often involve comfortingly concrete (and thus easily procured) technology, timelines, logistics, and deliverables.[27]

This is not a special problem of developing countries. In my experience, UK or US cities face many of the same challenges when working with outside foundations, as does a developing country government dealing with the World Bank. External funding exacerbates pressure to deliver quantifiable and report-able results in the lifetime of a given project, which in turn narrows the range

Table 8.1 **Summary of Route E strategies**

Level	Strategy	Summary
Manager (Direct to Subordinates)	Removing or Insulating Your Team from Red Tape	Collecting feedback on unhelpful rules; removing these or creating exceptions.
	Connecting Actions to Results	Connecting employees with clients or beneficiaries, allowing them to witness the positive consequences of their actions at work.
	Encouraging Self-Directed Development	Asking employees what they want to learn, do, and contribute.
	Treating Your Subordinates More Like Equals	Collectively discussing policy options and approaches alongside one's team.
	Establishing a Clear Mission Point	Defining a clear and widely understood mission point.
Manager (Peers and Empowering Team Culture)	Peer Reviews and Discussions	Regular peer discussions to foster collective sense of mission and peer accountability.
	Promoting Professionalism	Creating a sense of belonging within a professional community, for instance by utilizing mission symbols.
	Reinforcing an Empowerment-oriented Team Narrative	Developing a narrative of the team's identity, and actively communicating this purpose to employees.
Agency-Level Management	Setting Up Systems to Listen	Setting up channels for employees to offer their suggestions for improvements.
	Adding Green Tape	Adding or revising rules so that the rules more greatly empower and support employees.
	Cultivating Communities of Practice	Creating groups of employees who perform similar tasks or work toward a similar goal.

(continued)

Table 8.1 **Continued**

Level	Strategy	Summary
	Building "Better" Bosses	Encouraging managers to manage more thoughtfully.
	Formally Delegating Authority	Formally delegating decision-making authority to those lower down the hierarchy.
	Centering Citizen-Bureaucrat Interactions	Put the relationship between citizens and bureaucrats at the center of accountability and what it means to "perform well."
	Recognizing and Rewarding Mission Motivation	Celebrating employees who have shown exceptional mission motivation.
	Facilitating Downhill Managerial Trust	Setting an example of empowerment-oriented management toward one's direct subordinates.
Agency-Level Recruitment	Selecting for both Mission Motivation and Competence	Including mission motivation in the selection criteria for potential recruits.
	Instituting Fast-Stream Entry	Establishing fast-stream recruitment programs that attract the talented and mission-motivated.
	Paying People Better	Increasing salaries to signal greater respect.
	Utilizing Exit Interviews	Surveying departing employees on their decision to leave.

of possible solutions. This leads to capacity-strengthening efforts that focus too much on compliance-oriented management. External actors are hence partly to blame for our overabundance of compliance-oriented "screwdrivers."

That said, this dysfunction is particularly acute in foreign aid, as foreign donors are ultimately accountable to their own taxpayers, rather than to the citizens of developing countries. As a result, the aid industry tends to inefficiently focus on ensuring that every penny is accounted for to taxpayers "back home," rather than using those pennies most effectively and sustainably to improve the developing country's public sector performance. To crib from Charles Kenny, foreign aid industry actors are consequently even more likely than other external providers to focus on "receipts" rather than "results."[28]

Nevertheless, there is hope. There is an increasing recognition in international development circles that the previous generation of compliance-oriented development programs have failed.[29] The need for context-specific rather than cookie-cutter solutions is well-accepted rhetoric among development donors.[30] A new model is necessary—one that delivers sustainable performance improvements by recognizing the unique complexities of motivation, management, and employee empowerment.

Rather than offering solutions, I believe that outsiders hoping to support public sector reform in Leeds (UK), Lilongwe (Malawi), Luang Prabang (Laos), or anywhere else can help most with diagnostics. They can help the public sector explicitly examine whether managing for empowerment is an approach that might improve performance. When an external consultant is hired to assess an agency's needs, those assessments can and should include a section on current management practices, the motivation of current employees, and the potential gains of Route E.

The support of outsiders in these diagnostics can also act as a form of external endorsement of Route E strategies. This will help make empowering reforms to appear more legible and legitimate, "crowding in" domestic reformers who may also perceive external endorsement as increasing a given reform's prospects for success in overcoming internal skeptics. If, for example, the International Monetary Fund suggests to a country's finance minister that it might be a good idea to pursue an empowerment-oriented management philosophy, it will then encourage internal reformers who share that view to mobilize.[31]

Of course, an accurate diagnosis must be paired with effective implementation. If the diagnosis *does* suggest that managing for empowerment is likely to thrive in an organization, then it is important that future capacity-building programs not take the form of compliance-oriented tools or monitoring regimes. Capacity building efforts can focus instead on supporting the emergence of mission motivation and greater empowerment-oriented management. This can involve empowering groups of bureaucrats to work together to solve their own problems, directly allowing autonomy, cultivating a sense of competence, and cultivating connection to peers and purpose.

This direct empowerment approach is what undergirds Harvard's Building State Capability program, led by Matt Andrews and Salimah Samji, where I'm honored to be an associate. The program's core offering is not so much a "solution" as it is a method—a way of bringing bureaucrats together to collectively solve problems. They call this approach Problem Driven Iterative Adaptation

(PDIA). The benefits of direct empowerment are evidenced in the UK National Endowment for Science, Technology, and the Arts (Nesta)'s work on People Powered Results, which brought citizens and bureaucrats together to collectively brainstorm and solve problems.[32]

Route E cannot be implemented *quite* as rapidly as, say, a technological fix. But it does not have to take years, either, and certainly not longer than external funders' timelines. Key to Nesta's People Powered results were "100 day challenges," with intensive coaching and facilitation showing impressive results: for example, reductions in hospital admissions and improved clinical outcomes in the UK National Health Service.[33] There were also longer-term and broader impacts. As Nesta puts it, "successful small-scale tests turn into country-wide implementation" because "the momentum for front-line innovation and new ways of working lasts far beyond the initial 100 days."[34]

What outsiders may therefore offer best is an *approach*, not an answer. This must be an approach that gives those with real power and longer time horizons, like career civil servants, the tools to propose and pilot long-term Route E reforms. External players should offer support, not solutions.

Similar notes are struck by the recently established Local Capacity Strengthening (LCS) Policy at the US Agency for International Development (USAID), which seeks to guide USAID in their capacity-development projects in developing countries. LCS encourages a "new mindset and culture shift" that prioritizes partnering with local actors and leveraging their ability to create sustainable change.[35] As the policy puts it, "capacity encompasses the knowledge, skills, and motivations, as well as the relationships, that enable an actor—an individual, an organization, or a network—to take action to design and implement solutions to local development challenges, to learn and adapt from that action."[36]

If the significance of mission motivation and local leadership in finding solutions can even be recognized by USAID, an agency that in prior research I found to be highly steeped in compliance-oriented practices, then I have some hope that the "governance" sector as a whole may be able to similarly shift their orientation.[37] Outsiders can meaningfully facilitate organizational shifts toward management for empowerment. But doing so requires them to be advisors and supporters of locally led processes, rather than saviors providing a cookie-cutter fix.

Route E at Scale: Toward a Managerial Regime That's Fit for Purpose

The ultimate goal of public sector reform is often pretty simple, even if it can be very hard to achieve in practice: enhancing performance in order to improve citizen welfare. In many cases, the best way to do that is through empowerment-oriented management. This chapter has outlined a few of the many forms Route E reforms can take. The key now is to put them into practice.

This chapter has presented a set of strategies that are potential answers to the simple question at the heart of management for empowerment: "How can I make it easier for the people I work with to serve the agency's mission point?" The answer will depend on myriad factors, including whom you work with, your mission point, and your agency's norms and political leadership.

Here's the good news. Once that question is answered and managing for empowerment becomes part of your agency's culture, it tends to remain answered. Unlike Route C, Route E reforms do not require continued investments in external monitoring or rewards. While changes in culture might take longer to implement, Route E reforms take deep root. Scaling Route E means slowly building momentum as those roots spread, building Route E environments one team, and one agency, at a time. Just like successful political or social movements, Route E scales by generating "momentum," as Nesta put it, gathering force as it grows.[38]

The next chapter, Chapter 9, concludes with a focus on what we citizens can do to help direct that change in ways that ultimately allow our governments to best serve us. Before that, though, comes this book's final profile: Batool Asadi. Batool is dedicated to changing the state to better serve its laudable mission. Batool aims not just to change her own behavior, but that of other women in Balochistan, Pakistan, where she works. Mission Driven Bureaucrats like Batool can be catalysts of positive changes in their peers and the broader public.

Changing the bureaucracy, even a little bit, can seem like an impossible task. But on reflection, I think that it only appears to be that way. I think it's pretty well described by one of the most famous of philosophical paradoxes, Aristotle's Ship of Theseus. The wooden planks of a boat at sea are slowly replaced, one by one, as they begin to rot. Eventually, every single plank has been replaced and all of the boat's original wood has been discarded. Is the ship still the Ship of Theseus? How could it be, when every single part of it is different from the set of physical objects that originally constituted the ship? This thought experiment illustrates that what may at first seem unchangeable can be and in fact already is being altered. Even the most seemingly permanent objects change over time.

As ancient Greek ships go, so too do bureaucracies and states. "The state" may appear unchangeable and permanent. But it only *seems* that way. "States" are convenient fictions; they can do no more, and no less, than the individuals acting in their name. Zoom in and the state simply consists of groups of individuals led by their own missions. Changing a government just means changing what those people do. This not only *can* happen, it already *is* happening. Every day, in every state, individuals are changing in myriad ways, as we all do throughout our lives. All Route E needs to do is channel that change in mission-motivating directions.

Profile: Batool Asadi

Modeling Mission Motivation in Balochistan, Pakistan
(Assistant Commissioner)

"We all have to bring change."

Batool describes herself as "a bit rebellious—I am a rebellion."

She is close to her family and devout in her faith, but that has not stopped her from challenging the norms enshrined in both. "I come from a very conventional and traditional family. My father is a religious scholar, my brothers are religious. Being in a patriarchal society, we never had that agency that since childhood I felt that I needed."

Growing up, Batool faced many restrictions. "You cannot wear this, you cannot go there. . . . You cannot talk to males." This never sat well with Batool, who thought, "Whatever I want to wear, I should be able to wear it. If I want to study some subject that is forbidden, I should be able to do it unless I am convinced not to do that." With the stern clarity of someone who does not take this lightly, she said to her parents, "I *should* have this liberty," and "I should have liberty to distinguish as to what is wrong and what is right rather than being dictated 'do something.'"

She continues, "I always wanted something more for my life. I wanted to test myself. I wanted to know what I can do. I want people to know me, Batool, in her own capacities as a talented person." As a result, Batool has made "very, very different choices. I'm the first person [in my family] to be a civil servant through competitive exam. I was the first person to be in Oxford," where she is taking a career break to study for a master's degree at the time of this interview.[1]

She was attracted to the civil service because she wanted to change things for the better. "When I was in university, during our different talks, I used to criticize government policies. And usually, I used to think that, 'am I going to do this? The whole of my life talking with students and cribbing on what government is doing and I'm not able to do anything about it? I'm just an outsider?' So, apart from the prestige, I wanted to be part of civil service. I wanted to see if I could do anything." There is every reason to believe that she could in fact have done anything she put her mind to. Some quick research shows (she is far too modest to have brought this up herself) that the year Batool took Pakistan's civil service exam, she ranked twenty-first among approximately 14,000 test-takers.[2]

Once in the civil service, Batool sought an assignment back home in rural Balochistan, "nearer to my heart." Some of her classmates would call her home region "backward," and preferred to find more comfortable roles in stable, wealthier regions. Batool was motivated to go where things were hardest—where she could make the biggest impact. "When I criticize something, when I criticize corruption, when I criticize some social evil, personally, I believe that I will always think—what can I do about it?"

The few women who are employed in the Pakistani civil service are mostly in desk jobs. According to Batool, they often feel safer in those roles than going to the field. When she made known her intention of returning to the field in Balochistan, many in the civil service objected, "No, you are female, we can't do this. We can't take this risk." Everyone seemed to agree that it would be better if Batool would "just sign the files and help us with the file work."

Fueled by her desire to forward her organization's mission and her ambition to have an impact, Batool pushed to become the first female assistant commissioner to serve in the field in Balochistan's history. Batool's superiors and peers were initially reluctant to accept her at par with male colleagues. At first, she heard some people saying, "she will do something wrong, and then we will highlight, you know, psychology of downplaying her good things and you know highlighting her bad things. . . . She's a civil servant. She will make a wrong decision ultimately, she cannot take this much pressure." She remembers, "those five, six months were hell for me." Instead of seeking to support and utilize the talents of their new mission-driven employee, most of those surrounding Batool were waiting for her to fail. However, her willpower and enthusiasm helped her win the support of a few colleagues against the odds.

Fortunately for the Deputy Commissioner's Office and for the people of Balochistan, Batool remained mission-driven despite those difficult first months. In the absence of gender-sensitive official support and an empowerment-oriented environment, Batool turned to an alternative source of motivation: her connection to the citizens she was serving and inspiring through her work.

For every comment made to undermine her, a mother was saying, "we want our daughters and our sisters to be like you." When she saw the positive impact of her work, she was reminded that her actions mattered. Her tone shifts when she speaks about young girls who studied harder because they had seen her example. As we have discussed, cultivating mission motivation requires employees to believe in the value of their actions. The pride and responsibility Batool feels sustains her mission motivation. She is still amazed by the response she received from women in her community. "Young girls in Balochistan, when they are in their schools and they think that they can do something because I have been in those schools. They can relate to me, I've been there. They think, *'If she can do this, we can.'*" She remembers mothers asking her, "'Can you guide my daughter? Can I bring her to your office?' And that was my motivation each day."

This does not mean the job became easy. For Batool, being in the field means "you're directly implementing government policies and people *will* react if they see a female officer is coming to their shop and she is telling them they aren't doing it right or arresting them." In the extreme, reactions include "suicide bombings. I've seen people like that when I was in the field. People tried to shoot me at gunpoint. . . . It was insane, people are throwing stones at you. They are trying to torch your car and the police were always running here and there and being a female, you are all on your own. At that moment [I was confident] that I did the right thing. What is the worst that can happen to me? *I could die, people die. . . . If I don't die today, I'll die someday. But if I die, it will bring some change.* . . . People will start thinking that 'we were doing wrong. We were in the wrong.'"

We ask if Batool ever thinks it too difficult to serve as she does. She replied in her calm, quiet, yet firm tone, "*If you want to change something, you should be ready to take risks.*"

Batool's story highlights the power of mission motivation in driving individuals to maximize public performance despite extremely challenging and risky circumstances. But Batool's experience also shows that mission motivation is not endless. It needs to be sustained and encouraged by superiors, peers, and citizens.

Eventually, Batool's supervisors recognized and rewarded her mission motivation and competence, and they now support and empower her even when the job is still tough. "At times you forget your own inspiration. You forget why you are in civil service in the first place. There are days when you think, 'What the hell am I doing? People are chilling at their houses. They are home watching TV and at 9 A.M. or at 3 or at 2 at night, I'm standing on the street and making sure that the rubbish is removed or encroachments are removed.'"

Her response to these feelings is to refocus on the connection to the people she serves. "I never realized that I am inspiring girls. . . . I never realized that the intensity of inspiration would be this much. . . . When people started coming to me, I started feeling the intensity of my work, that it is echoing. People have their eyes on me, where she is going, what she is doing." Batool's connection with the women and girls in her community reinforces her mission motivation.

Her mission motivation is also rekindled by connecting with her peers. "I have a group of like-minded civil servants and friends and we keep pushing and supporting one another. I believe that in the later years, I felt the impact of the coalition, how important it is to have like-minded people around you and supporting you." As we know, peers who share a collective sense of mission empower and inspire each other to work harder. Peer networks can cultivate a broader sense of team and sustain Mission Driven Bureaucrats' commitment and mission focus. As Batool put it, "There are no individual successes. It is a bunch of, so many efforts, people from different quarters. I was very lucky to have supporting people."

Batool knows that she will have more moments of doubt about her ability to make an impact, but she will continue to draw on inspiration from her peers, from the little girls she knows are watching, and from her commitment to improving her nation. Her network will continue to remind her "that [it] is very important to keep pushing." What Batool feels her network reminds her of is something this book aspires to reminds us all: "*'You can do this. We all have to bring change.'*"

If You Build It, They Will Come

Why Management Practice Needs to Lead, Not Follow

> We have been so fearful that public servants will live down to our worst fears of them that we have also robbed them of the discretion and agency that might enable them to rise to their own best hopes for themselves.
>
> —Erin McDonnell, *Patchwork Leviathan*[1]

> Government bureaucracies are more bureaucratic than industrial ones in large part because we—the people and our political representatives—insist that they be.
>
> —James Q. Wilson, *Bureaucracy*[2]

This book is built on theory and empirical research. But when I personally recall the power of empowering management to motivate employees, I now think of Judy at the South African Revenue Service. When I think of the importance of retaining Mission Driven Bureaucrats, Tathiana in the Brazilian forest comes to mind. When I think of the impact of managing for empowerment, I think of Uma with her 125,000 frontline staff in Karnataka or Labanya leading the way to a successful census in South Sudan.

Mission Driven Bureaucrats can be headscarf-wearing women in rural Pakistan (Batool). They can be ex-US military officers in Washington, DC (Joseph). They can be senior staff boldly challenging power (Florence), or junior staff who find purpose in returning home (Preetam). Their mission can come from their childhood, almost like an inheritance (Uma, Joseph). It can come from their wishing to be nothing at all like their parents, instead forging a new path (Judy, Batool).

There are so, so, *so* many ways to be mission-driven. The profiles you have read are of people who are all very different from one another. But I suspect that if some room were fortunate enough to have two of these individuals in it, they would find connection and kinship across what divides them. Because in

Mission Driven Bureaucrats. Dan Honig, Oxford University Press. © Oxford University Press 2024.
DOI: 10.1093/oso/9780197641194.003.0009

perhaps the most fundamental way they are all the same: *they want to do the work they do*. They are Mission Driven Bureaucrats.

When my collaborator Sarah Thompson and I first started looking for people to profile, we thought it would be quite difficult. How many people could we actually find who had compelling personal stories that aligned with this book's messages? We wrote a few friends who had worked in or alongside bureaucracies in various countries for their recommendations, hoping that if we interviewed enough people, we would find the inspiring few who fit the narrative.[3] But finding Mission Driven Bureaucrats who were worthy of profiling proved to be shockingly, almost comically, easy. The response was overwhelming. Everyone had suggestions. And every person we talked to—*every single one*—had a compelling and inspirational story, which also fit the book in some way or another.

For a while, we thought we were just getting lucky. But we soon realized that it's the world that has gotten lucky. When we reached out to people to profile, it was as though we were playing darts, with Mission Driven Bureaucrats as our targets. We imagined the room had a very small dartboard, with a bullseye we'd be fortunate to find. But in fact we were at the county fair, throwing darts at a wall full of balloons. It turned out that our targets could be found literally *everywhere*. We ended up with more profiles than could fit in this book, and we would have ended up with many more if we hadn't stopped ourselves. A link to all the profiles can be found on my website, danhonig.info.[4]

As far as we can tell, the public sector has plenty of mission-driven Binas, and even more mission-motivateable Samirs. When you think about it, this isn't really very surprising at all. Why *wouldn't* bureaucrats, who willingly chose public sector careers, genuinely want to do their jobs?

The Elevator Pitch Version of Our Journey Together: This Book in 500 Words

This book has argued for a number of interrelated and perhaps seemingly complex claims. But the crux of my argument is ultimately simple. Lots of people want to do good things in the world. My suggestion is that we let them. Indeed, it's probably worth spending quite a lot of effort shifting our managerial approaches to support them (Chapter 1).

Reforms that manage for empowerment and manage for compliance both seek to improve performance, but they do so through different mechanisms (Chapter 2). Management for empowerment allows bureaucrats autonomy, cultivates their sense of competence, and creates connection to peers and impact. The first step to improving performance is usually diagnosis—identifying the most fruitful managerial approach for a given organization.

When it is likely to improve performance, management for empowerment can kindle the motivational flame of employees who are already there (Chapter 3). Management for empowerment can also help get the most competent, mission-motivated people in the door and keep them from walking out (Chapter 4). Savvy managers and leaders can tap on the power of team and peer effects, as well as seek to change norms, to sustain an empowerment-oriented environment (Chapter 5).

Shifting toward managing for empowerment will often yield better performance than an overly compliance-oriented status quo (Chapter 6). This is especially true where monitoring is "good but not great" or employees' motivation has not previously been considered in an organization's managerial approach. The motivation of bureaucrats indeed influences the quality of their work. The highest-performing bureaucrats, teams, and organizations are often the most mission-motivated. By cultivating Mission Driven Bureaucrats, an organization can nurture a workforce that is both dedicated *and* talented.

As more evidence is gathered, some of what is in these pages will likely be proved wrong or at the very least incomplete. As Clare Leaver and Lant Pritchett put it in a thoughtful discussion of teachers' pay-for-performance schemes, "the answer to any question requires a pause for thought about conditions and context rather than a presumption that there is an easy and universal answer."[5] We need to learn much more about the critical features that influence the best managerial approach. That in turn requires trying new managerial approaches— reforming systems and paying careful attention to the effects of reforms on motivation and performance.

When designing reforms, we must also consider the need to rethink accountability processes. Mission-driven bureaucrats thrive under an accountability framework that kindles, rather than suffocates, their motivational fire (Chapter 7). Almost every actor can do something useful to invest in empowerment-oriented management within the current system (Chapter 8). Possible reforms include altering recruitment processes, changing accountability routines, or just shifting one's managerial mindset (Chapters 7 and 8).

Empowerment-oriented reforms are not universally the best option; however, as it stands they seem to be substantially underutilized in our collective quest to improve performance. Policymakers, practitioners, scholars, and citizens would do well to give them greater attention.

This final chapter turns to our role as citizens—what we all can and should do to help unlock the full potential of Mission Driven Bureaucrats. If we think of bureaucrats as gears in the larger machine of the government, it's easy to forget that they, too, are people. Our collective failure to remember the humanity of our fellow citizens who work for the state is an important reason empowerment-oriented management is so underutilized.

The Harms of "Too Little" and "Too Much" Compliance

In 1997, Judith Tendler argued that mainstream approaches to governance reform seek to eliminate autonomy and discretion because these "provide opportunities for bureaucrats to exert undue influence."[6] A quarter-century later, it appears that little has changed. Erin McDonnell notes in her work (as first quoted in Chapter 2) that "current approaches [to improving public performance] advocate for abstract monitoring systems that can monitor across large scales and at a distance, assuming only a pinnacle principal can be trusted to monitor his interests."[7] As I wrote this book, I came to realize I was a small part of the reason we have seen so little progress—and I bet you, the reader, are too.

When I first described the demotivating and extremely compliance-oriented managerial environment at Detroit Child Protective Services (CPS) earlier, I did not dive into a key reason it emerged. In 2016, a few years before our study in Detroit took place, three-year-old Aaron Minor died while CPS was investigating his wellbeing. A forensic pathologist deemed the death a homicide, and his mother was charged with the crime.[8] The State of Michigan also charged the CPS specialist and her supervisor assigned to Aaron's case with manslaughter.[9] These charges, and the changes in CPS that resulted from them, were raised frequently by Detroit CPS employees in the interviews we conducted a few years after the event.

The managerial reaction to Aaron's death and the public scandal it brought was to tighten controls—tighter compliance, more oversight, and less room for workers to exercise judgment. Leadership's laudable intention with these measures was to prevent a tragedy like Aaron's from ever occurring again. Unfortunately, this came with dire consequences for the motivation and performance of CPS employees. The possibility that leaving a child in their home one day too long might lead to that child's death, or to the CPS worker "being called a killer," as one former employee put it, increased the pressure CPS specialists felt to close cases quickly. They felt pressured to "pull kids" from their homes and place them in foster care. As we saw, the experience of putting children into the overburdened state welfare system, even when specialists were not convinced that this was in the child's best interest, was incredibly demoralizing for CPS employees.[10]

This book's logic would suggest that Detroit CPS's managerial reaction likely harmed mission motivation, and ultimately the children CPS seeks to help. But it was also a reaction that I, and many others, supported at the time. Two years before Aaron's death I spent the summer renting a room right around the corner from Aaron's home. I remember reading of Aaron's death in the news and feeling helplessly angry. I had probably seen him in the neighborhood at some point, perhaps being pushed in a stroller. He reminded me of my own son, then only a toddler.

When the Detroit CPS employees were charged with manslaughter, I remarked to a friend that "boyslaughter" should carry even harsher penalties than "manslaughter." I was glad these charges had been filed. I could picture little Aaron's front door, never again to be crossed by his running feet. A child had died. It was only right that someone was held responsible, and that more compliance-oriented management be introduced to prevent such a thing from ever happening again.

My reaction, much like the state's, may have been natural in the face of such an unspeakable tragedy. But in retrospect, I believe I was very wrong. The courts ultimately found that those CPS employees held no responsibility for Aaron's death. But let's imagine for a second that these workers did indeed do something wrong. Were this the case, I *absolutely* believe they should have been punished. The public's desire for someone to be held responsible was justified. What I think I, and many others who followed this story, was wrong about was in believing that the system should have instituted more compliance-oriented management in response.

In the moment, we focused on the most obvious managerial error, the error of too little control. What we did not foresee were the consequences of a second kind of managerial error, the error of too *much* control. The managerial overcorrection after Aaron's death caused Detroit CPS to be struck by a second tragedy—its employees felt unable to fulfill their mission of protecting vulnerable children.

The consequences of this managerial error remain far less visible. To my knowledge, it has never been discussed in any public forum. Beyond anecdotal whispers and worries, I have no way whatsoever to estimate the impact of demotivation at CPS on the welfare of Detroit's children. But I have no doubt that the negative impact on Detroit's most vulnerable children has been very large indeed.

In the fairy tale "Goldilocks and the Three Bears," the title character reacts to foods that are "too hot" and "too cold," as well as beds that are "too soft" or "too hard," by finding alternatives that are "just right." Systems, too, will often benefit from a managerial equilibrium that is "just right"—somewhere in the middle, a balance between C and E. Unfortunately, the harms of too much control are often hidden. The harms of too little control are, by contrast, glaring. I choose "glaring" intentionally, because we in fact *over*-observe them, as in the case of the CPS workers in Aaron's tragedy.

When it turned out that those CPS employees were *not* at fault, Detroit CPS's additional compliance-oriented management did not go away. It remained to chase out those who cared the most and demotivate the rest. Agencies respond to what they and the public see, or think they see. But it's sometimes a mirage.

Compliance-oriented approaches may minimize bad actions while simultaneously undermining an agency's overall performance. Bad actions by unmotivated Peters, like fraud, are highly visible and easy to quantify. Good actions that are not taken by demotivated Samirs or Binas buried in paperwork are, by contrast, very hard to see. Good actions that are not taken by mission-motivated employees who depart an agency will never be seen. Ultimately, it's citizens who suffer as a result.

Overreliance on Compliance Begins with All of Us

A leader who wishes to empower Mission Driven Bureaucrats will often face political pressures not to do so. As Chapter 7 explored, shifting away from compliance-oriented management often increases the risk that bad actors might take advantage of reduced controls. Newspapers are much more likely to run the headline "Government Reform Leads to Fraud!" than "Reform Improves Performance Overall, but Not in All Cases."

It's easy to see why politicians and senior bureaucrats would think it unwise to risk bad press. Even the *possibility* of problems arising from too little compliance, such as fraud, often leads to increases in compliance-oriented management. Meanwhile, the near *certainty* of problems that arise from too much compliance rarely leads to its reduction. Hoping to constrain a minority of wrongdoers, many citizens default to demanding more accounting-based accountability and compliance-oriented regimes.

Here's where we could play a critical role as citizens: we can accept that the best managerial approach might also be accompanied by occasional bad behavior. While an empowerment-oriented approach increases the risk of a few bad actions, this risk alone does not prove that compliance-oriented management is the answer. Politicians and leaders of public agencies are only going to appreciate this truth if the people to whom they are ultimately accountable also appreciate it. We will get better public performance if we alter our mindsets, respect the nuance, and find more empathy for bureaucrats and their efforts. I think that begins with remembering that bureaucrats are people—and very frequently, people who want to do good.

At the risk of belaboring this in the way that only an academic can, I conducted a survey to see whether citizens view bureaucrats as people, particularly with regard to their motivation and responsiveness to management practices.[11] I asked for respondents' level of agreement with four statements. For half of the respondents, randomly chosen, the survey displayed the word "bureaucrat" in each statement, as written below; the other half saw the word "person" instead.[12]

(1) What a [bureaucrat] wants in the world—their goals—matters in predicting accurately what they're going to do when no one is looking. For example, if someone really cares intrinsically about doing a good job, they'll keep working hard even if their boss can't see what they do.

(2) What a [bureaucrat] wants isn't a fixed feature of a [bureaucrat]—especially at work. Yes, values, and character, and a lot else play an important role in determining how hard someone wants to work at their job. But how much a [bureaucrat] cares about the job they're doing *also* depends on their coworkers, and boss/how they're managed, and what the actual tasks of the job are.

(3) If a [bureaucrat] really cares about the thing the organization is trying to do but the way they're managed means they can't actually have any substantial impact they're much more likely to try to leave, to find a different job.

(4) The opposite's true, too. If a job seems like one where a person who holds it can really make a difference, then intrinsically motivated [bureaucrats] are more likely to apply.

I asked one final question at the end, which all respondents saw:

(5) Bureaucrats are people, human beings employed by a government.

Everyone agreed with the fifth statement, that bureaucrats are people. So we might imagine that there were no differences between "bureaucrat" and "person" on the other four items. But that was not the case. Respondents were substantially, and statistically significantly, more likely to agree with the first four statements if they referred to "people" rather than "bureaucrats."[13]

We know that individuals who work for the state are human beings. But when it comes to viewing these individuals through their professional identities, we somehow forget that this collective is composed of people. This is all the more a shame given Chapter 4's findings that bureaucrats tend to be even more mission-motivated than the average person. Our inability to see bureaucrats as good people impacts the way we talk about, think about, and actually manage bureaucrats.

The Alienating Downsides of Our Misunderstanding Bureaucrats

"Bureaucrat-bashing," or public criticisms of bureaucrats, can demotivate workers and lead them to exert less effort.[14] Employees who encounter these stereotypes are more likely to exit the bureaucracy.[15] As Lars Tummers puts it: "Ambitious professionals may not opt for a job in government because they, too, now think negatively about civil servants. It can also become a self-fulfilling prophecy: civil servants may work less hard if they are often portrayed negatively."[16]

In studying Ceará, Brazil's exceptional performance, Tendler and Freedheim ask, "What accounted for intense commitment and satisfaction expressed by many of the [health worker] agents and their supervising nurses, and the high performance associated with it?"[17] Their careful and thorough research boils down to a simple answer: "trust." If asked to describe empowerment-oriented management in one word, "trust" would be my answer, too. The core of empowerment-oriented management is encapsulated by the epigraph in Chapter 4 from Henry Stimson, a mid-twentieth-century statesman who variously served as US Secretary of State and Secretary of War under four presidents. Near the end of Stimson's esteemed career, he wrote: "The chief lesson I have learned in a long life [of public service] is that the only way you can make a man trustworthy is to trust him; and the surest way to make him untrustworthy is to distrust him, and show your distrust."[18]

We, the public, have been showing our distrust to the public sector for far, far too long. Compliance-oriented management and demotivated bureaucrats are the result. If mission-driven Binas think compliance-oriented management is preventing them from making an impact, they will look for other jobs. This might be fine for them—but it's really bad for all of us, as the public sector won't be able to benefit from their talents. We need to talk about the public sector in ways that empower it. We need to make the role of a bureaucrat aspirational for mission-driven young people. We also need to make public organizations environments that can make maximal use of those talents.

We need to change how we approach bureaucrats and accountability, to lessen those unproductive compliance-oriented pressures. We need to set clear missions for agencies. We need to support leaders to manage for empowerment—allowing autonomy, cultivating competence, and creating connection to peers and purpose. We need to change how we, the public, instinctively react to errors like fraud, corruption, incompetence, and other bad behavior. We owe it to our future to ensure that those who are protecting the vulnerable, educating the young, and keeping us healthy are able to do the best job they can. There is plenty that managers, agency leaders, and politicians can do to make this dream a reality. But each and every one of us can help, too.

One day in 2021 I opened my office mail and found a letter from a senior US foreign service officer I had never met, Chris Andino. The letter contained a lanyard that says "Bureaucrat": the last of 100 lanyards he'd had made for his team in Afghanistan a few years earlier, sent by Andino in response to public remarks I'd made praising Mission Driven Bureaucrats.[19] Andino explained the lanyards were tokens of inspiration, awarded to his staff after someone had done an exceptional job.[20] He wrote, "I'll be watching for your book. From 16 years in service . . . it looks to me that your thesis is the right one."[21] He later added, "very few see this [work in the US foreign service] as just a job. They see and understand a mission—both our main one and their role in the organization—and almost all are doing well, and often with great personal sacrifice, to accomplish their missions."[22]

I wear the lanyard with pride every day, my university ID hanging around my neck attached to the word "Bureaucrat."[23] Occasionally someone sees the lanyard and chuckles, thinking I'm wearing it ironically, noting my facelessness in the broader university bureaucracy. I correct them—for me being a bureaucrat is an honor, an aspiration.

When we see a bureaucrat acting in a "lazy" manner, it is certainly *possible* that they are an unmotivateable Peter, who will never work hard no matter the circumstances. But I think we should also entertain the possibility—indeed, the likelihood—that the "lazy" official is a motivateable Samir. He is not *un*motivated, but rather *de*motivated. We might ask ourselves what environment would lead Samir to act this way. We should ask what can be done to change his environment, to drive Samir to display the mission-driven behavior that we, as citizens, wish to see.

The status quo of inappropriate compliance-oriented management practices alienates bureaucrats, and builds a public sector that is less useful to citizens than it could be. *Compliance is making the world worse than it needs to be, and we are all part of the problem.*

Transforming the Landscape of Public Sector Management Will Require Some Pioneers

Route E reforms need to lead, not follow. Route E reforms will increase the mission motivation of today's workers and help Mission Driven Bureaucrats in their (and our) goal of serving their agency's missions. They will also attract and retain mission-driven employees tomorrow. As an epic line from the movie *Field of Dreams* puts it: "If you build it, they will come."

A world where Mission Driven Bureaucrats are valued and nurtured will not emerge on its own. It will only come into reality if bold reformers blaze the trail, accept the accompanied risks, and demonstrate the benefits of an alternative path. This book has explained why this is a tall order. Reformers face internal constraints, political pressures, and the punishing eye of public judgment. A shift toward empowerment-oriented management is not easy. It will take time, as well as trial and error. Every agency must begin by understanding the specific constraints they face. Changing ingrained organizational ways of working will often be a slow and tentative process. But change *can* happen, and in fact happens all the time.

Chapter 8 outlined a number of specific potential Route E reforms, but the best way forward depends on the unique context of each organization. There is also a great deal we need to learn about the "how"—about different ways of managing for empowerment, and the pathways from Route E reforms to improved performance.[24] Our theories should be informed and updated in light of data. I've tried in these pages to marshal all the relevant data I'm aware of in order to answer the question of when empowerment-oriented management is likely to benefit an organization, but much more is needed.

The only way we're ever going to find the answers we need is by trying. We live in a world of "pilot interventions," where people are keen to test new policies or technologies. Let's do the same for management. We should pilot managing for empowerment to see the results. The general direction that we should start traveling in is clear. It may seem a long road, but I'm with Lao Tzu on this one—a journey of a thousand miles begins with a single step. Let's all take it.

Let's Get Going

A government that empowers its citizens must be filled by bureaucrats who are themselves empowered. Focusing on monitoring, metrics, and compliance hasn't gotten us there. Given the complex and nuanced work we expect bureaucrats to perform, we never should have expected that it would. This book has argued that we should support the people who work for the government, rather than straitjacket them. From Detroit to Delhi, from London to Liberia, we can make a world of difference simply by helping mission-driven people to join and thrive in government service.

US President Ronald Reagan once famously said, "The nine most terrifying words in the English language are, 'I'm from the government, and I'm here to help.' "[25] I think our reaction should depend on what the person from the government says in their next sentence. If they say, "I have a bunch of forms to guide me created by people who don't trust me to assist you well," then I think Reagan's not far off. I'd be worried, too. But if they say, "Let me help you in any way I can, it's why I took the job," then I don't think there's any reason for fear. I think the more appropriate emotional reaction would be relief.

You know who I'm pretty sure would have agreed with me on this? Ronald Reagan. Reagan's "nine words" are part of remarks to farmers in his home state of Illinois at the state fair. His critique was of misguided *rules and procedures* that had failed to support farmers, not misguided bureaucrats themselves. Just a few seconds later in the speech, he announced an *increase* in government spending that could be used in more flexible ways than existing funds.

Reagan then added, "The government must act compassionately and responsibly."[26] Reagan wasn't decrying *all* uses of government. He was criticizing policies focused on compliance rather than what he thought government should do: help citizens in need. Government will only be compassionate and responsible if individual bureaucrats are compassionate and responsible. This requires management that allows autonomy, cultivates competence, and connects bureaucrats to peers and purpose.

I think there are countless people in the world—citizens, managers, politicians, and bureaucrats—who want to improve how government works. A great many of them already believe that empowerment-oriented management is an important part of improving performance or could, at least, be persuaded to give it a try. But we are held back by a collective fear. A fear of putting our trust in the wrong people and being punished for it. A fear that one headline-grabbing corrupt action by an employee will bring down their careers. A fear of the unknown.

Managing for empowerment will cultivate happier bureaucrats with more fulfilling work lives. But that's not what makes the effort worthwhile. We are losing out on the full support of the many Mission Driven Bureaucrats who want to help us.

Reforming the public sector will depend on managers, agency leaders, and bureaucrats themselves. But it will also depend on how we, the public, think about bureaucrats. The first step on the long journey of building a better public sector is not a physical step, but a mental one: a step we must take within ourselves.

Most of us know and like most of the individuals we have met who count as bureaucrats. Those we know personally are not the exception. They are on average very similar to those bureaucrats we do not know. All bureaucrats are people. Overwhelmingly, like most people, they mean well.

The first step on the long journey to more management for empowerment and Mission Driven Bureaucrats is each of us believing the truth: Mission Driven Bureaucrats exist. In fact, Mission Driven Bureaucrats are all around. If we empower them our lives, societies, countries, and world will be better.

ACKNOWLEDGMENTS

The weekend I sat down to write out this book's acknowledgments, in late June 2023, began with my son Dylan and I attending Shabbat services at our synagogue in Southwest London before heading to see Major League Baseball's London Series. The sermon that Saturday by our rabbi, Adrian Schell, was about the importance of community. Of our connection to each other as part of a shared, overlapping whole that has a different shape for each member, connected not just across space but also across time—across generations. This, it seemed to me, applied not just to the faith my son and I share but also to our shared love of baseball. I think Rabbi Schell's sermon applies to books, too.

A book isn't so much written by the author, but rather brought into being by the people with whom the author draws ideas, inspiration, energy. The hundreds whose written work the book draws upon. The thousands with whom I've had conversations that changed my thinking. Books, too, have rings of overlapping, interlocked communities.

Let me start with Sarah Thompson, who's credited "with contributions" on the title page. What, you might ask, are those contributions exactly? Sarah, then doing her MBA at Yale, wrote me in April 2020, asking to know more about *Mission Driven Bureaucrats* and to help if she could. There was something about her email, those first few paragraphs—her interest in "finding and supporting talented, mission-driven people to move public systems toward more equitable outcomes." Sarah had worked with Mission Driven Bureaucrats in global health and US education systems, and she saw the same things missing from the way we talk about bureaucrats as I did.

Over the past three years I've talked to Sarah, who now leads strategic growth for the nonprofit Evidence Action, most weeks—surely more than I've spoken to many family members and close friends. Having profiles in this book was an idea I'd had before I met Sarah, but one that never would have come to fruition without her—and that's the way I talk about her in the text when I refer to her, as the coauthor of the profiles. But Sarah's also played (among others) the roles of coach, advisor, project manager, and editor. She's not responsible for the research that underlies this book, nor for the words in the chapters, nor for the central points the book tries to make (which is why she, and I, didn't think it made sense to call her a coauthor—all errors or omissions of content are my responsibility alone). But I have no doubt that any good thing in this book would be much less so if I had not had the good fortune to have Sarah sit down at her desk in New Haven and write me an email one spring morning.

The bulk of the royalties generated from this book will go to supporting Mission Driven Bureaucrats.[1] That could mean a range of things in practice—supporting individuals, or nonprofits, or work directly with agencies seeking to change management practices. Sarah and I will decide together where these proceeds go.

Sarah and I have felt ourselves very much in community with those who generously agreed to be interviewed and profiled. We have many times felt ourselves to be in dialogue with, and drawn motivation from, Batool Asadi, Maria Bang, Kristina Björnberg, Tathiana Chaves de Souza, Florence Kuteesa, Uma Mahadevan, Labanya Margaret, Sara Newman, Judy Parfitt, Preetam Ponnappa, Joseph Roberts, Teresa Rovira, Josephine Sundqvist, and Liu Yong (a pseudonym, anonymized on request).

The next community around this book are those who have worked with me to help bring it into existence as research assistants: Miri Aung, whose sharp eye and editorial support (often in collaboration with Greg Larson) helped improve this book immensely. Lia Goldman, who supported the drafting of this book's profiles by Sarah and I. Alison Decker, who when Mission Driven Bureaucrats was just an idea helped me think about what it could mean. Henry Fung, who supported data collection and analysis of the large-N data that I use in this book. Archita Misra, who supported the data analysis of the Ghana and Liberia fellowship programs. Chau Hoang, who provided some critical inputs and structure during a short gap between professional roles. Each of these individuals did more things than I can articulate. They also all contributed to a sense of "us"; of team; of purpose.

I am also grateful to those whose minds were central to shaping this book via our discussions. Those who generously attended my book conference in March 2023 and offered brilliant feedback—Tugba Bozcaga, Ranil Dissanayake, Hahrie Han, Peter Harrington, Adnan Khan, Dan Rogger, and Christian Schuster. Jane Mansbridge and Jonathan Fox at early stages got very excited about this project in ways that suggested they saw value in it; I returned to their notes in moments of self-doubt and frustration. Those who generously provided endorsement blurbs. Jane Mansbridge, when asked to endorse this book, replied with a lovely endorsement—and also in-depth editorial comments, for which I am deeply grateful.

Sometimes I get the sense that others feel the world more generally, and academia specifically, is a place filled with competition rather than collaboration; people looking for strategic advantage, rather than approaching one another with a genuine desire to help. This is not my experience at all; a great many individuals have contributed ideas, energy, and comments that have made this book better. An entirely incomplete list: Yuen Yuen Ang, Oriana Bandiera, Lucy Barnes, Michael Barzelay, Kirill Bedenkov, Tim Besley, Kevin Bokaj, Kirsten Bound, Tony Bertelli, Lena Boraggina-Ballard, Sarah Brierley, Ryan Briggs, Derick Brinkerhoff, Jennifer Brinkerhoff, Salo Coslovsky, Kate Cronin-Furman, Fiona Davies, Tom DeLeire, Peter Dinesen, Clio Dintilhac, Alice Evans, Marc Esteve, Bob Gibbons, William Gormley, Duncan Green, Gus Greenstein, Susanna Hares, Mai Hassan, Martin Haus, Paul Heywood, Jennifer Hudson, Yue-Yi Hwa, David Jacobstein, Graham Kelly, Halima Khan, Mushtaq Khan, Molly Kinder, Rebecka Kitzing-Ivarsson, Greg Larson, Clare Leaver, Elizabeth Linos, Brian Levy, Akshay Mangla, Hardeep Matharu, Erin McDonnell, John McIntosh, Girish Menon, Brett Monson, Seth Palmer, Nealin Parker, Jim Perry, Mitch Pollack, Woody Powell, Lant Pritchett, Aidan Ricketts, Pallavi Roy, J-P Salter, Salimah Samji, Laura Savage, Colin Seals, Mike Sieferling, Joanne Sobeck, Paul Skidmore, Nick Thompson, Guillermo Toral, Lars Tummers, Chris Vanvalkenburgh, Bina Venkataraman, Martin Williams, Michael Woolcock, seminar participants, my students at SAIS and UCL, colleagues at SAIS, UCL, and Georgetown McCourt, anonymous reviewers at Oxford University Press and various journals, and many others I am sure over the coming months I'll wish I'd remembered to include here.

There is also a community around each of the individual empirical strands that I use in the book: Mae Chaladmanakul, Fai Tosuratana, and Ellie Woodhouse, for their collaboration on the manuscript that came from my research in Thailand. My co-investigators Tim Besley, Adnan Khan, Zeeshan Abedin, and Ferdous Sardar in Bangladesh. In Detroit my collaborators Joanne Sobeck and Lena Boraggina-Ballard. In supporting data collection, Dmitry Chakma, Tanapoom (Champ) Naratippakorn, Hathaichanok (Yok) Phengnu, the Wayne State interviewing team, and Mae Caladmanakul again (who served as research manager on the Thai work). Each project also had those who helped make them happen, who provided institutional access or support: for example, the BRAC Institute for Governance and Development (BIGD) and particularly Imran Matin; the Khon Kaen College of Local Administration (COLA) and particularly founding Dean Peerasit Kamnuansilpa; Wayne State University's School of Social Work; the Emerging Public Leaders program in Ghana and Presidents'

Young Professional Programme in Liberia and particularly Moses Cofie, Hh Zaizay, Caroline Kihato, Yawa Hansen-Quao, and Betsy Williams.

Those who generously shared data: the World Bank Bureaucracy Lab, particularly Kerenssa Kay Mayo and Dan Rogger. The Michigan Department of Health and Human Services. Nealin Parker, Trey Reffett, and Laura Hogshead from the US Department of Housing and Urban Development. Chris Andino, who sent me the lanyard (and some beautiful emails) referred to in the final chapter. In the UK, Mark Smith from Gateshead and Georgia Gould, Nick Kimber, and Tim Fisher from Camden.

My wife Özsel Beleli, as I note in the preface, is in many ways the one who got the seed of this book growing—and I am deeply grateful for our many conversations about it over the years. My thinking about bureaucracy would not be what it is without many—but particularly Matt Andrews and Antoinette Sayeh. Watching each of them work has provided object lessons I draw on weekly, if not daily.

There are so many names above, and it's still incomplete. A book is a small tip of a very large submerged iceberg of generous humans. Most of the people named above don't know most of the others named. I think that's beautiful, in that it speaks to the overlapping communities in which this book resides. Which brings me back to that Saturday morning in June, listening to Rabbi Schell's sermon next to my son Dylan.

Some months ago I asked Dylan, then nearly nine, what he knew about my mother's father, a man I barely knew myself (I was five when he passed away). Dylan said, "Sam Sloan? He's the guy with the bat and the books." The bat is the baseball bat that Hall of Famer Willie Mays used to hit his 3,000th hit, given by Mays to my grandfather, who gave it to me. It hangs on our wall (and is likely worth more than the rest of our possessions combined). As to the books: in his youth my grandfather, then living in Brooklyn, worked for the Haganah—supporting the Jewish community in Mandatory Palestine in their fight against the British ruling authorities. Sam's name appears in some books we own about the era (he was prominent enough to have a short obituary in the *New York Times*).

As I sat in synagogue that Saturday morning, I wondered what Sam Sloan would think if he could see us. Maybe Sam would be surprised by all the coincidences between his life and ours—us in synagogue, heading to see baseball, and sitting in the UK doing these things. But then it belatedly dawned on me: these weren't coincidences at all.

My being in synagogue surely had a fair bit to do with how he had raised my mother. The love of baseball was also, in a very tangible sense, the inheritance he gave me. I grew up in a house with many more books about the UK in it than I suspect was true of our neighbors in Detroit . . . likely some influence of Sam

Sloan there, too. These things I and I believe Dylan both treasure—our sitting in synagogue, our love of baseball, our fortunate life in the UK—had more than a little to do with Sam. This was community across generations.

Someday Dylan may have a child, and even a grandchild. To Dylan's grandchild I will be precisely as generationally distant as Sam Sloan is to Dylan. And perhaps I will be "the guy with the bat and the books"—or at least the books. If so, this book will be one of them. And maybe, if I'm fortunate, something about me or even this book will be connected to some things my great-grandchild treasures about themselves, too.

I suspect that the things in this book's pages will still matter to the world when my great-grandchild is old enough to read them. I don't really care if someone *actually* reads this book anymore—but I hope despite the odds that these ideas have some echoes, some positive ripples in the sea of experience and understanding in which our great-grandchildren's generation finds themselves. If human life persists for another century, our civilizations will likely still rely on people exercising judgment on behalf of some form of collective government, and those people will likely often respond better to being empowered and trusted than being managed for compliance.

If these words are of any use in navigating that future, it is a credit to the communities of which I've been incredibly fortunate to be a part in creating this book, and in my broader journey. These communities are also part of me. To the extent this work has any value, it is to the credit of those named above, and many more.

TECHNICAL APPENDIX

This appendix provides additional information on the empirical evidence utilized in this book. It includes descriptions of original empirical data that have not been made available or publicly associated with published work, including in online replication archives or pre-analysis plans.[1] By "original empirical material," I refer to both novel data that I have collected and my analysis of data collected by others. Table A.1 summarizes these empirical projects.

This appendix is organized by empirical project, then chapter. That is, it proceeds project-by-project; within each project it discusses the use of the data in each chapter in which that project's data appears.

Influences on Mission Motivation: Large-N Analysis of Civil Service Surveys

Chapter 3

Chapter 3 introduced a large-N database of public servant perceptions of their managerial environment and intrinsic motivation. In collaboration with my research assistant Henry Fung (to whom I am very grateful), I assembled a dataset of all existing nationally representative civil servant surveys that included questions on motivation and performance. The database comprised observations from over 4 million individuals and 2,000 government agencies across five countries. It measured bureaucrats' perceptions of various features of their work environment that could influence their motivation. Among others, these features included empowerment-oriented managerial practices, organizational culture, and the performance of fellow colleagues. The vast majority of the findings from the large-N analysis are present in the published paper by Honig (2021) in the *Proceedings of the National Academy of Sciences*, or its publicly available

Table A.1 **Describing the original empirical material employed in this book**

Country/ Setting	Population	Type of Study	Key Question(s)
Liberia	Fast-stream Civil Service Admits (PYPP)	Mixed Methods Regression Discontinuity (comparing admitted individuals to non-admitted)	How do talented and mission-motivated recruits impact the teams they work for and vice versa? How do fellows compare to non-fellows?
Ghana	Fast-stream Civil Service Admits (EPL)	Mixed Methods Regression Discontinuity (comparing admitted individuals to non-admitted) and within-person difference over time	How do talented and mission-motivated employees impact the teams they work for and vice versa? How do fellows change over time?
USA (Detroit)	Child Protective Services Workers	Qualitative Interviews Complemented by Surveys	What induces employees to exit, and how is this conditioned by management practice, motivation, and peers? (Article that draws from this empirical material: Boraggina-Ballard et al. 2021.)
Bangladesh	Public Engineers	Surveys of Bangladeshi Engineers	In a ministry with substantial malfeasance, who expects to benefit from changes in rules to allow greater autonomy? (Working paper that draws from this empirical material: Besley et al. 2020.)
Thailand	Centrally Appointed "Vertical Bureaucrats" in District Government	Qualitative Interviews Complemented by Surveys	How do managers who have no recourse to Route C rewards and sanctions manage employees? What impact does team level management have on employees? (Article that draws from this empirical material: Honig & Woodhouse 2023.)

Table A.1 **Continued**

Country/ Setting	Population	Type of Study	Key Question(s)
Civil Service Surveys (five countries)	Over 4 million individual and 2,000 agency observations	Econometric Analysis (Panel data by agency; repeated cross-section by individual)	Is mission motivation correlated with Route E management practices? How is their relationship affected by task type and monitorability? (Article that draws from this material: Honig 2021.)
M-Turk Survey of Public Perceptions	500 M-Turkers	Econometric Analysis (single-wave survey) and Qualitative Responses	How do talented and mission-motivated recruits impact the teams they work for and vice versa? How does this differ by task type and management style?
Prolific Survey of Public Sector Management Perceptions	1,354 public servants across twenty-eight countries	Econometric Analysis (single-wave survey)	What is the balance in public sector organizations between compliance-oriented and empowerment-oriented management practices? (Article that draws from this material: Dissanayake et al. 2023.)
Reanalysis of Existing Motivation Studies	Various (including 2014 International Social Survey Programme)	Econometric Analysis (mostly single observations for each study, but including International Social Survey Programme, with individual-level responses by country)	Does mission motivation differ between bureaucrats and non-bureaucrats? Does it differ between bureaucrats in the developing world and those in the developed? (Article that draws from this material: Honig "Bad Actors or Bad Actions.")

supplementary materials. However, I have modified some language from the paper to suit this book's vocabulary. For example, I have described what that paper calls "supportive management practices" as "managing for empowerment."

Chapter 3 described a series of regression analyses examining the relationship between motivation and various indicators of empowerment-oriented management. Figure A.1 shows the correlations from a series of regression analyses. The figure illustrates that empowerment-oriented management practices across a range of empowering managerial practices are correlated with greater mission motivation in individual-level data, drawing from a subset of the indicators used

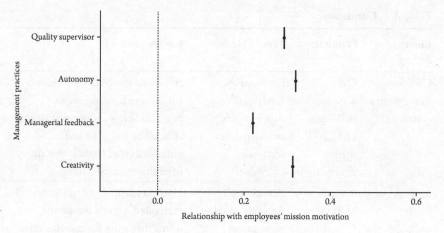

Figure A.1 Association of selected empowerment-oriented management practices and employees' mission motivation (individual-level data)

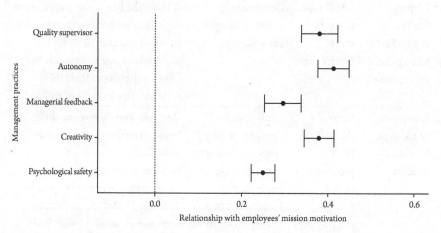

Figure A.2 Association of selected empowerment-oriented management practices and employees' mission motivation within an agency over time (agency-level data)

in Honig 2021. A 1-unit empowerment-oriented shift in each indicator was associated with 20–30 percent of a unit's improvement in employee mission motivation. Figure A.1 may appear as though it has lines, not points. This is a function of the large sample size and precisely estimated results, which have led the confidence interval lines to be very small—appearing almost as if they are single lines running through the point estimates.

Figure A.2 illustrates that empowerment-oriented practices also increase the mission motivation of the same agency's employees over time. This figure is a subset of Honig 2021, Figure 2, with the axes relabeled to be consistent with this book's use of terms. Honig 2021 contains the full underlying analysis.

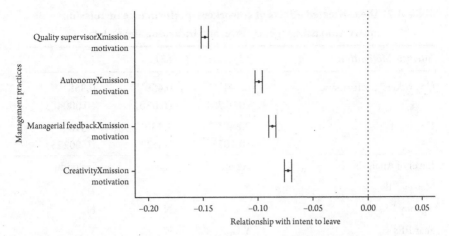

Figure A.3 Interaction of selected empowerment-oriented management practices with individual-level mission motivation on intent to leave

Chapter 4

Chapter 4 utilized the large-N database to examine the relationship between empowerment-oriented management and employee retention. Figure A.3 summarizes a subset of the data first reported in Honig 2021, demonstrating that empowerment-oriented practices are associated with lower intentions among bureaucrats to leave an agency. The mission-motivated are also more sensitive to these effects. Those with greater mission motivation are less likely to intend to leave an agency populated by empowerment-oriented practices.

Chapter 5

Chapter 5 used the large-N database to examine the relationship between perceptions of the performance of one's coworkers' and one's mission motivation and job satisfaction. This analysis does not appear in Honig 2021 and so is described in greater detail below.

Table A.2 illustrates that bureaucrats with greater regard for their coworkers' performance are more mission-motivated. Table A.3 highlights that they are also more satisfied with their jobs. These findings were true both across agencies and within agencies over time. On a 5-point scale, a 1-point increase in the perceived performance of one's coworkers is associated with more than a 0.7 point increase in job satisfaction and nearly a 0.5 point increase in mission motivation. Perceptions of the performance of one's coworkers is among, if not the, strongest predictor of one's job satisfaction and mission motivation.

Table A.2 **The estimated effects of coworkers' performance on mission motivation using agency-level and individual-level data**

Intrinsic Motivation	(1)	(2)	(3)
Coworkers' performance	0.441***	0.459***	0.358***
	(0.0270)	(0.0301)	(0.000483)
Constant	2.847***	2.356***	2.316***
	(0.107)	(0.122)	(0.00225)
Level of Analysis	Agency	Agency	Individual
Survey FEs	Y	Y	Y
Agency FEs	Y	N	N
Year FEs	Y	N	Y
R^2	0.940	0.676	0.210
Observations	2119	2119	4136029
Individual Surveys Included in Each Model			
US FEVS	Y	Y	Y
Canada PSES	N	N	N
UK CSPS	Y	Y	N
India CSS	Y	Y	N
Western Australia EPS	N	N	Y
Australia APS	N	N	Y

Linear regression model
Standard errors in parentheses
* p < 0.10, ** p < 0.05, *** p < 0.01

Chapter 6

Chapter 6 drew on the large-N database to identify the contexts in which empowerment-oriented management will most catalyze improvements in employee motivation and performance. It argued that empowerment-oriented management will particularly enable employees to thrive when monitoring employee actions is challenging.

Figure A.4 describes data from Honig 2021, where the underlying regressions are reported in its online appendix. Figure A.4 illustrates that the link between empowerment-oriented management and mission motivation is stronger in environments where verifiability is low—that is, monitoring is difficult. These are environments where it is more difficult to verify that tasks have been completed.

Table A.3 **The estimated effects of coworkers' performance on job satisfaction using agency-level and individual-level data**

Job Satisfaction	(1)	(2)	(3)
Coworkers' performance	0.737***	0.720***	0.688***
	(0.0378)	(0.0271)	(0.000621)
Constant	0.872***	0.622***	1.099***
	(0.15075)	(0.1090)	(0.00365)
Level of Analysis	Agency	Agency	Individual
Survey FEs	Y	Y	Y
Agency FEs	Y	N	N
Year FEs	Y	N	Y
R^2	0.7927	0.3706	0.2686
Observations	1708	1708	4009025
Individual Surveys Included in Each Model			
US FEVS	Y	Y	Y
Canada PSES	Y	Y	N
UK CSPS	N	N	N
India CSS	N	N	N
Western Australia EPS	N	N	N
Australia APS	N	N	Y

Linear regression model
Standard errors in parentheses
* $p < 0.10$, ** $p < 0.05$, *** $p < 0.01$

Motivation in a Second Choice Agency: Bangladeshi Public Service Agency (Chapter 3)

Chapter 3 introduced a survey of Bangladeshi civil servants that Tim Besley, Adnan Khan, Ferdous Sardar, and I conducted in July 2019. The civil servants were employed in an agency that Chapter 3 termed the Bangladesh Public Service Agency (BPSA). The agency's real name has been anonymized to keep within confidentiality provisions of our agreement with the agency.

The original aim of our study was to examine who might benefit from rule changes that offer employees greater autonomy. This was intended to be a baseline survey for broader policy engagement, but COVID-19 interrupted those plans. There is no public paper reporting the results. However, they do appear in

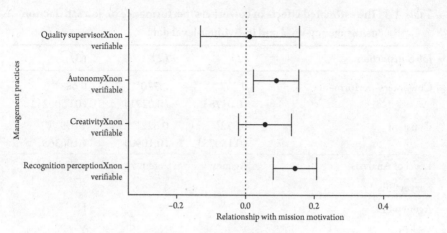

Figure A.4 Effect of non-verifiability on the relationship between empowerment-oriented management practices and intrinsic motivation

a (non-anonymized, and thus not publicly disclosable) report provided to BPSA (Besley et al. 2020). I am happy to provide bits of the underlying analysis on request in anonymized form.

Our survey involved nearly 500 key Bangladeshi district and sub-district (*upazila*) staff. The sample was nationally representative of the anonymized agency, except for sixteen districts that were experiencing flooding when the survey was conducted. Our survey asked employees a series of questions about their motivation, their decision to join BPSA, and their job satisfaction.

The findings indicated that compliance-oriented management can repel BPSA's mission-motivated workers. Fifty-five percent of these employees reported that if they were to choose again, they would not join this agency. Of 413 respondents, 79 would not rejoin the public sector at all and 147 would join the public sector but avoid BPSA. The primary reason for their unwillingness to rejoin BPSA was the prominence of compliance-oriented management. Employees most strongly desired more individual authority, including more control over the design and revision of projects. Those with greater mission motivation were most desirous of greater authority and recognition of their good performance. They overwhelmingly supported policy changes that would offer them more freedom in their decision-making at work.

Attracting the Mission-Motivated: Fast-Stream Civil Service Program in Liberia

Chapter 4 introduced two fast-stream civil service programs in Liberia and Ghana. The first was the Presidents' Young Professionals Program (PYPP) in

Liberia. A sister program was launched in Ghana, named the Emerging Public Leaders (EPL) program. Both aim to recruit talented and mission-motivated employees to the public sector. Fellows embark on a two-year fellowship with direct mentorship from experienced civil servants.

I partnered with EPL and PYPP to understand the impacts of their programs in Ghana and Liberia. I assisted EPL and PYPP to design an impact evaluation exercise of their fast-stream programs in 2019 and 2020. In exchange, I was provided with full access to its quantitative and qualitative results under a Data Use Agreement. I did not conduct the evaluation personally, but I did have access to the raw data.

In Liberia, evaluators surveyed current fast-stream fellows and alumni fellows, and interviewed civil servants who were not in the PYPP program. They particularly sought out non-fast-stream civil servants who were comparable in age and background to the PYPP group. The surveys asked participants a set of questions about their experience in the civil service. Topics included their satisfaction with their job placement, perceptions of the performance of fast-stream fellows, and how long they planned to remain employed at the civil service. The sample size was relatively small, since fast-stream cohorts consist of approximately twenty fellows per year.

My research assistant Archita Misra (to whom I am deeply grateful) and I used the survey results to examine the effects of various organizational influences on the mission motivation of employees. We examined mission motivation based on three different scores: extrinsic motivation, intrinsic motivation, and public service motivation. Though the study followed the basic logic of a regression discontinuity design, it should be noted that the modest sample size limited what quantitative analysis alone could tell us with confidence. Data memos describing both the EPL and PYPP data analysis are available on request with further detail.

Chapter 4

Chapter 4 used the evaluation results to demonstrate that the mission-motivated individuals in our sample did desire to remain in the Liberian civil service. Chapter 4 identified that bureaucrats who were mission-motivated planned to remain the civil service for a longer period of time. For both PYPP fellows and non-fellows, higher levels of mission motivation were associated with a longer plan to remain in the civil service. The effect size was 0.6 points on a 5-point scale, statistically significant at the 95 percent level. This indicated that Liberia's civil service was not, in fact, repelling the mission-motivated.

However, there was suggestive evidence that exposure to the Liberian civil service slightly reduced the mission-motivation of PYPP fellows compared to non-fellows. The effect size was 0.26 points on a 5-point scale, statistically significant at the 99 percent significance level.

Chapter 4 also described the positive influence that mission-motivated Liberian PYPP fellows had on the performance of their teams. As Khana Group's Phase II Impact Evaluation (2022) reported, 75 percent of the supervisors of PYPP fellows in Liberia considered them to be higher-performing than their coworkers. Eighty-five percent considered their fellow a leader within their team, and 100 percent believed that the fellows and the fast-stream program was a positive influence on their organizational culture. These findings indicate that recruiting the mission-motivated may be a meaningful way to improve agency performance.

Chapter 7

Chapter 7 used the PYPP and EPL evaluation results to highlight the importance of citizen engagement to bureaucratic mission motivation. Citizen accountability relies on strong connections forged between bureaucrats and citizens, which positively influences their mission motivation. Indeed, the results indicated that greater community immersion was linked to higher levels of motivation among bureaucrats. On average, fast-stream fellows reported 0.6-unit higher levels of community immersion than did civil servants. This was significant at the 99 percent significance level. Fast-stream fellows also reported higher levels of motivation as a result of greater community immersion.

Attracting the Mission-Motivated: Fast-Stream Civil Service Programs in Ghana

Under the same Data Use Agreement with EPL, I gained access to the results of the EPL evaluation in Ghana, conducted by the Ghana Institute of Public Administration (GIMPA).

The evaluation in Ghana was conducted in two waves in 2019 and 2020. It incorporated the first two cohorts of EPL fellows in Ghana, as well as some applicants who had not been selected for the fellowship. I termed the former Cohort 1 and 2, recruited in 2018 and 2019 respectively. The first wave of the survey occurred when Cohort 1 were in the middle of their two-year fellowship (a midline), while Cohort 2 was just beginning their fellowship (close to a true baseline). The second wave of the survey occurred when Cohort 1 was just completing their fellowship (an endline) while Cohort 2 was in the middle of their fellowship.

The same individuals were surveyed at two separate times, allowing us to observe within-person changes in their answers between waves of the survey. The survey included a varied set of questions about the experience of EPL fellows so far in the civil service, including their intended length of employment and job satisfaction.

Chapter 4

Chapter 4 used the evaluation results to demonstrate that in the sample, joining the Ghanaian civil service did not demotivate EPL fellows. In fact, the mission motivation of EPL fellows rose slightly between waves of the survey. These effect sizes were small, and the change not statistically significant. Cohort 1 displayed an average change in extrinsic motivation of 0.04 and an average change of intrinsic motivation of 0.05. Cohort 2 displayed an average change of extrinsic motivation of 0.27 and an average change of intrinsic motivation of 0.17.

There was also no evidence that joining the civil service led EPL fellows to shorten their desired careers in the Ghanaian civil service. Indeed, for some fellows, the placement seemed to increase intended public sector career length. Four fellows in Cohort 1 and one fellow from Cohort 2 increased their planned length of stay in the civil service from 5–10 years to over 20 years. As fellows became more satisfied with their job placement, their mission motivation also increased by 0.45 points on a 5-point scale, significant at the 95 percent level. Their intrinsic motivation also increased by 0.627 points on a 5-point scale, statistically significant at the 99 percent level.

Chapter 4 also highlighted that Ghanaian EPL fellows improved the performance of the public sector agencies to which they were assigned. Seventy-four percent of supervisors of EPL fellows considered fellows' performance superior to that of their co-workers and 82 percent of supervisors agreed that fellows strengthened public service delivery. Overall, the results suggest that the public service can be improved with the recruitment of mission-motivated and talented fast-stream fellows. Not only did the fellows perform better individually than non-EPL fellows, EPL fellows also triggered a series of transformations in the work environment that positively influenced the performance of their peers.

Chapter 7

Chapter 7 illustrated that closer engagements with citizens can increase bureaucrats' motivation. This can be attributed to a deeper sense of citizen accountability. In Ghana, respondents reported that greater community immersion was linked to feeling more accountable to citizens and finding creative opportunities for performance improvement. Community immersion was found to be positively correlated with extrinsic motivation, with a coefficient of 0.24. This was statistically significant at the 95 percent level. Community immersion was also positively correlated with intrinsic motivation, with a coefficient of 0.2. This was also statistically significant at the 90 percent level. A 1-point increase in one's community immersion score was approximately associated with a 0.2-point increase in extrinsic and intrinsic motivation. The change in a bureaucrat's community immersion over time was one of the best predictors of changes in their mission motivation.

Reanalysis of Existing Public Survey Motivation Studies and International Social Survey (ISSP) Data
Chapter 4

Chapter 4 discussed my explorations of mission motivation from existing studies. To form this sample, my research assistant Henry Fung and I first identified a number of existing studies of motivation in developing and developed countries, which publicly reported Public Service Motivation scores, which as discussed in Chapter 2 I consider one measure of mission motivation.[2] Chapter 4 used this sample to compare the mission motivation of public and private sector workers. Figure A.5 illustrates that bureaucrats generally display higher levels of mission motivation than do non-bureaucrats. Figure A.6 illustrates that this is true for both developed and developing countries. This finding does not vary by either the income level or the level of corruption in a country. In fact, bureaucrats in developing countries are, if anything, slightly more mission-motivated than their counterparts in developed countries.

Henry Fung and I also gathered data from the 2014 wave of the International Social Survey Programme (ISSP). The ISSP is a cross-country survey that is conducted annually on topics related to social science research. The theme for the 2014 survey was "citizenship." The survey asked citizens about their employment status and their beliefs, which we aggregated to measures of some form of mission motivation (public service motivation). The 2014 ISSP contained 49,807 survey responses from thirty-four countries.

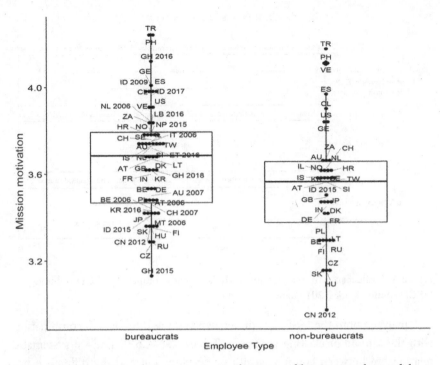

Figure A.5 Comparison of mission motivation between public sector workers and the general public, existing studies

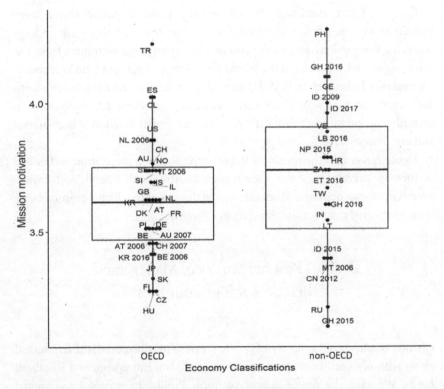

Figure A.6 Mission motivation in OECD as compared to non-OECD countries, existing studies

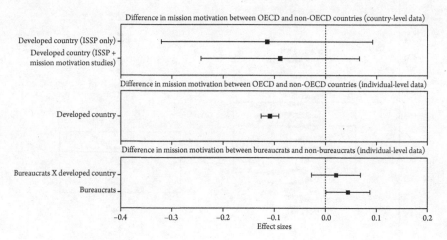

Figure A.7 Effect sizes from regression analysis formally comparing OECD and non-OECD countries, ISSP 2014 data

I analyzed both the ISSP data on its own and the ISSP data in combination with the sample of existing studies in Tables A.4–A.6.[3] I find no systematic relationship between country wealth or development and the difference between the motivation of bureaucrats and non-bureaucrats in these countries. Figure A.7 summarizes key findings from these analyses.

Chapter 4 also discussed the relationship between public sector wage premiums and the mission motivation of bureaucrats. I combine the findings regarding the gap between public and private sector wage premiums from the prior analysis with data from the World Bank Bureaucracy Lab (the Worldwide Bureaucracy Indicators, or WWBI) on wage premiums in the public sector from the closest matching year. There were seven countries where data were available on both wage premiums and the difference in mission motivation of bureaucrats and non-bureaucrats.

Figure A.8 graphs the relationship between the gap in motivation and public sector wage premiums for these seven cases, illustrating that public sector wage premiums are associated with an increase in the extent to which bureaucrats are more motivated than non-bureaucrats in a given country.

Online (Prolific) Survey of Management Practices across Countries

Chapter 8

Chapter 8 introduced a survey of public servants' motivation that I conducted along with my coauthors Ranil Dissanayake, Sarah Thompson, and Elizabeth Linos. We used the online survey platform Prolific to survey 1,354 public servants across twenty-eight countries. Respondents drew from a wide range

Table A.4 **Bureaucrats' motivation in developed and developing countries, country-level data**

PSM	(1)	(2)	(3)	(4)	(5)	(6)	(7)	(8)
Developed Country	-0.0896 (0.0780)		-0.0284 (0.132)	-0.370 (0.341)	-0.115 (0.103)		-0.101 (0.160)	-0.246 (0.535)
Corruption Perception Index		-0.0243 (0.0164)	-0.0193 (0.0288)	-0.0684* (0.0396)		-0.0216 (0.0267)	-0.00487 (0.0413)	-0.0265 (0.0698)
Developed Country × Corruption Perception Index				0.0690 (0.0539)				0.0290 (0.0863)
Constant	3.681*** (0.0670)	3.722*** (0.120)	3.759*** (0.137)	3.958*** (0.182)	3.716*** (0.0904)	3.769*** (0.197)	3.737*** (0.218)	3.830*** (0.362)
R^2	0.029	0.038	0.040	0.067	0.042	0.025	0.042	0.047
Observations	52	52	52	52	34	34	34	34
Data Source								
ISSP 2014 (country level)	Y	Y	Y	Y	Y	Y	Y	Y
PSM studies	Y	Y	Y	Y	N	N	N	N

Linear regression model
Standard errors in parentheses
* $p < 0.10$, ** $p < 0.05$, *** $p < 0.01$

Table A.5 **Bureaucrats' motivation in developed and developing countries, individual-level data**

PSM	(1)	(2)	(3)	(4)	(5)	(6)
Developed Country	−0.0971***		−0.109***		−0.0648***	−0.0231
	(0.0780)		(0.00871)		(0.0119)	(0.0376)
Corruption Perception Index		−0.0201***		−0.0277***	−0.0165***	−0.0104*
		(0.00207)		(0.00221)	(0.00302)	(0.00595)
Years of Education			0.00423***	0.00509***	0.00525***	0.00525***
			(0.000960)	(0.0000974)	(0.000976)	(0.000976)
Male			−0.0835***	−0.0839***	−0.0836***	−0.0835***
			(0.00745)	(0.00745)	(0.00744)	(0.00745)
Age			0.00234***	0.00244***	0.00250***	0.00249***
			(0.000221)	(0.000222)	(0.000222)	(0.000233)
Developed Country × Corruption Perception Index						−0.00816
						(0.00682)
Constant	3.677***	3.735***	3.563***	3.646***	3.617***	3.590***
	(0.00714)	(0.0140)	(0.0180)	(0.0198)	(0.0208)	(0.0305)
R^2	0.003	0.002	0.008	0.008	0.008	0.008
Observations	49297	49297	47042	47042	47042	47042
Data Source						
ISSP 2014 (country level)	Y	Y	Y	Y	Y	Y
PSM studies	N	N	N	N	N	N

Linear regression model
Standard errors in parentheses
* p < 0.10, ** p < 0.05, *** p < 0.01

Table A.6 **Comparing bureaucrats and non-bureaucrats in developed and developing countries, individual-level data**

PSM	(1)	(2)	(3)	(4)	(5)	(6)
Bureaucrats	0.0695***	0.0695***	0.0600***	0.0536**	0.0442**	0.0442**
	(0.00986)	(0.00986)	(0.0102)	(0.0218)	(0.0220)	(0.0220)
Bureaucrats × Developed Country				0.0207	0.0209	0.0209
				(0.0244)	(0.0245)	(0.0245)
Developed Country				−0.219***	−0.364***	1.832***
				(0.0368)	(0.0379)	(0.281)
Corruption Perception Index		−0.0347***	−0.0583***			−0.360***
		(0.00582)	(0.00599)			(0.0484)
Years of Education			0.0169***		0.0169***	0.0169***
			(0.00109)		(0.00109)	(0.00109)
Male			−0.0844***		−0.0841***	−0.0841***
			(0.00773)		(0.00774)	(0.00774)
Age			0.00481***		0.00482***	0.00482***
			(0.000247)		(0.000247)	(0.000247)
Constant	3.684***	3.962***	3.673***	3.902***	3.569***	4.253***
	(0.0210)	(0.0382)	(0.0418)	(0.0302)	(0.0349)	(0.0979)
Country Fixed Effect	Y	Y	Y	Y	Y	Y
R^2	0.088	0.088	0.099	0.088	0.099	0.099
Observations	41544	41544	39737	41544	39737	39737
Data Source						
ISSP 2014 (individual level)	Y	Y	Y	Y	Y	Y
PSM studies	N	N	N	N	N	N

Linear regression model

Standard errors in parentheses

* p < 0.10, ** p < 0.05, *** p < 0.01

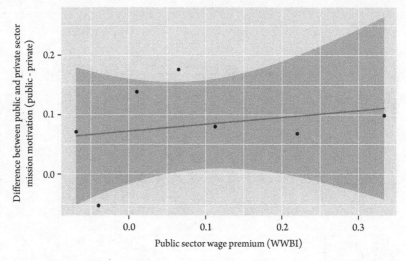

Figure A.8 Public wage premiums and gap between public and private sector mission motivation scores by country

of sectors and jobs within the public service. More information can be found in "What Motivates Public Sector Workers to Form Peer Networks? Evidence From a Survey Experiment." (Dissanayake et al. 2023).

Our survey partly sought to investigate bureaucrats' perceptions of public sector management. As Chapter 8 discussed, the survey included the question: "In your opinion, what is the balance in your organization between providing freedom for staff to pursue organizational goals (however they are defined) as they see fit on the one hand, and tightly controlling staff through targets, monitoring, oversight and incentive schemes?" The respondents answered on a 0–100 scale, where 0 represented "complete freedom for staff" (heavily empowerment-oriented management) and 100 represented "complete control of staff action" (heavily compliance-oriented management).

Figure 8.1 presented the cross-country distribution of the answers to this question. The distribution of answers was roughly bimodal, with a larger peak at the compliance-oriented end of the scale. Public sector organizations tend to be managed in either compliance-oriented or empowerment-oriented ways in the view of staff, though the former is more common. Figure A.9 presents the within-country distribution of answers. Though countries do differ one from another, Figure A.9 highlights that a range of management practices can be found in every country. However, more respondents tend to experience compliance-oriented management practices. Figure A.9 utilizes the original scale of the survey, with 0 full empowerment and 100 full compliance (rather than vice versa, as in the reversed scale of Figure 8.1).

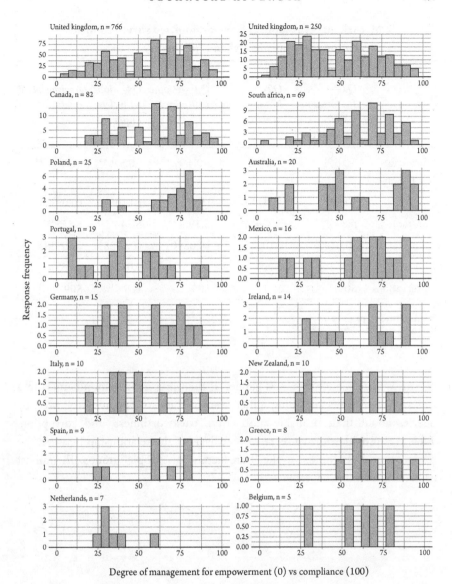

Figure A.9 Within-country distribution of empowerment-oriented and compliance-oriented management practices

Perceptions of Bureaucrats: An M-Turk Survey

Chapter 9

Chapter 9 discussed a survey I conducted on the online platform M-Turk concerning public perceptions of bureaucrats. I recruited 509 respondents for the M-Turk survey in very early 2020. The survey first inquired about respondents'

Table A.7 **M-Turk survey responses from randomized survey comparing perceptions of "bureaucrats" and "people"**

	(1) Q1—Performance when unmonitored	(2) Q2—Management practice	(3) Q3—People who care	(4) Q4—Jobs with clear impact	(5) Average of all questions
Bureaucrats (v-v People)	−0.611***	−0.186	−0.456***	−0.579***	−0.458***
	(0.105)	(0.116)	(0.126)	(0.105)	(0.0791)
Constant	5.844***	5.324***	5.195***	5.844***	5.552***
	(0.0740)	(0.0815)	(0.0890)	(0.0738)	(0.0558)
R^2	0.063	0.005	0.025	0.057	0.062
Observations	509	509	509	509	509

Standard errors in parentheses
* $p < 0.10$, ** $p < 0.05$, *** $p < 0.01$

countries of residence, age, and gender. It then presented respondents with a series of statements regarding either "bureaucrats" or "people," followed by queries about their probable motivation, trustworthiness, and corruption. Table A.7 provides formal regression analysis of the relationship between the responses and assignment to the "bureaucrats" or "people" groups. The full list of statements is in Chapter 9.

NOTES

Preface

1. In particular, we'd been discussing Herzberg's hygiene factors. Hygiene factors are in Herzberg's theorizing features, such as company policy and management practice, which are required for employees to maintain motivation. I debated not including this detail, as it seems too pat to be true. But it is.

Acknowledgments

1. Oxford University Press would not accept a nonprofit entity (from which funds could then be donated) as royalty recipient, so I mean here net proceeds after personal income tax.

Chapter 1

1. "The Ezra Klein Show" podcast, Vox 2019.
2. Wilson (1989), p. 159.
3. Foreign government evacuation flights were exempt from the Senegalese border closures, as they arrived empty and removed only foreign citizens.
4. This section is based on my immediate recollection of the conversation, as it was originally written while still on the plane. However, the conversation is not reproduced verbatim.
5. As outlined by the Office of Personnel Management at the time: "Those who are reporting to work, but aren't receiving a paycheck, don't qualify [for unemployment benefits]" (Smith 2019). It was widely expected, and indeed came to pass, that once the shutdown was resolved, all workers would receive back pay post-furlough; but this did mean effectively that these bureaucrats worked even when they could have taken what in the end proved to be paid days off.
6. Trish Gilbert, as quoted in Tankersley & Kaplan 2019.
7. Jacqueline Smith, director of public policy, as quoted in Tankersley & Kaplan 2019.
8. There are important exceptions to "laudable," of course. To take the most extreme case, bureaucrats in the Nazi regime were, on some accounts, *very* mission-driven. They autonomously acted in pursuit of agency goals that they were intrinsically motivated to fulfill (Yeşilkağıt 2018). Chapter 5 will discuss that the fact that a bureaucrat means well—and even

advances their agency's mission—does not necessarily mean that all members of the society agree with that mission. Many citizens or politicians might sincerely wish to change the direction of the government, making Mission Driven Bureaucrats a hindrance for these reformers.

9. Here, and throughout this work, I use "autonomy" in a way that comports to its common use (as a synonym for "decision latitude"), rather than using the term as scholars of bureaucracy often do. I am concerned principally with actions individuals take of their own prerogative and will call that "autonomy" rather than being concerned with whether a given decision latitude is formally delegated (discretion, in scholarly terms) or stems from another source (autonomy, in scholarly terms).

10. In my view, selecting for Mission Driven Bureaucrats is one of the key building blocks to answer important questions such as, "If monitoring is not possible, then what (if anything) sustains good bureaucratic performance?" (Pepinsky et al. 2017, p. 263).

11. This is a treatment effect, in the language of economics—a within-person change. The claim is that people are capable of change, with behaviors, preferences, and even identities that can be shaped and reshaped by management practice. Bureaucrats' objective functions are not fully exogenous but rather partially endogenous to management practice.

12. If management says, "you'll be rewarded if you produce ten widgets, but the method to do so is flexible," they're practicing compliance-oriented management inasmuch as management is trying to induce employees to do something they would not otherwise do. This is not to say the flexibility is irrelevant; indeed, it may be a critical part of ensuring a given compliance-oriented approach is successful. There are many flavors of compliance-oriented management, just as there are many flavors of empowerment-oriented management.

13. *Oxford English Dictionary*, https://www.oed.com/view/Entry/24906?redirectedFrom=bureaucrat&.

14. *Mechanic's Magazine*, March 31, 1832. As cited in the *Oxford English Dictionary*, https://www.oed.com/view/Entry/24906?redirectedFrom=bureaucrat&. The earliest known use of any closely related word is "bureaucratic" in 1800 and is similarly pejorative: "Bureaucratic luxury aims at devouring the republic. We tremble when we consider what legions of persons employed, and factors we have, and that they are equal in number to our soldiers" (https://www.oed.com/view/Entry/24907#eid11931627).

15. Residents also benefit from public services, of course; I use the term "citizens" throughout but in almost all cases mean for the argument to apply to all individuals who do or could benefit from services, irrespective of their legal status.

16. Quote from Goetzmann 2017, p. 170; see Liao 1939 for the original. One key element of what Han Feizi advocated was a pay-for-performance approach, rewarding individuals for a job done well via *Xing-Ming*.

17. From Jackson 2009's able summary of the debate (p. 69); see also Bertelli 2012, chapter 6, and Stewart 1985.

18. These are usually examined in "pairs"—for example, motivation and mission (Christensen & Wright 2011; Kim 2012); motivation and exit (Bright 2008; Moynihan & Pandey 2008); motivation and management practice in the public sector (e.g., Moynihan & Pandey 2007; Perry 2020); and management practice and performance (e.g., Boyne 2003; Moynihan & Pandey 2005). Nor am I the first to frame organizational missions as reference points (e.g., Goodsell 2010; Grindle 1997; DiIulio 1994; Akerlof & Kranton 2010; Brewer & Selden 1998) or to suggest that there are such things as bureaucrats motivated by passion and public purpose in developed (e.g., Riccucci 1995; Goodsell 2010; DiIulio 1994; O'Leary 2019; Miller & Whitford 2016) and developing (e.g., Tendler & Freedheim 1994; Grindle 1997; McDonnell 2020) countries. Many of these pieces will be referenced in more detail later in this volume. To my knowledge there is little existing scholarship that combines these various threads into a single whole.

19. This book does not provide a comprehensive summary of the existing literature on motivation and management practice in the public sector. James Perry, arguably the dean of scholars on motivation in the public service, recently written a masterly volume, *Managing Organizations to Sustain Passion for Public Service* (Cambridge University Press, 2020), which surveys this literature, particularly focusing on public service motivation. I think his is a wonderful

complement to this book. While our books have different foci and scopes, they share a view that "sustaining passion for the public service" will lead to better performance.

20. A sampling of this wide literature finds Mission Driven Bureaucrats among US Forest Rangers (Kaufmann 1960), Brazilian health workers in the state of Ceará (Tendler & Freedheim 1994), mid-level bureaucrats in Ghanaian ministries and agencies (McDonnell 2020), procurement officers in Pakistani Punjab (Bandiera et al. 2020), the Nigerian civil service (Rasul & Rogger 2018), and far beyond (Grindle 1997). This book will say much more about these examples, as well as many others.

21. Goodsell 2006, p. 631. To be clear, the claim here is not that there is *never* such a laudable mission point in the private sector—indeed, many private sector firms have such mission points. But it is still less frequently true in the private than the public sector.

22. That is, with more frequency/more unambiguously; this is true for many private sector firms, but nearly all public sector firms.

23. This distortion between monitorable and unmonitorable is the well-documented multitask problem in organizational economics (Holmstrom & Milgrom 1991). See Honig 2019 and Honig 2022 for a fuller discussion. Chapter 2 will delve into these monitorability challenges in more detail.

24. The private sector literature on organizational culture and behavior as it relates to prosocial motivation is voluminous and just the tip of the iceberg; management consultants earn substantial fees thinking carefully about management practice, including the ways in which it relates to motivation.

25. By "telemarketers" I have in mind Adam Grant's pioneering work on prosocial motivation, e.g., Grant 2008.

26. See acknowledgments for more detail. These profiles are not "research"—they make no claims to representativeness or systematic selection. The profiles are illustrations, meant to make more concrete—more "human"—some of the book's core messages.

27. Tendler 1997, p. 5; for those interested in reading more but not able to acquire the book, see Tendler & Freedheim 1994's wonderful description of public health workers in Ceará.

28. Tendler 1997, pp. 14–15.

Chapter 2

1. Goodsell 2010, p. 1; emphasis in original.
2. Scott 1990, pp. 193–195.
3. McDonnell 2020, p. 205.
4. The lone exception in my experience is the Netherlands, where I did not feel compliance was the default in quite the same way as everywhere else.
5. In the sense of philosophy and sociology, I mean that mission points are intersubjectively verifiable; they are understood by a collective and *could* be verified (e.g., by asking lots of people what the mission point of the agency was/comparing answers), even if they are not formally codified or communicated. The bounds of who shares this understanding vary. Mission points may and are contested between employees, the public, politicians, and beyond. Chapter 7 returns to contestation of mission points.
6. This is not far from an organization's reputation; see, e.g., Carpenter 2001, 2014; Carpenter & Kruse 2012. See Moore 1995 on serving the public and "creating public value."
7. Many private firms have goals beyond profits, including generating public welfare.
8. Mullan 2002; Williams 2008. A mission statement has multiple roles. For instance, it is also in part about projecting—"selling" what an organization does to the outside world.
9. https://www.greeningdetroit.com/member/michigan-department-of-environmental-quality/.
10. https://www.moe.gov.sg/about.
11. https://dwss.punjab.gov.in/.

12. That is, being mission-motivated is not the same as being generally "public-spirited," in the sense usually employed in the literature on Public Service Motivation.

13. See, e.g., Caillier 2014; Rainey & Steinbauer 1999. There is also suggestive evidence that those who believe in the mission will be most likely to sustain their effort; see Resh et al. 2018.

14. This stickiness can be a good thing (by preserving public value) or a barrier to reform. It is also possible for agencies to have non-public value-creating missions; see Chapter 5's discussion of Mission Driven Nazis. There is no necessary normative valence to these terms; I just mean to establish an organizational purpose to which employees may be aligned. Mission points are, importantly, independent of the individuals who happen to be supervisors or even agency leadership. For instance, a low-level employee can be more aligned to an agency's mission point than is their supervisor.

15. Goodsell 2010, p. 250. Mission points may evolve over time for any number of reasons, especially when they are contested in implementation. Citizens, legislators, the courts, executives, and even bureaucrats within an agency may disagree about the actions that the organization ought to perform. While many employees who disagree are likely to exit, some may attempt to change the agency's mission point to align with their own idea of its true purpose. Some of the Mission Driven Bureaucrats profiled in this book—e.g., Batool Asadi and Tathiana Chaves de Souza—are mission-driven *not* because they do what their organization tells them to. Rather, they act in service of a welfare-enhancing mission point that they personally believe in. Chapter 7 further explores mission contestation.

16. Goodsell 2010.

17. Grindle 1987, p. 486.

18. This conception of accountability as more than just "accounting" metrics and targets, but rather about giving account—about perceptions, discourse, justification—is described in Honig & Pritchett 2019 and is expanded on in Chapter 7.

19. This occurs in part through elections. In the view of many scholars, public legitimacy is necessary regardless of whether elections are being held, and in any case elections do not constitute the only form of public accountability even where they're present. See, e.g., Gandhi 2008; Gandhi & Przeworski 2007; Mansbridge 2009, 2014; Sabel & Zeitlin 2012.

20. McDonnell 2020, p. 206.

21. My central deviation from conventional wisdom is to solve problems not from the "top" of the chain (from the principal's perspective) but from the "bottom" (the bureaucrat and the citizens with whom they interact). There is nothing in the "math" of principal-agent models that *requires* them to be "solved" from the principal's perspective.

22. DiIulio 1994, p. 227.

23. This is in contrast with much that seems to be focused on motivation but sees "down" from the principal's perspective. One such example is Besley and Ghatak 2005's well-known mission match framework, which "emphasizes the role of matching the mission preferences of principals and agents in increasing organizational efficiency" (p. 616). The abstract of Besley and Ghatak 2005 notes that "mission-oriented organizations are frequently staffed by motivated agents who subscribe to the mission," but in practice, the paper focuses on principal-agent agreement.

24. This is not to suggest that whistleblower laws are uniformly successful in protecting those who do come forward; see Vaughn 2012.

25. Schuster et al. 2020, 2021; greater public service motivation (and thus mission motivation) predicts greater use of voice and other means of thwarting what they term "unprincipled principals."

26. Slotnik 2020.

27. Bogage 2020.

28. Miller & Whitford (2016) make a somewhat parallel argument that bureaucrats can be custodians of the public good, at times even preventing politicians from deviating from it. In my view, being mission-driven need not mean in this (or any) case that the bureaucrats are "right" and the management "wrong" about their interpretation of the mission, or that the mission of the agency is itself laudable; Chapter 7 will discuss these issues further.

29. A stylized Mission Driven Bureaucrat is, then, a form of what DiIulio and others call a principled agent; DiIulio 1994.

30. McGregor 1960. This is not an obscure work, particularly for scholars of private sector management and organizational behavior. As of late 2022, it had nearly 22,000 citations (21,749 on December 8, 2022). However, there has been vanishingly little practical application of McGregor's ideas in the study and management of government.

31. This builds off Brandsma & Schillemans 2013's use of "hierarchical accountability" as accountability that pulls "up" an administrative hierarchy.

32. Ryan & Deci 2000.

33. Ryan & Deci 200, p. 73. I'm reframing because I don't find "relatedness" an intuitive label for this feeling of connection—and focusing on peers and purpose (including beneficiary benefits) as these are the people with whom bureaucrats most frequently experience this motivating sense of connection.

34. That is, being mission-motivated is not the same as being generally "public-spirited," in the sense usually employed in the literature on Public Service Motivation.

35. Esteve & Schuster 2019, p. 14.

36. This includes motivations not easily incorporated into this schema, such as religious conviction. See Akerlof & Kranton 2011 for a wider range of "identity-based" motivations, all of which are mission motivations in my view.

37. I find the term "mission motivation" to be more relevant to this book's themes than alternatives like "intrinsic" or "internal" motivation. There many other ways to differentiate types of motivation. For instance, organizational scholar Amy Wrzesniewski and psychologist Barry Schwartz distinguish between "instrumental" and "internal" motivation (Schwartz & Wrzesniewski 2019). Amabile 2018 defines "as *intrinsic* any motivation that arises from the individual's positive reaction to the task itself" and "as *extrinsic* any motivation that arises from sources outside of the task itself (p. 115). The exact labels are less important than the core message: mission-motivated employees will genuinely want to fulfill their mission. Mission motivation is also associated with other benefits, including creativity (Amabile) and greater fulfilment at work (Schwartz & Wrzesniewski).

38. One can be mission-motivated and still respond to incentives. However, mission-motivated people aren't primarily driven by these incentives to do their jobs.

39. Salaries are a tricky case. Sometimes salaries—and particularly bonuses—are compliance-oriented managerial tools. If an employee performs certain actions in the hopes of getting a higher salary, then the salary is acting as an incentive. However, simply desiring more pay does not preclude an employee being mostly, or even entirely, mission-driven. Even among the most mission-driven, there are few who would choose to remain at a job whose salary is insufficient for their needs. Salaries can also be a sign of respect, appreciation, and trust.

40. This begs the question how you would know if someone was mission-motivated. What measurement strategy could capture this range of motivators? Perhaps unsurprisingly, scholars have very different, if overlapping, ways of thinking about workplace motivation. Psychology's Self-Determination Theory may be my conceptual base, but it is far from the only candidate. The major frameworks currently in use—prosocial motivation, public service motivation, Herzberg's dual factor theory, ERG theory, etc.—share many similarities. Unhelpfully, each of these potential measures has its own set of measurement strategies and scales. I could decide to throw out all data that do not map precisely onto the concept of mission motivation that I use, but that would leave out a lot of relevant existing research. Instead, I do the opposite—using anything and everything I can that captures a subset of mission motivation, thus allowing me to draw on the wise work of a broad range of scholars. I'm copying this strategy from the guru of public service motivation, James Perry. In a recent book he writes, "My goals are instead pragmatic and applied. Waiting for all the conceptual and theoretical questions to be answered should not deter us from exploiting opportunities and improvements" (Perry 2020, pp. 30–31). Like Perry, I employ prosocial motivation (Grant 2008), the work preference inventory (Amabile et al. 1995), and public service motivation (Perry & Wise 1990) as measures of mission motivation.

41. Bina is named for my friend Bina Venkataraman, whom I happened to speak to the day I was trying to come up with these names. Bina's a fantastic human whom I've seen maintain mission motivation in a variety of jobs, public and private. When you're done reading this book it's worth picking up her excellent *The Optimist's Telescope*.

42. Accountability Lab is sometimes referred to as an "American NGO"; but while its founder is indeed American, it is separately incorporated in many of the countries in which it works. See https://accountabilitylab.org/our-governance/. Quote from https://accountabilitylab.org/integrity-idol-how-a-reality-tv-show-is-changing-minds-about-public-service/. Integrity Idol has now been rebranded "Integrity Icon."

43. Peter comes from the film *Office Space*'s character Peter Gibbons, who explains he'll do just enough to avoid being fired and no more (though this does seem to be linked in the film to his experiences with management with the red tape of "TPS Reports"—it is possible Peter is in fact demotivated, not unmotivateable).

44. It's possible that some *other* unexplored channel could increase the mission motivation of a given individual. I don't actually believe there are any "true" Peters in the world, only Samirs we haven't found yet. Nevertheless, in this thought experiment, Peters represent those employees who managers would find exceedingly difficult to motivate.

45. Following "Peter," Samir is also drawn from *Office Space*. Samir works diligently at his job until he feels mistreated by management, which demotivates him.

46. I remember hearing her say this in an interview but can't find the reference. The wording might be slightly off, but I think the thrust is correct.

47. Those few exceptions are where monitorability is highest and trust is appropriately 0 between supervisors and workers. Forced labor or slavery come to mind—morally reprehensible environments where performance may be best under the most extreme compliance-oriented management.

48. This then crowds out tacit knowledge and soft information (Honig 2018), which will not be cultivated by an employee who cannot make use of them (Aghion & Tirole 1997).

49. I have in mind here the Lucas Critique or Goodhart's Law. Among many other descriptions of this phenomenon, I have one in Honig 2018.

50. Kerr 1975.

51. Holmstrom & Milgrom 1991; this is known as a multitask problem in contract theory.

52. Bernstein 2012.

53. Aghion & Tirole 1997.

54. Nguyen 2022, p. 333.

55. Polanyi 1966; Scott 1998.

56. Rasul et al. 2021.

57. Rasul et al. 2021; personal communication. See Chapter 2 of Williams 2023 for related discussion.

58. In my practical work with governments, I often begin by asking, "What does good performance look like?" After all, the question of "how do we get there?" is something we can only ask when we have somewhere to head toward. As baseball great Yogi Berra wisely noted, "If you don't know where you are going, you'll end up someplace else."

59. While there are plenty of historical accounts on this point, my favorite one is fictional— Francis Spufford's *Red Plenty*.

Chapter 3

1. Aiyar et al. 2021, p. 18.

2. Stimson 1945.

3. See, e.g., Esteve & Schuster 2019; Herzberg 1959; Moynihan & Pandey 2007; Wright & Pandey 2008.

4. Christensen et al. 2017, p. 529. James Perry's book *Managing Organizations to Sustain Passion for Public Service* reviews the public management literature on this point (Perry 2020).

5. I served first as a Scott Fellow/special assistant to finance minister Antoinette Sayeh, then as aid management advisor to her successor, Augustine Ngafuan.

6. This is the National Transitional Government of Liberia (2003–2005).

7. See, e.g., Ebo 2005 for this problem in the context of the security sector; Friedman 2012 and Government of Liberia 2008 on the civil service more broadly.

8. See, e.g., Friedman 2012.

9. World Bank quote from https://www.worldbank.org/en/country/thailand/overview, accessed May 27, 2021; number of coups and constitutions are author's calculations building from various sources, e.g., Farrelly 2013.

10. E.g., Dunleavy 1995; this is also an implication of transaction cost economics' approach to understanding government function (e.g., Williamson 1981).

11. See Honig & Woodhouse 2023 for more detail on these indicators.

12. Semi-structured interviews covered bureaucrats' motivation, career trajectory, experience of management, and behavior; surveys included standard measures of motivation and job satisfaction. See Honig & Woodhouse 2023 for more detail.

13. Interviews; Honig & Woodhouse 2023.

14. Interviews; Honig & Woodhouse 2023.

15. Hasnian et al. 2022. The GSPS contains motivation scores but no link between management practice and motivation (to explain the difference between the claims on database size made in this chapter regarding the GSPS and the Honig 2021 data). This claim is made with the caveat that we measure prosocial motivation in the Thai survey, not public service motivation as included in the GSPS. As available end 2022. Prosocial motivation (Grant 2008) averages 6.68 on a 7-point likert-type scale; job satisfaction averages 6.28/7 on a 7-point likert-type scale. This high level of satisfaction is also seen in the qualitative data; see Honig & Woodhouse 2023 for a more complete analysis of the data underlying this and all other claims in this section, as well as a more complete description of data.

16. Honig & Woodhouse 2023.

17. "Adapt" in this context includes accounts of, for example, doing one thing in practice and reporting another—that is, actively deceiving their Bangkok-based superiors. A number of interviewees note that strong civil service protections mean they are unlikely to be dismissed, even if identified as refusing or adapting orders. While interviewees were given anonymity, this is surely an undercount. If 40 percent would admit this in an interview, I suspect the true number is still higher.

18. Honig & Woodhouse 2023.

19. Honig & Woodhouse 2023.

20. As with all the statements in this section, there is significant variation. Some district heads do not use a Route E approach, some vertical bureaucrats do not report feeling supported, and so forth. See Honig & Woodhouse 2023 for more information.

21. E.g., Bellé 2013; Moynihan & Pandey 2017; Vogel & Willems 2020.

22. Jensen & Bro 2018. This is part of a broader body of work on "transformational leadership" led by Lotte Bøgh Andersen and others centered on Danish public administration. This rich literature demonstrates that leadership training does influence how managers manage, which in turn alters employee motivation and action. See, e.g., Andersen et al. 2018a, 2018b, 2018c; Bro & Jensen 2020; Bro et al. 2017; Jensen & Bro 2018; Jacobsen et al. 2022.

23. Gailmard and Patty 2007, 2012. Gailmard and Patty discuss "grants of discretion" to bureaucrats. In economics terms, this is arguably an extension of Aghion & Tirole 1997's work regarding the returns to "real" authority.

24. On professional accountability see Jackson 2009; Brehm & Gates 1999; Mulgan 2000.

25. Kuper & Marmot 2003.

26. I mean by this to incorporate the job crafting literature (see Perry 2020, Chapter 4, for an overview) as well as experimental work such as Bellé 2013. The beneficiary exposure work has a clear and well-known private sector parallel in Grant (2008)'s work on prosocial motivation.

27. When one American social worker was asked, "What do you make?," she responded "I make a difference. . . . What do you make?" Arrington 2008, as quoted in Perry 2020, p. 87.

28. Chowdhury 2020.

29. Chowdhury 2020. Chowdhury credits this framework to Pink 2009, and Pink in turn credits his framework to Deci and Ryan's self-determination theory.

30. Quote from https://stireducation.org/what-we-do/, accessed July 2022. Two hundred thousand teachers and 109 districts from STiR 2022, p. 16. I am a member of STiR's Partner Strategy Group; I receive updates and are sometimes called upon to offer them feedback.

31. STiR Theory of Change; STiR 2022, p. 7.

32. Interview with Sharath Jeevan, March 2020; Jeevan was then director of STiR but stepped down in 2020. In 2022, Jeevan was awarded an Order of the British Empire (OBE) for his efforts with STiR.

33. Tummers 2012; see Usman et al. 2021 for a developing world example from Pakistan.

34. Thomann et al. 2018.

35. George et al. 2021; half a dozen countries is an estimate based on Table 1's description of administrative traditions.

36. Khemani 2020, describing the research in Khemani et al. 2020.

37. Khemani et al. 2020; Khemani 2020. The measures are "Irrespective of my efforts, the system will not allow health outcomes to improve" (inverse of connection to impact) and "In my work, I have to obtain permission for every little thing" (inverse of autonomy).

38. Boraggina-Ballard et al. 2021. Lena and Joanne are scholars at Detroit's Wayne State University, in the School of Social Work. This section draws on data on the published article but also on qualitative data collected as part of this joint effort that was not included in the final publication. Interviews are with former and current CPS employees who entered CPS through a special program called Wayne Together; see the published article for more detail. Some readers might note that there is no such thing as "Detroit CPS"; CPS is a county responsibility in Michigan. My references to Detroit CPS are to the Wayne County, Michigan, CPS offices located in Detroit. As to "hometown," I was born in Detroit but grew up just outside the city border Eminem made famous in his film *8 Mile*, in Oak Park, Michigan.

39. See Michigan Department of Health and Human Services guidelines at https://www.michi gan.gov/mdhhs/0,5885,7-339-73971_7119_50648_7193-159484--,00.html.

40. The state tracking system is the Michigan Statewide Automated Child Welfare Information System (MiSACWIS), operated by the Michigan Department of Health and Human Services (MiSACWIS).

41. Boraggina-Ballard et al. 2021; Interviews. The response time regulation is MCL 722.628.

42. McDonald 1996. These statistics surely demonstrate that state care is not necessarily a pathway to "normal" childhood or adulthood. In fact, some studies have found that care-eligible children sometimes fare better when allowed to remain with their families. See, e.g., Doyle Jr. 2007.

43. Interview 201501.

44. Interview 201708.

45. Though far from all, some CPS employees report they can make a difference on the job, and do not feel overly burdened by incentives to remove children.

46. Boraggina-Ballard et al. 2021; Interviews.

47. Boraggina-Ballard et al. 2021; Interviews.

48. Boraggina-Ballard et al. 2021; Interviews.

49. Boraggina-Ballard et al. 2021, p. 5.

50. Majid & Ali 2023, p. 4.

51. Majid & Ali 2023, p. 22.

52. Australia, Canada, India, the United States, and the United Kingdom. These data also undergird my 2021 paper in *Proceedings of the National Academy of Science* (Honig 2021). Full information about the dataset and specifications can be found in the article, its 50-page online appendix, and 120-page pre-analysis plan. One set of surveys is from the Australian state of Western Australia. This survey is representative at the state (rather than the national) level.

53. More information can be found in Figure A.1 of the Technical Appendix.

54. There is both a selection effect and a treatment effect, where "treatment" with more Route E–compatible management practices independently influences motivation.

55. More information can be found in Figure A.2 of the Technical Appendix.

56. The measures available at the agency and individual level are different, as some measures do not have enough coverage in surveys at a given level of measurement. See the pre-analysis plan associated with Honig 2021 for more detail.

57. Empowerment-oriented management practices are not the only management practices that influence motivation. However, Honig 2021 finds that while other management practices are also associated with changes in motivation, Route E management practices are particularly influential.

58. I mean to imply here the standard econometric caveats; relative to the mean, and with all of the standard concerns regarding measurement error and scale construction and interpretation. See Honig 2021 and the associated pre-analysis plan and online appendix for further detail, discussion, and robustness checks.

59. More information can be found in the Technical Appendix.

60. This is unpublished work, intended as the first stage of a larger project that never found traction. We thank the International Growth Centre (IGC) for their financial support for this research, the BRAC Institute of Governance and Development (BIGD), and particularly Imran Matin, Zeeshan Abedin, and Dmitry Chakma for their partnership in this research.

61. In 2018, 10,964 candidates passed both the preliminary and final written BCS exams of 412,532 candidates. Daily Star 2022.

62. In 2018, 1,963 were ultimately recruited of 412,352 candidates. Daily Star 2022.

63. While Samir is fictionalized, this account draws upon and combines conversations with a number of BPSA staff.

64. Survey reported in Besley et al. 2020. The sampling was nationally representative of BPSA, with the exception of sixteen districts experiencing flooding when the survey was conducted in July 2019. Both prosocial motivation and public service motivation scores (Besley et al. 2020, p. 9) higher than the PSM (self-sacrifice) reported in the GSPS (Hasnian et al. 2022, as accessed in July 2022; online at globalsurveyofpublicservants.org).

65. Of 413 respondents, 79 would not rejoin the public sector at all and 147 would join the public sector but avoid BPSA.

66. All statistics in this paragraph are from Besley et al. 2020. The statement on "mission motivation" is true whether conceived of as prosocial motivation, public service motivation, or intrinsic motivation in the work preference inventory (Besley et al. 2020, Table 9). "More authority" includes more control over design and revision; initial project budgets and amendments as circumstances change. Support for greater recognition is also strongest among those with greater levels of mission motivation.

67. See Harford 2022 for an engaging summary of relevant research.

68. Harford 2022; Graeber 2018.

69. Graeber 2018.

70. See Grant & Berg 2010 for an overview of this literature, and Grant 2013 for a (*New York Times* bestselling) accessible overview of Grant's research.

71. Quotes from Stillman 2013, describing the research in Dutton et al. 2016; Wrzesniewski & Dutton 2001.

72. Stillman 2013.

73. This account in substance and (in many cases) phrasing repeated from my prior book, *Navigation by Judgment* (Honig 2018), with permission of the copyright holder, Oxford University Press.

74. This American Life 2010. The quote is from Bruce Lee, then regional manager for the United Auto Workers, the union that represented the Fremont plant.

75. Adler 1993.

76. Shook 2010.

77. Adler 1993.

78. Shook 2010; Adler 1993; This American Life 2010.

79. Adler 1993.

80. Shook 2010.

81. Aiyar et al. 2021, p. 48.

82. Aiyar et al. 2021, p. 44.

83. Aiyar et al. 2021.

84. Brooks 2019, drawing on Cottam 2018.

85. Aiyar et al. 2021; see, e.g., the description of Chunauti in Section 6.2.

Chapter 4

1. Lincon's notes for a law lecture dated July 1, 1850. See https://www.abrahamlincolnonline. org/lincoln/speeches/lawlect.htm for more detail.
2. This is a widely quoted translation into English; see, e.g., Barks 2005
3. Many thanks to Lucy Barnes for inspiring this section.
4. The single largest source of data are the International Social Survey Programme (Gesis 2014)—a large, cross-national survey that asked respondents if their employers were public or private, and also asked a series of questions regarding the extent to which respondents were motivated to help others in their country and the rest of the world. These data are augmented by additional publicly available studies. Excluding either the ISSP or focusing only on the ISSP yields the same stylized result as the data presented here. More information can be found in the Technical Appendix.
5. See Technical Appendix Figure A.5.
6. See, e.g., Houston 2000, which pursues a similar strategy with the General Social Survey that we do with the ISSP.
7. Allegretto & Mishel 2020.
8. Baig et al. 2021, p. 570, Figure 6b. A public sector wage premium is an additional amount an employee could expect to get in the public sector, relative to outside options. Figure 6b draws from 79 countries or the 132 countries in the overall dataset, according to the article.
9. Schuster et al. 2020, p. 829. They come to this conclusion on the basis of a conjoint experiment involving a quite large number of bureaucrats (6,500) in three developing countries and one OECD country.
10. I do not intend to question the internal validity of Schuster et al. 2020a, but rather its generalizability across countries. This analysis follows Schuster et al. 2020 and Bertelli et al. 2020, among others, as defining OECD countries as "developed" and non-OECD countries as "developing." Using alternate definitions—e.g., World Bank or IMF income groupings—does not change the stylized conclusions below.
11. See Technical Appendix Figure A.6.
12. Mikkelsen et al. 2021 raise just this kind of cross-national comparability issue regarding public service motivation surveys, suggesting that this is not just a hypothetical concern but a real threat to validity in this context.
13. While there was no formal pre-analysis plan for this, I did work with a research assistant (Henry Fung) to assemble an aggregate measure of mission motivation without any knowledge of the results, which we then used without alteration, to avoid "garden of forking paths" issues in the sense of Gelman & Loken 2013.
14. See Technical Appendix Figure A.7 and Tables A.4–A.6 for the results.
15. There may well be exceptions at the agency and unit level, but my personal experience in Liberia, described in Chapter 3, makes me think even these are few and far between.
16. Transparency International 2022.
17. The Indonesia study is Banuri & Keefer 2016; the Russia study is Gans-Morse et al. 2020. This is not to suggest that there is *never* an environment in which there is adverse selection, with, for instance, differentially dishonest people more attracted to the public sector. Hanna & Wang 2017 document just such a case in India, also noting that screening on high ability will not weed out the differentially dishonest. That said, a selection mechanism that specifically focused on mission motivation—as I advocate for below and in Chapter 8—might well do so.
18. Russia; Gans-Morse et al. 2020.
19. Indonesia; Banuri & Keefer 2016.
20. See, e.g., Bertelli 2012 for a discussion of this literature, or Gailmard & Patty 2012 for a well-known example of a model depending on differential selection into the public sector.
21. Zarychta et al. 2020.
22. See, e.g., Ashraf et al. 2020; Deserranno 2019; Linos 2018. For more of the literature and theory on attracting the differentially motivated see Perry 2000, particularly Chapter 3.
23. Quote from their website; https://www.broadcenter.org/broad-residency/.

24. All quotes in this paragraph are from Sarah Thompson's email, March 2, 2021. When Sarah started talking about this, I asked her to write it down so I could cite it.

25. Sarah reports that no fewer than three people described her outreach as "divine intervention" or "sent by the lord" but is quite confident that in fact many more of those Sarah and her colleagues contacted would report feeling this way if asked.

26. Banuri & Keefer 2016; Deserranno 2019; Ashraf et al. 2020.

27. Pay-for-performance schemes are compliance-oriented managerial practices as I describe them. However, I do not consider one's salary to be a compliance-oriented managerial tool. It is an extrinsic motivator, but one that is not directly tied to specific actions.

28. I draw here on personal conversations. I am not aware of any research/empirical evidence on this point.

29. E.g., Van Veldhuizen 2013.

30. Dal Bo et al. 2013.

31. Ashraf et al. 2020 find that emphasizing career concerns in a nationwide recruitment job in Zambia leads to lower levels of prosocial motivation among applicants. However, they detect no net reduction of prosocial motivation among those hired following an active selection process (e.g., interviews). Dal Bo et al. 2013 also find that higher wages attract a more competent and mission-motivated pool of applicants in Mexico. Higher salaries are not always a good thing for recruiting the mission-motivated, but salaries often complement mission motivation. See also Ashraf et al. 2014.

32. See Technical Appendix Figure A.8. The relationship is weak, as there are only seven countries where data are available both on the wage premium and both public and private mission motivation, hence the tentative language employed here. Wage premium uses the closest matching year (2013 or 2014) from the WB's Worldwide Bureaucracy Indicators (WWBI), https://datacatalog.worldbank.org/search/dataset/0038132.

33. Foreword to the National Civil Service Reform Strategy (Government of Liberia 2008), p. iii.

34. Government of Liberia 2008, p. iii; emphasis on "motivated" added by me.

35. I have known PYPP since its earliest days in Liberia, when it emerged out of the program (the Scott Fellows Liberia) that initially employed me in Monrovia.

36. In exchange for assisting EPL with the design of impact evaluations and feedback/guidance as they employed consultants to do the work, EPL provided me with full anonymized primary quantitative and qualitative data from the evaluation under a data use agreement. This gives EPL a right of review, but no ability to restrict my use of the data for scholarly purposes. I did not conduct this research but do have access to the raw data.

37. This is the basic logic of a regression discontinuity design, but due to the small sample size I am not describing it that way, to avoid implying a level of confidence and rigor that is not possible in this setting. EPL cohorts are small (approximately twenty fellows per year), limiting what quantitative analysis alone can tell us with confidence.

38. More information can be found in the Technical Appendix.

39. The effect size is 0.6 points on a 5-point scale (significant at the 95% level); see Technical Appendix.

40. The effect size is 0.26 points on a 5-point scale (significant at the 99% level).

41. As reported by Khana Group Phase II Impact Evaluation (2022).

42. This is a within-person comparison (i.e., individual-level panel data). The effect sizes are small, and the change not statistically significant; reported here as there certainly is no evidence of decreases (which is what the Liberia data suggest).

43. 0.45 points on a 5-point scale (significant at the 95% level) with WPI_intrisic as "mission motivation" for PSM 0.627 points on a 5-point scale (significant at the 99% level).

44. Reported in the Khana Group's Phase II Impact Evaluation (2022).

45. Reported in the consultants' final report: Taabazuing & Honu-Siabi for EPL Ghana, 2021, p. 45.

46. Borragina-Ballard et al. 2021.

47. Also quoted in Chapter 3. Interview 201708.

48. Interview ID 201708. I have indicated all quotes not used in the original paper using their anonymous interview ID. I've also used female pronouns irrespective of the speaker's true gender to protect anonymity.

49. Interview ID 201603.

50. Boraggina-Ballard et al. 2021.

51. Data provided by the Michigan Department of Health and Human Services in April 2022 in response to Freedom of Information Act (FOIA) Request H015210-041122. Special thanks to MDHHS for their incredibly prompt and thorough response. These data are for the Wayne County Child and Family Services North Central Office, but the pattern is very similar at the other Wayne CFS Offices (South Central and Western Wayne). Data provided are for the maximum period available, from October 7, 2017, to April 2, 2022, so just short of 54 months/4.5 years. I am reporting here figures for the "front line" job of Services Specialist-E, rather than the supervisory Services Specialist-A, but combining them makes little difference (there were two supervisor roles in the 2022 data).

52. US Bureau of Labor Statistics Series JTS920000000000000QUR; JTS920000000000000TSR, available from data.bls.gov. Detroit turnover rate as calculated by MDHHS at 153.1 percent; BLS total turnover drawn from monthly total separations rate over the months closest to the MDHHS start and end dates (BLS October 2017 through March 2022, inclusive), which total 90.1 percent.

53. Three retirements and 3 involuntary departures out of 118, for whom cause of exit is listed at CFS North Central. BLS data is quits as a proportion of all exits.

54. Tummers et al. 2015.

55. Our evidence in Bangladesh (joint with Tim Besley, Adnan Khan, and Ferdous Sardar) is also consistent with this even for those who remain. That is, among those who intend to remain in a very compliance-oriented agency, mission motivation is associated with lower job satisfaction, though not at conventional levels of statistical significance. Many thanks to Ferdous Sardar for secondary/additional data analysis on this front.

56. See Honig 2021 and Technical Appendix Figure A.3 for more detail.

57. Quote from van Loon et al. 2015.

58. See Esteve & Shuster 2019, Footnote 1. This follows directly from Self-Determination Theory. Those thwarted in their desire to care for others (low in feelings of relatedness or connection), unable to make the impact they desire (low in feelings of autonomy), and lacking feelings of mastery or control (low in feelings of competence) are unlikely to feel satisfied at their jobs. They are thus most likely to leave.

59. Greenstein & Honig 2022; Moore 2019.

60. Moore 2019, p. i; also quoted in Greenstein & Honig 2019.

61. More information can be found in Technical Appendix Figure A.3 and Honig 2021.

62. Vogel & Willems 2020.

63. Kaufmann et al. 2022, p. 1441.

64. Zarychta et al. 2020.

65. Piza et al. 2021.

66. This is a paraphrase based on best memory. I've also altered language to make it less clear what country this took place in.

67. US Department of Health and Human Services 2023.

68. This conversation convinced me that this book needed profiles.

69. Clark 2017.

70. This was not quite a conference, but rather a summer institute as part of the Organizations & Their Effectiveness community at Stanford CASBS, led by Bob Gibbons and Woody Powell.

71. This and all quotes in this section are from memory and may not be exactly accurate.

Chapter 5

1. Pahlka 2023, p. 100.

2. Public remarks at the 2023 ODDO Conference at London School of Economics, May 18. Cleared for citation via personal communication, May 31, 2023.

3. Emerging Public Leaders 2021. Evaluation led by Dr. Taabazuing, Ghanaian Institution of Management and Public Administration (GIMPA), supplemented by my own additional analysis of the underlying data. More information can be found in the Technical Appendix.

4. Esteve et al. 2016, p. 1. This is part of a broader process of socialization and work identity formation, which has long been recognized in organizational sociology and increasingly in organizational economics as well. See, e.g., Akerlof & Kranton 2005; Besley & Ghatak 2017; Besley & Persson 2022.

5. Manning 1991.

6. As these analyses do not appear in Honig 2021, where these data are primarily utilized, this analysis can be found in the Technical Appendix Tables I.2–I.3. On a 5-point scale, a 1-point increase in the perceived performance of coworkers within an agency is associated with a greater than 0.7-point increase in job satisfaction and nearly a 0.5-point increase in mission motivation.

7. Jackson & Bruegmann 2022.

8. Ho 2017. The study in fact covers all of King County, which extends beyond Seattle proper.

9. Ho 2017.

10. Ho 2017, p. 79.

11. This has echoes, in my experience, of how a smart ministry of finance uses internal auditors, with a focus not on "catching" malfeasance but rather on improving processes through long-term relationships of trust.

12. Mansbridge 2014, p. 56. In this section I also draw on Honig & Pritchett 2019, which introduces this way of thinking about the problem. Chapter 7 will return to this.

13. Gartenberg et al. 2019.

14. Carter 2021. As Carter puts it, "accountabilities within these SIB projects are . . . a shared project for the pursuit of social outcomes with co-dependencies between stakeholders. Trust-led, relational 'network' governance begins to emerge as a distinguishing, and arguably crucial, differentiator of SIBs" (p. 91). Carter is referring to collaborations around Social Impact Bonds (SIBs), where payment is tied to delivery of a social outcome. This makes the finding particularly striking, as SIBs are normally conceived of as working through an "incentives" channel; Carter argues convincingly that it is often in fact the collective reshaping of peer accountability among collaborators that leads to good performance.

15. Mikkelsen et al. 2022, p. 1.

16. Brehm & Gates 1999, p. 23.

17. Brehm & Gates 1999, p. 196.

18. Wenger 2011.

19. Pyrko et al. 2017.

20. Pyrko et al. 2017.

21. Pyrko et al. 2017; Wenger 2011.

22. E.g., Schein 1990; Hatch 1993.

23. Mangla 2022.

24. Mangla 2022.

25. Mangla 2022, p. 17.

26. Mangla 2022.

27. Zacka 2017.

28. Mangla 2022, p. 17.

29. Presentation at Relational Public Services conference, Newcastle (UK), June 14, 2023.

30. Honig 2018, 2019; Pahlka 2023.

31. Pahlka 2023.

32. NYT 2023.

33. Pahlka 2023.

34. Pahlka 2023; NYT 2023.

35. Pahlka 2023; NYT 2023.

36. NYT 2023.

37. Pahlka 2023.

38. The Netflix film *Home Team*, which I recently watched with my son Dylan, is what first prompted this link—but it's pretty common. Disney's *Miracle*. *The Bad News Bears*. *Mighty Ducks*. Many, many others.

39. When the series is airing, I also get asked if I'm doing a Ted Lasso impression once a week or so in London, particularly in moments where I'm speaking positively about something. I find this just delightful, to be totally honest. I feel chuffed each time. Perhaps uncoincidentally, fictional Ted, the real-life actor who plays him (Jason Sudeikis), and I are indeed all from the American Midwest, broadly defined.

40. Trent Crimm; Season 3, Episode 8, *Ted Lasso*. Ted changes his team's tactical approach mid-season to "Total Football"—a strategy that requires mutual trust between players and devolves decision-making. This is a tactical outgrowth of the larger cultural transformation.

41. Trent Crimm; Season 3, Episode 8, *Ted Lasso*.

42. Impact as reported by STiR; see, e.g., STiR 2022.

43. Pahlka 2023.

44. NYT 2023 quote, example from Pahlka 2023.

45. NYT 2023.

46. Pahlka 2023.

47. Pahlka 2023.

48. Presentation at Relational Public Services conference, Newcastle (UK), June 14, 2023.

49. Smith 2022.

50. Smith 2022.

51. Smith 2022.

52. Smith 2022; Lowe et al. 2022.

53. Smith 2022, p. 1.

54. Smith presentation at Newcastle Relational Public Services conference, June 2023.

55. Loew et al. 2022, p. 39.

56. Mangla 2022, Chapter 4.

57. Mangla 2022, Chapter 7.

58. Mangla 2021, p. 1.

59. As they articulate it, "public servants and residents [do] come together, do things together and decide things together." Camden Centre for Collaborative Practice 2022.

60. Early Intervention Foundation 2018. These conferences are not limited to children's services support, but that is one of the main foci of conferences for families with children.

61. Merkel-Holguin 2004, p. 165. This research is about FGCs more broadly as a model, not Camden-specific application of the model. The second quote is from Merkel-Holguin 2004, p. 160, in reference to Buford 2001.

62. Early Intervention Foundation 2018.

63. Merkel-Holguin 2004, p. 165.

64. Merken-Holguin 2004.

65. UK Department for Education 2023.

66. UK Department for Education 2023, p. 40. I am converting the language here from UK to US (Detroit CPS) English—by "pulled" I mean "children referred for statutory social care," which has fallen from 522 to 280 per 100,000 children; by "foster care" I mean "children in care" has fallen by 48 percent.

67. It also appears that Camden has improved exceptionally in this regard compared to other areas in the UK, as evidenced by the UK Department for Education (2023) highlighting Camden's success. Camden may of course—likely is—systematically different from other areas in myriad other ways, but it does suggest the need for a Camden-specific cause of the performance gains, for which the change in approach seems the most likely candidate.

68. https://www.youtube.com/watch?v=n53hW-0r3c0.

69. https://www.youtube.com/watch?v=n53hW-0r3c0.

70. https://www.youtube.com/watch?v=n53hW-0r3c0.

71. McDonnell 2020, book subtitle.

72. McDonnell 2020, p. 14.

73. McDonnell 2020, p. 206.

74. McDonnell 2020, Chapter 3.

75. McDonnell 2020, Chapter 3.
76. McDonnell 2020, Chapter 4.
77. Zak 2014.
78. Zak 2014.
79. Wright et al. 2012, p. 212.
80. As noted in Chapter 3, prosocial motivation (Grant 2008) averages 6.68 on a 7-point likert-type scale; job satisfaction 6.28. Using the Global Survey of Public Servants (Fukuyama et al. 2022) as a comparison, this would make the Thai bureaucrats (if national sample) first overall on motivation and second of seventeen on job satisfaction.
81. See Honig 2022b for more on this.
82. McDonnell 2020.
83. I have in mind cases like the duly elected Netanyahu government's (in my view incredibly troubling) civil service and judicial reforms in Israel in 2023. I think these put two democratic principles—majority rule and minority rights—in opposition to one another.
84. See, e.g., Strobel & Veit 2021; Yeşilkağıt 2018; Yeşilkağıt & Christensen 2022.
85. Strobel & Veit 2021; Yeşilkağıt 2018.
86. Strobel & Veit 2021; Yeşilkağıt 2018.
87. My agreement stems from the statistics and protests, but also from my own experience. It's pretty hard to grow up in Detroit and not be very, very aware of racial discrimination by police.
88. Brehm & Gates 1999, Chapter 6.
89. See Lum et al. 2019 for a summary of empirical research/meta-analysis showing the null result, and thus "on average" no effect. There are individual studies that find effects in particular settings, including some after the meta-analysis was conducted, e.g. Williams et al. 2021 (and thus it is possible that an updated meta-analysis might find positive effects, on average, though also might not). 80% figure from National Institute of Justice 2022.
90. As Canice Prendergast put it in a careful causal study of civilian accountability boards in Los Angeles, "The arrest-to-crime rate fell [by] 40% after accountability to the public rose, then rebounded to its original level when accountability fell. For the 'victimless' crimes of narcotics and prostitution, arrests fall [by] almost 50% and then rebound" (Prendergast 2021); see also Prendergast 2001.
91. Headley et al. 2021; Headley & Wright 2020; Headley 2022. Some of these are coauthored, of course; I describe these as Headley's papers as she is the common author across the set. I also follow Headley/these papers in describing the officers as "Black" rather than "African American," and also in capitalizing both "Black" and "White" in this context. This is an active discursive debate in the United States.
92. Headley & Wright 2020.
93. Headley & Wright 2020, p. 1057.
94. Headley 2022.
95. See, e.g., Fox 1993, 1996 or more generally the Sandwich Strategy Research page of the Accountability Research Center, which Fox directs (https://accountabilityresearch.org/sandwich-strategy-research/).
96. See, e.g., Moe 1989's seminal work and many of the (as of late 2022) 1,500+ papers that cite it.

Chapter 6

1. McGregor 1960, p. 60.
2. Aiyar et al. 2021, p. 28.
3. Kaufman 1960.
4. DiIulio 1994.
5. What Goodsell calls "internal commitment" to the agency's "central mission purpose" is a close equivalent—indeed, essentially an alternative wording—of my "mission motivation." Goodsell 2010.
6. Goodsell 2010.

7. Carpenter 2014.
8. See Bertelli et al. 2020 for an overview of my coauthors' and my concerns on this front and our view of how the study of public administration in developing countries might proceed.
9. Tendler 1997.
10. These agencies were responsible for elements of macroeconomic management, agricultural extension services, and maternal and child health in Bolivia, Central African Republic, Ghana, Morocco, Sri Lanka, and Tanzania.
11. Grindle 1997. Grindle refers to this sense of mission as "organizational mystique," in an echo of Goodsell 2010. It is interesting that two scholars seemingly independently (as Goodsell does not cite or refer to Grindle) felt the word "mystique" appropriate here, suggesting there does seem to be something somewhat mystical, or magical, about the culture of a high-performing agency where empowerment-oriented management has taken hold.
12. Clarey 2017.
13. Honig 2022a explores the education sector in further depth.
14. Bold et al. 2017.
15. Piper et al. 2018; see Stockard et al. 2018 for a recent meta-analysis. The most effective scripts still appear to be those that allow "teachers [to] adapt the lessons to make them their own." This is consistent with the idea that even in environments that benefit from control-heavy C reforms, the optimal level of empowerment-oriented management is rarely zero.
16. Perhaps the best evidence of this comes from Rwanda via Leaver et al. 2021. This lovely RCT found that both teachers recruited with the knowledge that they would be involved in a pay-for-performance scheme linked to student test scores, and teachers recruited through normal channels, increased their efforts and improved student learning.
17. Ganimian & Murnane 2016.
18. E.g., Popham 2001.
19. Ganimian & Murnane 2016, p. 740.
20. Ganimian & Murnane 2016.
21. Dhaliwal & Hanna 2017.
22. Banerjee et al. 2008.
23. Gulzar et al. 2023.
24. Williams 2023.
25. Acemoglu et al. 2020; casualty count from Table 4.
26. Transparency International 2022.
27. Rasul & Rogger 2018, p. 1.
28. Rasul et al. 2021, pp. 3, 27.
29. Rasul & Rogger 2018, Figure 1.
30. Rasul et al. 2021, p. 1.
31. This graph draws from Honig 2021 as well. See Technical Appendix for more detail.
32. Honig 2019.
33. Honig 2018, 2019.
34. Khan 2023.
35. Khan 2023.
36. Khan 2023. There is also a combined treatment arm, which also outperforms the finance-only arm of the study.
37. Bandiera et al. 2021.
38. There is also a combined treatment arm, which also outperforms the finance-only arm of the study.
39. Transparency International 2022.
40. Bandiera et al. 2021.
41. Azulai et al. 2023. It constituted one day of training in a ten-day training program; the other nine days are the same between treatment and control groups. Interestingly, another treatment arm that delivered the same training to teams, including directors who manage these bureaucrats, had no detectable effect.
42. Azulai et al. 2023, Table 5.
43. Azulai et al. 2023, Table 6.
44. Aiyar et al.

45. Aiyar et al. 2021, p. 72.
46. Burgess et al. 2017.
47. Crouch 2020.
48. Crouch 2020.
49. Mbiti et al. 2019.
50. McAlpine 2018, p. 23.
51. McAlpine et al. 2018, p. 4.
52. Mbiti & Schipper 2021.
53. Lohmann et al. 2018.
54. Lohmann et al. 2018.
55. De Walque et al. 2022. The core of the empirics are data from RCTs in Cameroon, Nigeria, Zambia, Zimbabwe, and Rwanda. There are also data from the Kyrgyz Republic and Tajikistan employed in Chapter 5 that look at the effects of PBF on health worker motivation.
56. De Walque et al. 2022, p. xxxix.
57. See the discussion of Zimbabwe, De Walque et al. 2022, p. 121. This is consistent with other empirical work, e.g., Ashraf et al. 2014's finding that financial incentives are more effective for more prosocially motivated agents in HIV prevention/condom distribution work in Zambia.
58. Ashraf et al. 2020.
59. Ashraf et al. 2020.
60. The shape of the curve in Figure 6.1 is thus the "ridge"—the slope in three dimensions that captures maximal possible performance (the z-dimension) in the combination of E and C managerial practices.
61. Duflo et al. 2012. I draw on Honig & Pritchett 2019 here, which frames this as a case of accounting-based accountability.
62. Duflo et al. 2012.
63. By "many other cases" I have in mind, e.g., Dhaliwal & Hanna 2017 and Banerjee et al. 2008.
64. Aiyar et al. 2021. The authors study the public system, which by reputation is even more focused on C-style compliance than are NGO schools.
65. "If implemented" is critical here; there were a number of attempts to spread the camera technology in India, all to my knowledge ineffective in actually rolling out this policy. These attempts were thwarted by parents groups, teachers unions, politicians, and technical limitations.
66. To reiterate, this figure is based on no data—it simply maps the argument.
67. By "tractable," I mean observable and attributable with sufficient frequency and without distortions.
68. Based on a normal distribution. Discussed in slightly greater detail in Honig & Pritchett 2019.
69. These are 2008 India ASER scores to match the 2007 endline of Duflo et al. 2012; ASER results are India-wide, not in the specific locations Duflo et al. study (and so may be higher- or lower-performing on average). ASER results as summarized in Pritchett 2013, p. 29. Grade 4 in UK/India is equivalent to US 3rd grade, Grade 2 in UK/India equivalent to US 1st grade.
70. Duflo writing in Pritchett & Murgai 2007, p. 170.
71. See programs that focus on teachers' motivation; e.g., the Broad Residency (broadfoundation.org) and STiR Education (stireducation.org). Evidence from Indonesia supports this general claim. Banuri and Keefer (2015) find that a pay-for-performance scheme in Indonesia spurred public sector workers to put in greater effort at work than a flat payment approach—but only among the initially unmotivated. The intervention also cost more than its alternatives and failed to result in any net performance improvement.
72. E.g., Decarolis 2020.

Profile: Labanya Margaret

1. Labanya is the only profiled individual whom we were unable to contact to confirm the details in their profile after it had been written. As such, this account is drawn entirely from Sarah Thompson's and my conversation with Labanya on November 17, 2020.

Chapter 7

1. Rich 2022, p. 837.
2. https://jobs.netflix.com/culture.
3. I use "citizens," but for many of these cases I mean "citizens and residents"—that is, all people who live in a place and interact with the government, irrespective of their legal status.
4. I use the word "corruption" here with some hesitancy. I suspect former students of mine reading this have already thought, "Hold on now, Dan would *never* let us get away with that word," and they're 100 percent right. I almost always ask my students to clarify or rephrase the term. One of the main ways in which I think the term is unhelpful is in the implication that all corruption is equal. Yuen Yuen Ang does us a great service by differentiating between corruption that involves elites as opposed to non-elites, and that which involves theft (e.g., an elite politician stealing money from a budget for personal use) as opposed to exchange (e.g., a citizen paying a bribe to a non-elite clerk to expedite an administrative process). For more information see, e.g., Ang 2020.
5. For the record, Nealin is one of the most capable, generous, giving, and mission-motivated people I've ever encountered. If she's not a mission-driven Bina, I'm not sure who is.
6. US Public Law 113-2, p. 38.
7. US Public Law 113-2, p. 38. The sum is 10 million USD—small by US government standards, of course, but illustrative of the broader phenomenon.
8. Communications with Laura Hogshead, Nealin Parker, and Trey Reffet.
9. Private communication, July 2023.
10. I borrow this phrasing from Julian Legrand. See Legrand 2003.
11. Rothstein 2021b.
12. Rothstein 2021a; Rothstein 2021b.
13. Bandiera et al. 2021.
14. Aneja & Xu 2023.
15. Brierley 2020, p. 1.
16. See, e.g., Folke et al. 2011 on the United States; Aspinall & Sukmajati 2016 on Indonesia; Clifton 2015 on Victorian England. Brierley 2021 finds that in Ghana, patronage occurs primarily in low-level jobs less likely to undermine the core functions of the state.
17. Schuster et al. 2020.
18. Figueroa 2020.
19. Miller & Whitford 2016.
20. Miller & Whitford 2016.
21. Schuster et al. 2020.
22. Thomson 2022. Luckily there do seem to still be plenty of mission-driven politicians in the United Kingdom, in my personal experience—and that of many far more expert observers. John Bercow, the UK Speaker of the Commons during the tumultuous years of the Brexit debates, described Parliament as "a wonderful place, filled overwhelmingly by people who are motivated by their notion of the national interest."
23. Gulzar & Khan 2021.
24. Gulzar & Khan 2021.
25. Seim et al. 2020.
26. The Apolitical Foundation and conversations with Lisa Witter, Apolitical Foundation CEO.
27. Klitgaard 1998.
28. This framework drawn from Ang 2020.
29. Toral 2023 on "Patronage Delivers"; e.g., Schuster et al. 2020 and Brierley 2021, among many others, on the downsides to performance of political patronage.
30. Ang 2020.
31. Weaver 2021.
32. Peiffer et al. 2021. This is in a sense the qualitative complement to the statistical findings in Peiffer & Armytage 2019.
33. Peiffer et al. 2021, p. 721.
34. Mansbridge 2014, p. 55.

35. Bandiera et al. 2009.
36. Bandiera et al. 2009.
37. Sometimes, of course, this attempt is beneficial. For example, it appears that attempts by the US government to vet firms asking for COVID-era financial support reduced fraud, saving over 700 million USD (Aman-Rana et al. 2022). The authors called this "the trade-off between administrative ordeals and fraud." However, the fact that attempts to reduce active waste *can* be net-beneficial does not mean they always are. Indeed, US federal procurement does appear to be a domain where passive waste often outweighs active waste. (Carril 2021).
38. 80 percent is four times 20 percent.
39. Rich 2022.
40. Honig 2018, 2019.
41. Rich 2022, p. 848.
42. Tu & Gong 2021, p. 271.
43. Khan on the podcast "In Pursuit of Development," Season 2, Episode 8. Khan and collaborators pursue this broader systems strategy in their work on Anti-Corruption Evidence (ACE); see, e.g., Khan & Roy 2022.
44. Marquette Twitter thread, November 14, 2020, https://twitter.com/hamarquette/status/1327635592860094465?s=20&t=9ccJ9wS5EbRhiTUOS499Pw.
45. Mansbridge 2009, as quoted in Mansbridge 2014, p. 59.
46. This does not apply only to democracies. In full democracies, citizens ultimately elect the politicians and are in that sense principals, but others (including myself) would argue that all governments can and do rely on the consent of the governed for their legitimacy. In that sense, citizens always are the "principals" of politicians, even where they have limited ability to control their "agents" who lead a country.
47. World Bank 2004.
48. World Bank 2004.
49. See Khemani 2016 for an excellent overview of when, where, and how "short-route compliance" can and does work, and the interaction between this channel and deeper/broader political considerations.
50. See Reinkka & Svensson 2005, 2011 for details of the intervention, and Reinkka & Svensson 2004 for a description of the diversion from students prior to the intervention.
51. Reinkka & Svensson 2005, 2011.
52. E.g., Heywood & Rose 2014 on corruption. See Fischer-Mackey & Fox 2022 for a nice extension of this to studies of community monitoring itself. They find that the indicators used to assess the quality of community monitoring are *themselves* also subject to this basic problem.
53. Lowe et al. 2022. The quote is from the report's foreword by Dee Fraser (p. 2).
54. I think this is important enough that it's where my future work is heading. I call this "relational state capacity." If you're interested in learning more, please visit my website, danhonig.info.
55. Drawing from my personal experience, and that of others; e.g., conversation with Halima Khan (ex-Nesta), July 2023.
56. Garg & Pande 2018.
57. Garg & Pande 2018; by "other cases" I have in mind, e.g., Mangla 2021, 2022.
58. See Ehren & Baxter (eds.) 2021, particularly Chapters 3 (by Frederique Six), 4 (by Baxter), and 14 (by Ehren & Baxter).
59. Ehren & Baxer (eds.) 2021.
60. See, e.g., Heywood & Rose 2015a; Heywood & Rose 2015b; and Heywood et al. 2017.
61. See Heywood et al. 2017 for a summary. These ideas are gaining practical traction. The OECD program on anti-corruption and integrity in the public sector (https://www.oecd.org/gov/ethics/) also works toward "integrity promotion."
62. I mean here something like "decision support tools"; see, e.g., Hazır 2015 for an overview of decision support tools in project monitoring.
63. Moynihan et al. 2020.
64. Honig & Pritchett 2019.
65. Sabel & Zeitlin 2012.
66. Dehart-Davis 2009, 2009b; Dehart-Davis et al. 2015.

67. Dehart-Davis 2009a, 2009b.
68. Dehart-Davis et al. 2015. The study tests for job satisfaction; extension to mission motivation is my conjecture, not that of the authors.
69. https://jobs.netflix.com/culture.
70. https://jobs.netflix.com/culture.
71. https://www.etymonline.com/search?q=Mission.
72. As a practicing Jew (a religion that prohibits actively seeking new converts) and someone who works in many countries with colonial legacies, I feel far from supportive of missionaries who saw proselytizing as their mission. On Jesuit proselytizing in "native communities," see Prieto 2017. Jesuits appear to have been particularly attuned to adapting, rather than imposing, elements of Church doctrine (see, e.g., Brockey 2007). Nonetheless, even if Jesuits did not forcefully convert anyone, structural power differences surely exist when developed world organizations proselytize in the developing world.
73. Quattrone 2004, 2015.
74. Quattrone 2015.
75. Quattrone 2004, 2009, 2015.
76. Quattrone 2004, 2009.

Chapter 8

1. Schleicher 2019.
2. I develop this argument more fully in collaboration with coauthors in Bertelli et al. 2020.
3. McGregor 1966.
4. Conversations with change management consultants and scholars who focus on private sector organizations suggest senior staff ignorance of the actual managerial environment lower-level employees experience is not a public sector–only phenomenon.
5. Survey conducted via the online platform Prolific; see Dissanayake et al. 2023 for full details. Original survey had 0 as full empowerment/100 as full compliance. The scale is reversed here so as to match the PPF graphs in more empowerment being to the "right" and more compliance the "left" of the graph.
6. Figure from Dissanayake et al. 2023. See Technical Appendix for more information.
7. This doesn't need to be a big formal exercise, to be clear, and should only be done if it feels useful. The Performance Possibility Frontier's primary purpose is to aid in systematic thinking, not to create paperwork and complexity that itself adds layers of red tape.
8. Michael Woolcock once told me this was one of the world's best and most meaningful moments for an academic. He's 100 percent right about this (and much more).
9. See, e.g., George et al. 2021 for a meta-analysis and review of this literature. As the authors put it, "red tape imposed by one's own organization is—to some extent—within a public manager's control. This form of red tape is not externally imposed but results from the organization's internal rules, regulations, and procedures, and can thus be actively managed, although reducing it might be challenging" (p. 638).
10. Christensen et al. 2018 for a summary; see also Grant 2007.
11. Vogel & Willems 2020.
12. See McDonnell 2020, as described in Chapter 5.
13. Hwa 2022, p. 81.
14. Wright et al. 2012, p. 206.
15. Khan 2023.
16. Grindle 1997. Managers seeking to instil this professionalism might utilize "mission symbols"—tokens that cultivate a sense of communal pride. For instance, some organizations distribute "challenge coins," small metal coins that bear the agency's mission statement. Canadian-trained engineers often wear "iron rings," which are meant to evoke pride, professional obligations, and ethics. Tapping on the power of mission symbols may be a useful strategy to encourage professional pride.

17. Azulai et al. 2020; Williams & Yecalo-Tecle 2020. Quotes from Azulai (both studies of the same intervention).
18. Williams & Yecalo-Tecle 2020, p. 1.
19. https://jobs.netflix.com/culture. As Netflix puts it (in reference to the expense policy and a collection of others): "You might think this much freedom would lead to chaos. Instead, it has created an extremely successful business model over the last 25 years. The lesson is you don't need policies for everything. You can be groundbreaking without them. Freedom can (and does) lead to chaos when we fail to couple it with a strong sense of responsibility. That is why freedom and responsibility go together."
20. Those interested in cultivating communities of practice may find Wegner et al. 2002 of interest. In my experience, this is little-read among those interested in improving public systems, despite having over 15,000 Google Scholar citations as of June 2021.
21. Of course, employees' feedback will rarely be completely unbiased. Subordinate evaluations will only elicit accurate information if employees believe they will be treated confidentially, which tends to be unlikely for many government agencies. Even where the information is biased, these evaluations signal to employees that their perspectives on and satisfaction with their bosses carry weight with agency leadership.
22. Miller & Whitford 2016.
23. See, e.g., Ashraf et al 2020.
24. Khana Group 2022, p. 19. As Khana Group 2022 puts it more broadly, "Taken in tandem with the agreement of nearly all of the interviewed supervisors that the presence of Fellows helped improve their team's work, evidence from this survey suggests that the PYPP program may not only be improving the performance of these ministries, commissions, and departments solely through their performance, but also by serving as a leader and model capable of improving collective performance within each team" (p. 19).
25. See, e.g., Ashraf et al. 2020 and the broader discussion of these issues in Chapter 6. As discussed in Chapter 4, public sectors with higher wages (relative to the private sector) also may have higher levels of mission motivation, further suggesting pay and motivation are complements, as tentatively suggested in the Technical Appendix.
26. Chapter 9 will turn to discuss a different type of outsider—citizens, and their role in improving public sector performance.
27. My previous book (Honig 2018) is partly about the appeal of these kinds of easily quantifiable solutions in foreign aid projects. It finds that these solutions often undermine performance, especially when it is hard to measure the important things in a given area.
28. Kenny 2017.
29. E.g., Andrews et al. 2017; Honig 2018; Williams 2023.
30. In addition to my work (e.g., Honig 2018, 2019; Honig & Gulrajani 2018), see Andrews 2013; Andrews et al. 2017; Ang 2020; Israel 1987; Levy 2014.
31. This follows from Vreeland 2006's arguments about the IMF more broadly (and is echoed by my lived experience). Offloading "responsibility" for a reform to an IMF condition (e.g. a government official asking for a desired reform to be included in an IMF program so that they can then overcome internal objections by arguing "we need to do this because the IMF is requiring it") is often an excellent way for domestic actors to achieve policy reforms they seek.
32. See, e.g., https://www.nesta.org.uk/project/people-powered-results/.
33. Nesta 2019, 2023.
34. Quote from Nesta 2019; see also Nesta 2023, p. 16, for more detail on both short- and long-term impacts.
35. USAID Website 2022.
36. USAID Website 2022.
37. By previous work, I have in mind Honig 2018. USAID's LCS strategy recognises this culture change by remarking, "At its core, the LCS Policy is a mindset and culture shift towards embracing capacity strengthening that supports local actors' ability to deliver and sustain development results—rather than focusing on local actors' capacity to qualify for and manage awards." USAID 2022.
38. Nesta 2019.

Profile: Batool Asadi

1. November 2020.
2. See http://www.cssforum.com.pk/css-datesheets-results/previous-css-results-datesheets/css-2012-exam/68943-ce-2012-result-announced.html.

Chapter 9

1. McDonnell 2020, p. 206.
2. Wilson 1989, p. 133.
3. I am not suggesting that the selection of profilees was random or representative. We were intentionally seeking out Mission Driven Bureaucrats to illustrate this book's arguments, not to serve as an independent source of data in their own right.
4. If readers find themselves inspired to write profiles of Mission Driven Bureaucrats on their own, I'd love to post them, too.
5. Leaver & Pritchett 2019.
6. Tendler 1997, p. 2. Tendler meant this as a criticism, not an endorsement, of the mainstream.
7. McDonnell 2020, p. 206.
8. Allen 2016.
9. Allen 2016.
10. Personal conversation between author and CPS employee in 2019 (not part of the formal data collection of Boraggina-Ballard et al. 2021).
11. This was funded out of my personal research account while I was employed by Johns Hopkins University. I thank JHU for the support. More information about the survey can be found in the Technical Appendix.
12. The survey explicitly defined a bureaucrat as "an official in a government department" and asked respondents "for the purposes of the following questions, please use that definition—that is, someone receiving their paycheck from their government."
13. The difference in agreements with the statements is significant at the 99 percent level for statements 1, 3, and 4; the average of all 4 statements is also significant at the 99 percent level. See Technical Appendix Table A.7.
14. Lipsky 1983; Abner et al. 2020; Tummers et al. 2016; Hershcovis & Barling 2010. "Bureaucrat bashing" also lowers perceptions of agency performance by the public; see, e.g., Caillier 2018.
15. Hershcovis & Barling 2010; Tummers et al. 2016. US police have been quitting in record numbers as well, plausibly linked to the George Floyd protests; see, e.g., NYT 2021 ("Why Police Have Been Quitting in Droves in the Last Year"). Whether this exodus of police is useful in shifting mission points in useful directions depends, in my view, on who is departing, who is replacing them, and management practice.
16. Quote from Tummers's website; https://en.larstummers.com/vidi.
17. Tendler & Freedheim 1994, p. 1776.
18. Stimson 1945.
19. Andino initially emailed me in response to remarks I'd made on Twitter, and I'd given him my address; the lanyard was sent subsequent to the email exchange I quote immediately below.
20. Personal email of April 8, 2020, 18:18 P.M.
21. Personal email of April 8, 2020, 18:18 P.M.
22. Personal email of July 3, 2023, 14:12 P.M., sent in response to my request for Andino's permission to quote and publicly acknowledge him. The quote is in reference to reviewing files for promotion in the foreign service, and thus considering the motivation of applicants.
23. The careful reader will note that I am not, in fact, a bureaucrat by my own definition; my paycheck does not come from a government institution. I raised this with Andino—that I was no bureaucrat, and I didn't want to pretend to be something I'm not, especially something that

I hold in high regard. "If bureaucrats are people," he replied, "then people can be bureaucrats with no 'honorary' stickers needed." (Personal email of April 8, 2020, 20:15 p.m.).

24. The Performance Possibility Frontier (PPF) discussed in Chapters 6 and 8 can be a helpful conceptual tool here, but it is not even close to enough for agencies seeking a fine-tuned reform agenda. If a PPF was a topographical map, I think there's enough data to show the valleys, and to point the direction to the summit. But the precise shape of the peaks? The precise "ridge line" where it's a close call whether Route C or E will be the best strategy for a given agency? It's impossible to predict or define these details from the outside for any specific context, certainly not based on the global knowledge we have to date. Agencies must map their own paths to the summit.

25. August 12, 1986. https://www.reaganfoundation.org/ronald-reagan/reagan-quotes-speeches/news-conference-1/.

26. https://www.reaganlibrary.gov/research/speeches/081286d.

Technical Appendix

1. As such, no sections for the Detroit CPS or Thailand studies are included, as these details are covered in published papers (Detroit) or working papers that are publicly available (Thailand).

2. Full details about this sample, including a list of the studies included, are available on request in the appendix of my working paper "Bad Actors or Bad Actions? Developing Country Public Sector Bureaucrats, Character, and Corruption." There are many more studies of motivation than those included; however, I am limited to including those studies that report scores or whose authors were willing to share such measures upon request. Most notably, perhaps, Meyer-Sahling et al. (2018b) survey 23,000 civil servants in developing countries; however, the data are not publicly available nor are country or agency scores reported in the published work.

3. See "Bad Actors or Bad Actions" for further detail on these analyses.

BIBLIOGRAPHY

Abner, G., Perry, J. L., & Fucilla, L. (2020). Experiments on the effects of positive and negative perceptions of a public sector profession. *Public Performance & Management Review, 43*(5), 1025–1052.

Acemoglu, D., Fergusson, L., Robinson, J., Romero, D., & Vargas, J. F. (2020). The perils of high-powered incentives: Evidence from Colombia's false positives. *American Economic Journal: Economic Policy, 12*(3), 1–43.

Adler, P. (1993). Time-and-motion regained. *Harvard Business Review.* https://hbr.org/1993/01/time-and-motion-regained.

Aghion, P., & Tirole, J. (1997). Formal and real authority in organizations. *Journal of Political Economy, 105*(1), 1–29.

Aiyar, Y., Davis, V., Govindan, G., & Kapur, T. (2021). Rewriting the grammar of the education system: Delhi's education reform (a tale of creative resistance and creative disruption). Research on Improving Systems of Education (RISE). DOI: https://doi.org/10.35489/BSG-RISE-Misc_2021/01

Akerlof, G. A., & Kranton, R. E. (2011). *Identity economics: How our identities shape our work, wages, and well-being.* Princeton University Press.

Allegretto, S., & Mishel, L. (2020). Teacher pay penalty dips but persists in 2019: Public school teachers earn about 20% less in weekly wages than nonteacher college graduates. Economic Policy Institute.

Allen, R. (2016, November 14). 2 social workers charged with manslaughter in Detroit toddler's death. *Detroit Free Press.*

Amabile, T. M. (2018). *Creativity in context: Update to the social psychology of creativity.* Routledge.

Amabile, T. M., Hill, K. G., Hennessey, B. A., & Tighe E. M. (1994). The Work Preference Inventory: Assessing intrinsic and extrinsic motivational orientations. *Journal of Personality and Social Psychology, 66*(5), 950–967.

Aman-Rana, S., Gingerich, D., & Sukhtankar, S. (2022). Screen now, save later? The trade-off between administrative ordeals and fraud. National Bureau of Economic Research. DOI: https://doi.org/10.3386/w31364

Andersen, R., Thingstrup, S. H., & Schmidt, L. S. K. (2018). The purpose of education: Pedagogues' and teachers' negotiations in Danish primary schools. *Educational Action Research, 26*(3), 354–364.

Andrews, M. (2013). *The limits of institutional reform in development: Changing rules for realistic solutions.* Cambridge University Press.

Andrews, M., Pritchett, L., & Woolcock, M. (2017). *Building state capability: Evidence, analysis, action.* Oxford University Press.

Aneja, A., & Xu, G. (2023). Strengthening state capacity: Civil service reform and public sector performance during the Gilded Age. Working paper.

Ang, Y. Y. (2016). *How China escaped the poverty trap.* Cornell University Press.

Ang, Y. Y. (2020). *China's gilded age: The paradox of economic boom and vast corruption.* Cambridge University Press.

Ashraf, N., Bandiera, O., Davenport, E., & Lee, S. S. (2020). Losing prosociality in the quest for talent? Sorting, selection, and productivity in the delivery of public services. *American Economic Review, 110*(5), 1355–1394.

Ashraf, N., Bandiera, O., & Jack, B. K. (2014). No margin, no mission? A field experiment on incentives for public service delivery. *Journal of Public Economics, 120,* 1–17.

Aspinall, E., & Sukmajati, M. (Eds.). (2016). *Electoral dynamics in Indonesia: Money politics, patronage and clientelism at the grassroots.* NUS Press.

Austin, R. D. (2013). *Measuring and managing performance in organizations.* Addison-Wesley.

Azulai, M., Fornasari, M., Rasul, I., Rogger, D., & Williams, M. G. (2020). Can training improve organizational culture? Experimental evidence from Ghana's civil service. Working paper.

Baig, F. A., Han, X., Hasnain, Z., & Rogger, D. (2021). Introducing the Worldwide Bureaucracy Indicators: A new global dataset on public sector employment and compensation. *Public Administration Review, 81*(3), 564–571.

Bandiera, O., Best, M. C., Khan, A. Q., & Prat, A. (2021). The allocation of authority in organizations: A field experiment with bureaucrats. *Quarterly Journal of Economics, 136*(4), 2195–2242.

Bandiera, O., Prat, A., & Valletti, T. (2009). Active and passive waste in government spending: Evidence from a policy experiment. *American Economic Review, 99*(4), 1278–1308.

Banerjee, A., Duflo, E., & Glennerster, R. (2008). Putting a band-aid on a corpse: Incentives for nurses in the Indian public health care system. *Journal of the European Economic Association, 6*(2–3), 487–500.

Banuri, S., & Keefer, P. (2012). Pro-social behavior where we least expect it? The selection and socialization of intrinsically-motivated government (tax!) officials. World Bank Working Paper, Development Economics Research Group.

Banuri, S., & Keefer, P. (2015). Was Weber right? The effects of pay for ability and pay for performance on pro-social motivation, ability and effort in the public sector. World Bank Policy Research Working Paper 7261.

Banuri, S., & Keefer, P. (2016). Pro-social motivation, effort and the call to public service. *European Economic Review, 83,* 139–164.

Barfort, S., Harmon, N. A., Hjorth, F., & Olsen, A. L. (2019). Sustaining honesty in public service: The role of selection. *American Economic Journal: Economic Policy, 11*(4), 96–123.

Barks, C. (2005). *Rumi: The book of love: Poems of ecstasy and longing.* Deckle Edge.

Bass, B. M., & Riggio, R. E. (2006). *Transformational leadership.* Psychology Press.

Baumeister, R. F., & Leary, M. R. (2007). The need to belong: Desire for interpersonal attachments as a fundamental human motivation. *Interpersonal Development, 117*(3), 57–89.

Beaman, L., Duflo, E., Pande, R., & Topalova, P. (2012). Female leadership raises aspirations and educational attainment for girls: A policy experiment in India. *Science, 335*(6068), 582–586.

Bellé, N. (2013). Experimental evidence on the relationship between public service motivation and job performance. *Public Administration Review, 73*(1), 143–153.

Bellé, N. (2015). Performance-related pay and the crowding out of motivation in the public sector: A randomized field experiment. *Public Administration Review, 75*(2), 230–241.

Berg, J. M., Grant, A. M., & Johnson, V. (2010). When callings are calling: Crafting work and leisure in pursuit of unanswered occupational callings. *Organization Science, 21*(5), 973–994.

Bernstein, E. S. (2012). The transparency paradox: A role for privacy in organizational learning and operational control. *Administrative Science Quarterly, 57*(2), 181–216.

Bertelli, A. M. (2012). *The political economy of public sector governance.* Cambridge University Press.

Bertelli, A. M., Hassan, M., Honig, D., Rogger, D., & Williams, M. J. (2020). An agenda for the study of public administration in developing countries. *Governance, 33*(4), 735–748.

Bertram, I., Bouwman, R., & Tummers, L. (2022). Socioeconomic status and public sector worker stereotypes: Results from a representative survey. *Public Administration Review, 82*(2), 237–255.

Besley, T., & Ghatak, M. (2005). Competition and incentives with motivated agents. *American Economic Review, 95*(3), 616–636.

Besley, T., & Ghatak, M. (2018). Prosocial motivation and incentives. *Annual Review of Economics, 10*(1), 411–438.

Besley, T., Honig, D., Khan, A., Sardar, M., Abedin, Z., & Chakma, D. (2020). *Improving [agency name redacted] performance by considering management practice, motivation, and the mission match of employees.* Working paper.

Besley, T. J., & Persson, T. (2022). Organizational dynamics: Culture, design, and performance. CEPR Discussion Paper No. DP17382. CEPR Press.

Bevan, G., & Hood, C. (2006). What's measured is what matters: Targets and gaming in the English public health care system. *Public Administration, 84*(3), 517–538.

Bogage, J. (2020, July 14). Postal Service memos detail "difficult" changes, including slower mail delivery. *Washington Post.*

Bogage, J., & Ingraham, C. (2020, August 20). Here's why the Postal Service wanted to remove hundreds of mail-sorting machines. *Washington Post.*

Bold, T., Filmer, D., Martin, G., Molina, E., Rockmore, C., Stacy, B., & Wane, W. (2017). What do teachers know and do? Does it matter? Evidence from primary schools in Africa. World Bank Policy Research Working Paper 7956.

Bond, D. (2019). Full text of John Bercow's resignation speech. *Politics Home.* https://www.polit icshome.com/thehouse/article/full-text-of-john-bercows-resignation-speech

Boraggina-Ballard, L., Sobeck, J., & Honig, D. (2021). What motivates highly trained child welfare professionals to stay or leave? *Children and Youth Services Review, 124.* DOI: https://doi.org/10.1016/j.childyouth.2021.105958

Boyne, G. A. (2003). What is public service improvement? *Public Administration, 81*(2), 211–227.

Brandsma, G. J., & Schillemans, T. (2013). The accountability cube: Measuring accountability. *Journal of Public Administration Research and Theory, 23*(4), 953–975.

Brehm, J. O., & Gates, S. (1999). *Working, shirking, and sabotage: Bureaucratic response to a democratic public.* University of Michigan Press.

Brewer, G. A., & Selden, S. C. (1998). Whistle blowers in the federal civil service: New evidence of the public service ethic. *Journal of Public Administration Research and Theory, 8*(3), 413–440.

Brierley, S. (2021). Combining patronage and merit in public sector recruitment. *Journal of Politics, 83*(1), 182–197.

Bright, L. (2008). Does public service motivation really make a difference on the job satisfaction and turnover intentions of public employees? *American Review of Public Administration, 38*(2), 149–166.

Bro, L. L., Andersen, L. B., & Bøllingtoft, A. (2017). Low-hanging fruit: Leadership, perceived prosocial impact, and employee motivation. *International Journal of Public Administration, 40*(9), 717–729.

Brockey, L. M. (2007). *Journey to the East: The Jesuit mission to China, 1579–1724.* Harvard University Press.

Brooks, D. (2019, May 27). The welfare state is broken. Here's how to fix it. *New York Times.*

Burgess, S., Propper, C., Ratto, M., & Tominey, E. (2017). Incentives in the public sector: Evidence from a government agency. *The Economic Journal, 127*(605), F117–F141.

Caillier, J. G. (2014). Toward a better understanding of the relationship between transformational leadership, public service motivation, mission valence, and employee performance. *Public Personnel Management, 43*(2), 218–239.

Caillier, J. (2018). The priming effect of corruption and bureaucracy bashing on citizens' perceptions of an agency's performance. *Public Performance & Management Review, 41*(2), 201–223.

Camden Centre for Collaborative Practice. (2022). *Slide deck: Overview of the center.*

Carpenter, D. (2001). *The forging of bureaucratic autonomy: Reputations, networks, and policy innovation in executive agencies, 1862–1928*. Princeton University Press.

Carpenter, D. (2014). *Reputation and power: Organizational image and pharmaceutical regulation at the FDA*. Princeton University Press.

Carpenter, D. P., & Krause, G. A. (2012). Reputation and public administration. *Public Administration Review*, 72(1), 26–32.

Carpenter, J., Doverspike, D., & Miguel, R. F. (2012). Public service motivation as a predictor of attraction to the public sector. *Journal of Vocational Behavior*, 80(2), 509–523.

Carril, R. (2021). *Rules versus discretion in public procurement*. Barcelona GSE Working Paper 1232.

Carter, E. (2021). More than marketised? Exploring the governance and accountability mechanisms at play in social impact bonds. *Journal of Economic Policy Reform*, 24(1), 78–94.

CFS North Central. (2022). North Central—Children & Family Services. https://www.michi gan.gov/mdhhs/inside-mdhhs/county-offices/wayne/north-central-children-family-services

Chowdhury, A. (2020). Public sector innovation transforming a country." TEDx Talks. https://www.youtube.com/watch?v=-9RGb7S4lq4

Christensen, R. K., Paarlberg, L., & Perry, J. L. (2017). Public service motivation research: Lessons for practice. *Public Administration Review*, 77(4), 529–542.

Christensen, R. K., & Wright, B. E. (2011). The effects of public service motivation on job choice decisions: Disentangling the contributions of person-organization fit and person-job fit." *Journal of Public Administration Research and Theory: J-PART*, 21(4), 723–743.

Clarey, C. (2017, November 12). The secret to Roger Federer's success is this man. *New York Times*.

Clark, C. 2017. Deconstructing the Deep State. *Government Executive*. https://www.govexec.com/feature/gov-exec-deconstructing-deep-state/

Clerkin, R. M., & Coggburn, J. D. (2012). The dimensions of public service motivation and sector work preferences. *Review of Public Personnel Administration*, 32(3), 209–235.

Clifton, G. (2015). *Professionalism, patronage and public service in Victorian London: The staff of the Metropolitan Board of Works, 1856–1889*. Bloomsbury Publishing.

Cottam, H. (2018). *Radical help: How we can remake the relationships between us and revolutionise the welfare state*. Hachette UK.

Crewson, P. E. (1997). Public-service motivation: Building empirical evidence of incidence and effect. *Journal of Public Administration Research and Theory*, 7(4), 499–518.

Crouch, L. (2020). *System implications for core instructional support: Lessons from Sobral (Brazil), Puebla (Mexico), and Kenya*. RISE Insight Note.

Daily Star. (2022, March 31). 1,963 recommended for recruitment under 40th BCS. *Daily Star*.

Dal Bó, E., Finan, F., & Rossi, M. A. (2013). Strengthening state capabilities: The role of financial incentives in the call to public service. *Quarterly Journal of Economics*, 128(3), 1169–1218.

Decarolis, F., Fisman, R., Pinotti, P., & Vannutelli, S. (2020). *Rules, discretion, and corruption in procurement: Evidence from Italian government contracting* (No. w28209). National Bureau of Economic Research.

Deci, E. L., & Vansteenkiste, M. (2003). Self-determination theory and basic need satisfaction: Understanding human development in positive psychology. *Ricerche di Psicologia*, 27(1), 23–40.

DeHart-Davis, L. (2009a). Green tape: A theory of effective organizational rules. *Journal of Public Administration Research and Theory*, 19(2), 361–384.

DeHart-Davis, L. (2009b). Green tape and public employee rule abidance: Why organizational rule attributes matter. *Public Administration Review*, 69(5), 901–910.

DeHart-Davis, L., Davis, R. S., & Mohr, Z. (2015). Green tape and job satisfaction: Can organizational rules make employees happy? *Journal of Public Administration Research and Theory*, 25(3), 849–876.

Deserranno, E. (2019). Financial incentives as signals: Experimental evidence from the recruitment of village promoters in Uganda. *American Economic Journal: Applied Economics*, 11(1), 277–317.

De Walque, D., Kandpal, E., Wagstaff, A., Friedman, J., Neelsen, S., Piatti-Fünfkirchen, M., Sautmann, A., Shapira, G., & Van de Poel, E. (2022). *Improving effective coverage in health: Do financial incentives work?* World Bank.

Dewatripont, M., Jewitt, I., & Tirole, J. (1999). Economics of career concerns, Part II. *Review of Economic Studies, 66*, 199–217.

Dhaliwal, I., & Hanna, R. (2017). The devil is in the details: The successes and limitations of bureaucratic reform in India. *Journal of Development Economics, 124*, 1–21.

DiIulio, J. D., & DiIulio, J. J. (1994). Principled agents: The cultural bases of behavior in a federal government bureaucracy. *Journal of Public Administration Research and Theory, 4*(3), 277–318.

DiIulio, J. J. (2011). *Deregulating the public service*. Brookings Institution Press.

Di Maro, V., Evans, D. K., Khemani, S., and Scot, T. (2021). Building state capacity: What is the impact of development projects? Center for Global Development Working Paper 598.

Dissanayake, R., Honig, D., Thompson, S., & Linos, E. (2023). What motivates public sector workers to form peer networks? Evidence from a survey experiment. Working paper.

Dixit, A. (1997). Power of incentives in private versus public organizations. *American Economic Review, 87*(2), 378–382.

Dixit, A. (2002). Incentives and organizations in the public sector: An interpretative review. *Journal of Human Resources, 37*(4), 696–727.

Doyle Jr., J. J. (2007). Child protection and child outcomes: Measuring the effects of foster care. *American Economic Review, 97*(5), 1583–1610.

Duflo, E., Hanna, R., & Ryan, S. P. (2012). Incentives work: Getting teachers to come to school. *American Economic Review, 102*(4), 1241–1278.

Dunleavy, P. (1995). Policy disasters: Explaining the UK's record. *Public Policy and Administration, 10*(2), 52–70.

Dunsch, F. A., Evans, D. K., Eze-Ajoku, E., & Macis, M. (2017). Management, supervision, and healthcare: A field experiment. *Journal of Economics & Management Strategy, 32*(3), 583–606.

Dutton, J. E., Debebe, G., & Wrzesniewski, A. (2016). Being valued and devalued at work: A social valuing perspective. In B. A. Bechky & K. D. Elsbach (Eds.), *Qualitative organizational research: Best papers from the Davis Conference on Qualitative Research* (pp. 9–51). IAP Information Age Publishing.

Early Intervention Foundation. (2018). Family group conferencing, Camden. EIF Case Study.

Ebo, A. (2005). The challenges and opportunities of security sector reform in post-conflict Liberia. Geneva Centre for the Democratic Control of Armed Forces, Occasional Paper 9.

Ehren, M., & Baxter, J. (2021). *Trust, accountability and capacity in education system reform*. New York: Routledge.

Ehren, M., Paterson, A., & Baxter, J. (2020). Accountability and trust: Two sides of the same coin? *Journal of Educational Change, 21*, 183–213.

Emerging Public Leaders. (2021, January). Process evaluation of the EPL Programme in Ghana.

Esteve, M., & Schuster C. (2019). *Motivating public employees*. Cambridge University Press.

Esteve, M., Urbig, D., Van Witteloostuijn, A., & Boyne, G. (2016). Prosocial behavior and public service motivation. *Public Administration Review, 76*(1), 177–187.

Evans, D., & Piper, B. 2020. Guiding teachers rather than scripting them. Blog, Center for Global Development.

Farrelly, N. (2013). Why democracy struggles: Thailand's elite coup culture. *Australian Journal of International Affairs, 67*(3), 281–296.

Figueroa, V. (2020). Political corruption cycles: High-frequency evidence from Argentina's notebooks scandal. *Comparative Political Studies, 54*(3–4), 482–517.

Fischer-Mackey, J. & Fox, J., (2022). Pitfalls of "slippery indicators": The importance of reading between the lines. *Development in Practice, 33*(6), 665–674.

Fisher, E. A. (2009). Motivation and leadership in social work management: A review of theories and related studies. *Administration in Social Work, 33*(4), 347–367.

Folke, C., Polasky, S., Rockström, J., Galaz, V., Westley, F., Lamont, M., & Walker, B. H. (2021). Our future in the Anthropocene biosphere. *Ambio, 50*, 834–869.

Fox, J. (1993). *The politics of food in Mexico: State power and social mobilization.* Cornell University Press.

Fox, J. (1996). How does civil society thicken? The political construction of social capital in rural Mexico. *World Development, 24*(6), 1089–1103.

Frean, A. (2017, August 2). Peterborough prison test proves that bonds can have a real impact. *The Times of London.*

Friedman, J. (2012). Building civil service capacity: Post-conflict Liberia, 2006–2011. Innovations for Successful Societies Case Study. Princeton University.

Fukuyama, F. (2013). What is "governance?" *Governance, 26*(3), 347–368.

Gailmard, S., & Patty, J. W. (2007). Slackers and zealots: Civil service, policy discretion, and bureaucratic expertise. *American Journal of Political Science, 51*(4), 873–889.

Gailmard, S., & Patty, J. W. (2012). *Learning while governing: Expertise and accountability in the executive branch.* University of Chicago Press.

Gandhi, J. (2008). *Political institutions under dictatorship.* Cambridge University Press.

Gandhi, J., and Przeworski, A., (2007). Authoritarian institutions and the survival of autocrats. *Comparative Political Studies, 40*(11), 1279–1301.

Ganimian, A. J., & Murnane, R. J. (2016). Improving education in developing countries: Lessons from rigorous impact evaluations. *Review of Educational Research, 86*(3), 719–755.

Gans-Morse, J., Kalgin, A. S., Klimenko, A. V., Vorobyev, D., & Yakovlev, A. A. (2020). *Public service motivation and sectoral employment in Russia: New perspectives on the attraction vs. socialization debate.* Higher School of Economics Research Paper No. WP BRP, 26.

Garg, S., & Pande, S. (2018). Learning to sustain change: Mitanin community health workers promote public accountability in India. *Accountability Note 4.*

Gartenberg, C., Prat, A., & Serafeim, G. (2019). Corporate purpose and financial performance. *Organization Science, 30*(1), 1–18.

Gazette. (1999, November). Is this Heaven? Maybe, once MLB finishes field of dreams stadium in Dyersville. *The Gazette.*

Gelles, D., & Yaffe-Bellany, D. (2019, August 19). Shareholder value is no longer everything, top C.E.O.s say. *New York Times.*

Gelman, A., & Loken, E. (2013). The garden of forking paths: Why multiple comparisons can be a problem, even when there is no "fishing expedition" or "p-hacking" and the research hypothesis was posited ahead of time. Department of Statistics, Columbia University.

George, B., Pandey, S. K., Steijn, B., Decramer, A., & Audenaert, M. (2021). Red tape, organizational performance, and employee outcomes: Meta-analysis, meta-regression, and research agenda. *Public Administration Review, 81*(4), 638–651.

GESIS. (2014). www.gesis.org. Available at: https://www.gesis.org/en/issp/modules/issp-modules-by-topic/citizenship/2014

Gibbons, R., & Henderson, R. (2012a). Relational contracts and organizational capabilities. *Organization Science, 23*(5), 1350–1364.

Gibbons, R., & Henderson, R. (2012b). What do managers do?: Exploring persistent performance differences among seemingly similar enterprises. Harvard Business School.

Gindling, T. H., Hasnain, Z., Newhouse, D., & Shi, R. (2019). Are public sector workers in developing countries overpaid? Evidence from a new global dataset. *World Development, 126*, 104737.

Giné, X., Mansuri, G., & Shrestha, S. A. (2022). Mission and the bottom line: Performance incentives in a multigoal organization. *Review of Economics and Statistics, 104*(4), 748–763.

Goetzmann, W. N. (2017). *Money changes everything.* Princeton University Press.

Goodsell, C. T. (2006). A new vision for public administration. *Public Administration Review, 66*(4), 623–635.

Goodsell, C. T. (2010). *Mission mystique: Belief systems in public agencies.* CQ Press.

Government of Liberia. (2008). "Smaller government, better service"—Liberia's civil service reform strategy, 2008–2011.

Graeber, D. (2018). *Bullshit jobs: A theory.* New York: Simon & Schuster.

Grant, A. M. (2007). Relational job design and the motivation to make a prosocial difference. *Academy of Management Review, 32*(2), 393–417.

Grant, A. M. (2008). Does intrinsic motivation fuel the prosocial fire? Motivational synergy in predicting persistence, performance, and productivity. *Journal of Applied Psychology, 93*(1), 48–58.

Grant, A. M. (2013). *A revolutionary approach to success: Give and take.* Penguin Books.

Greenstein, G., & Honig, D. (2022). Managing aid personnel. In preparation for R. Desai, S. Devarajan, & J. Tobin (Eds.), *The Elgar handbook of aid and development.*

Grindle, M. S. (1997). Divergent cultures? When public organizations perform well in developing countries. *World Development, 25*(4), 481–495.

Gulzar, S., & Khan, M. Y. (2021). "Good politicians": Experimental evidence on motivations for political candidacy and government performance. Available at https://ssrn.com/abstract= 3826067

Gulzar, S., Ladino, J. F., Mehmood, M. Z., & Rogger, D. (2023). Command and can't control: An evaluation of centralized accountability in the public sector. Working paper.

Hanna, R., & Wang, S. Y. (2017). Dishonesty and selection into public service: Evidence from India. *American Economic Journal: Economic Policy, 9*(3), 262–290.

Hasnain, Z., Kay, K., Rogger, D., Bersch, K., Mistree, D., Mikkelsen, K. S., Schuster, C., Fukuyama F., & Meyer-Sahling, J. (2022). The Global Survey of Public Servants. Available from www. globalsurveyofpublicservants.org

Harford, T. (2022). What Le Corbusier got right about office space. Available at https://timharf ord.com/2022/04/what-le-corbusier-got-right-about-office-space/

Hatch, M. J. (1993). The dynamics of organizational culture. *Academy of Management Review, 18*(4), 657–693.

Hazır, Ö. (2015). A review of analytical models, approaches and decision support tools in project monitoring and control. *International Journal of Project Management, 33*(4), 808–815.

Headley, A. M. (2022). Accountability and police use of force: Interactive effects between minority representation and civilian review boards. *Public Management Review, 24*(11), 1682–1704.

Headley, A. M., & Wright, J. E. (2020). Is representation enough? Racial disparities in levels of force and arrests by police. *Public Administration Review, 80*(6), 1051–1062.

Headley, A. M., Wright, J. E., & Meier, K. J. (2021). Bureaucracy, democracy, and race: The limits of symbolic representation. *Public Administration Review, 81*(6), 1033–1043.

Hershcovis, S., & Barling, J. (2010). Towards a multi-foci approach to workplace aggression: A meta-analytic review of outcomes from different perpetrators. *Journal of Organizational Behavior, 31*(1), 24–44. DOI: https://doi.org/10.1002/job.621

Herzberg, F. (1964). The motivation-hygiene concept and problems of manpower. *Personnel Administration, 27*(1), 3–7.

Heywood, P., Marquette, H., Peiffer, C., & Zúñiga, N. (2017). *Integrity and integrity management in public life.* European Union.

Heywood, P. M., & Rose, J. (2014). "Close but no cigar": The measurement of corruption. *Journal of Public Policy, 34*(3), 507–529.

Heywood, P. M., & Rose, J. (2015a). Curbing corruption or promoting integrity? Probing the hidden conceptual challenge. In P. Hárdi, P. M. Heywood, & D. Torsello (Eds.), *Debates of corruption and integrity* (pp. 102–119). Palgrave Macmillan.

Heywood, P. M., & Rose, J. (2015b). The limits of rule governance. In A. Lawton, Z. Van der Wall, & L. Huberts (Eds.), *Ethics in public policy and management* (pp. 181–196). Routledge.

Ho, D. E. (2017). Does peer review work? An experiment of experimentalism. *Stanford Law Review, 69*(1–119).

Holmstrom, B., & Milgrom, P. (1991). Multitask principal-agent analyses: Incentive contracts, asset ownership, and job design. *Journal of Law, Economics, and Organization, 7*(special), 24–52.

Hong, J. S., Choi, J., Espelage, D. L., Wu, C.-F., Boraggina-Ballard, L., & Fisher, B. W. (2020). Are children of welfare recipients at a heightened risk of bullying and peer victimization? *Child & Youth Care Forum, 50*(3), 547–568.

Honig, D. (2018). *Navigation by judgment: Why and when top-down management of foreign aid doesn't work*. Oxford University Press.

Honig, D. (2019). When reporting undermines performance: The costs of politically constrained organizational autonomy in foreign aid implementation. *International Organization, 73*(1), 171–201

Honig, D. (2021). Supportive management practice and intrinsic motivation go together in the public service. *Proceedings of the National Academy of Sciences, 118*(13).

Honig, D. (2022). *Managing for motivation as public performance improvement strategy in education & far beyond*. CID Faculty Working Paper Series.

Honig, D., & Gulrajani, N. (2018). Making good on donors' desire to do development differently. *Third World Quarterly, 39*(1), 68–84.

Honig, D., Lall, R., & Parks, B. C. (2022). When does transparency improve institutional performance? Evidence from 20,000 projects in 183 countries. *American Journal of Political Science*. DOI: https://doi.org/10.1111/ajps.12698

Honig, D., & Pritchett, L. (2019). *The limits of accounting-based accountability in education (and far beyond): Why more accounting will rarely solve accountability problems*. Working paper No. 510. Center for Global Development.

Honig, D., & Woodhouse, E. (2023). The strength of weak tools and clear missions: Management practice & the tension between citizens' welfare and formal instructions in Thai districts. Working paper.

Hood, C., & Dixon, R. (2015). What we have to show for 30 years of new public management: Higher costs, more complaints. *Governance, 28*(3), 265–267.

Hossain, N., & Hickey, S. (2019). The problem of education quality in developing countries. *The Politics of Education in Developing Countries: From Schooling to Learning, 1*, 1–21.

Houston, D. J. (2000). Public-service motivation: A multivariate test. *Journal of Public Administration Research and Theory, 10*(4), 713–728.

Hwa, Y.-Y., et al. (Eds.). (2022). *Purpose, pressures, and possibilities: Conversations about teacher professional norms in the Global South. Research on improving systems of education*. Research on Improving Systems of Education.

Israel, A. (1987). *Institutional development: Incentives to performance*. Johns Hopkins University Press.

Jackson, C. K., & Bruegmann, E. (2009). Teaching students and teaching each other: The importance of peer learning for teachers. *American Economic Journal: Applied Economics, 1*(4), 85–108.

Jackson, M. (2009). Responsibility versus accountability in the Friedrich-Finer Debate. *Journal of Management History, 15*(1), 66–77.

Jacobsen, C., Hvitved, J., & Andersen, L. (2013). Command and motivation: How the perception of external interventions relates to intrinsic motivation and public service motivation. *Public Administration, 92*(4), 790–806.

Jeevan, S. (2021). *Intrinsic: A manifesto to reignite our inner drive*. Hachette UK.

Jensen, U. T., & Bro, L. L. (2018). How transformational leadership supports intrinsic motivation and public service motivation: The mediating role of basic need satisfaction. *American Review of Public Administration, 48*(6), 535–549.

Kaufmann, D., & Wittwer, S. (2022). Public policy and small and medium-sized towns. In H. Mayer & M. Lazzeroni (Eds.), *A research agenda for small and medium-sized towns* (pp. 163–178). Edward Elgar Publishing.

Kaufmann, H. (1960). *The forest ranger: A study in administrative behavior*. Routledge.

Kaufmann, W., Borry, E. L., & DeHart-Davis, L. (2022). Can effective organizational rules keep employees from leaving? A study of green tape and turnover intention. *Public Management Review, 25*(8), 1–22.

Kenny, C. (2017). *Results not receipts: Counting the right things in aid and corruption*. Brookings Institution Press.

Kerr, S. (1975). On the folly of rewarding A, while hoping for B. *Academy of Management Journal*, *18*(4), 769–783.

Khan, M. (2021). Corruption and political settlements. Simplecast.com. Available at https://in-pursuit-of-development.simplecast.com/episodes/mushtaq-khan

Khan, M., & Roy, P. (2022). *Making anti-corruption real: Using a "Power Capabilities and Interest Approach" to stop wasting money and start making progress.* SOAS Anti-Corruption Evidence Research Consortium.

Khan, M. A. S., Sayeed, S., Kader, M. A., & Hawlader, M. D. H. (2021). Healthcare workers' knowledge, attitude, and practice regarding personal protective equipment for the prevention of COVID-19. *Journal of Multidisciplinary Healthcare, 14*, 229–238.

Khan, M. Y. (2023). Mission motivation and public sector performance: Experimental evidence from Pakistan. Working Paper.

Khana Group. (2022, February). *President's Young Professional Program. Phase II impact evaluation—Final report.*

Khemani, S. (2020a). How India can lead the world to build a functioning public health system. Ideas 4 India. Available at https://www.ideasforindia.in/topics/human-development/how-india-can-lead-the-world-to-build-a-functioning-public-health-system.html

Khemani, S. (2020b). Ideas 4 India blog. Available at https://www.ideasforindia.in/topics/human-development/how-india-can-lead-the-world-to-build-a-functioning-public-health-system.html

Khemani, S. (Ed.). (2016). *Making politics work for development: Harnessing transparency and citizen engagement.* World Bank Group.

Khemani, S., Chaudhary, S., & Scot, T. (2020). Strengthening public health systems: Policy ideas from a governance perspective. World Bank Policy Research Working Paper No. 9220.

Kim, S. (2012). Does person-organization fit matter in the public-sector? Testing the mediating effect of person-organization fit in the relationship between public service motivation and work attitudes. *Public Administration Review, 72*(6), 830–840.

Klein, E., & Lewis, M. (2019). US government bureaucrats in the age of Trump. Podcast, The Ezra Klein Show.

Klitgaard, R. (1998). International cooperation against corruption. *Finance & Development*, *35*(1), 3–6.

Kuper, H., & Marmot, M. (2003). Job strain, job demands, decision latitude, and risk of coronary heart disease within the Whitehall II study. *Journal of Epidemiology & Community Health*, *57*(2), 147–153.

Lam, L., Nguyen, P., Le, N., & Tran, K. (2021). The relation among organizational culture, knowledge management, and innovation capability: Its implication for open innovation. *Journal of Open Innovation: Technology, Market, and Complexity, 7*(1), 66.

Leaver, C., Ozier, O., Serneels, P., & Zeitlin, A. (2021). Recruitment, effort, and retention effects of performance contracts for civil servants: Experimental evidence from Rwandan primary schools. *American Economic Review, 111*(7), 2213–2246.

Leaver, C., & Pritchett, L. (2019, November 6). Should "pay for performance" be used for teachers? (With a plea to pause before you answer). RISE Programme. Available at https://riseprogramme.org/blog/pay-for-performance-plea-pause

Le Grand, J. (2003). Knights and knaves in the public sector: What do we mean and what do we know? In J. Le Grand (Ed.), *Motivation, agency, and public policy: Of knights and knaves, pawns and queens* (pp. 23–38). Oxford University Press.

Levine, C. B., & Smith, M. J. (2018). Clawbacks and earnings management. *Journal of Management Accounting Research, 31*(3), 129–151.

Levy, B. (2014). *Working with the grain: Integrating governance and growth in development strategies.* Oxford University Press.

Lewis, D. E. (2019). Deconstructing the administrative state. *Journal of Politics, 81*(3), 767–789.

Liao, W. K. (1939). *The complete works of Han Fei Tzu.* Stephen Austin & Sons, Ltd., Oriental and General Printers.

Liljegren, A., Berlin, J., Szücs, S., & Höjer, S. (2021). The police and "the balance"—Managing the workload within Swedish investigation units. *Journal of Professions and Organization*, *8*(1), 70–85.

Linos, E. (2018). More than public service: A field experiment on job advertisements and diversity in the police. *Journal of Public Administration Research and Theory*, *28*(1), 67–85.

Lipsky, M. (1980). *Street-level bureaucracy: Dilemmas of the individual in public services*. Russell Sage Foundation.

Liu, B., Hui, C., Hu, J., Yang, W., & Yu, X. (2011). How well can public service motivation connect with occupational intention? *International Review of Administrative Sciences*, *77*(1), 191–211.

Lohmann, J., Wilhelm, D., Kambala, C., Brenner, S., Muula, A. S., & De Allegri, M. (2018). "The money can be a motivator, to me a little, but mostly PBF just helps me to do better in my job." An exploration of the motivational mechanisms of performance-based financing for health workers in Malawi. *Health Policy and Planning*, *33*(2), 183–191.

Lowe, T., Padmanabhan, C., McCart, D., & McNeill, K. (2022). *Human learning systems: A practical guide for the curious. Full version 1.1*. Center for Public Impact, Healthcare Improvement Scotland, Iriss.

Lum, C., Stoltz, M., Koper, C. S., & Scherer, J. A. (2019). Research on body-worn cameras: What we know, what we need to know. *Criminology & Public Policy*, *18*(1), 93–118.

MacFarquhar, N. (2021, June 25). Why police have been quitting in droves in the last year. *New York Times*.

Majid, M. A., & Ali, S. A. M. Teachers and their monitors: Negotiating disciplinary regimes in Pakistan. In S. M. Zavattarao, J. E. Sowa, A. C. Henderson, & L. H. Edwards (Eds.), *Portraits of public service: Untold stories from the front lines*. State University of New York Press, 67–90 (inclusive).

Mangla, A. (2021). Social conflict on the front lines of reform: Institutional activism and girls' education in rural India. *Public Administration and Development*, *42*(1), 95–105.

Mangla, A. (2022). *Making bureaucracy work: Norms, education and public service delivery in rural India*. Cambridge University Press.

Manning, F. J. (1991). Morale, cohesion, and esprit de corps. In R. Gal and A. D. Mangelsdorff (Eds.), *Handbook of military psychology* (pp. 453–470). John Wiley & Sons.

Manoharan, K., Dissanayake, P. B., Pathirana, C., Deegahawature, D., & Silva, K. R. R. (2023). A labour performance score and grading system to the next normal practices in construction. *Built Environment Project and Asset Management*, *13*(1), 36–55.

Mansbridge, J. (2009). A "selection model" of political representation. *Journal of Political Philosophy*, *17*(4), 369–398.

Mansbridge, J. (2014). A contingency theory of accountability. In M. Bovens, R. E. Goodin, & T. Schillemans (Eds.), *The Oxford Handbook of Public Accountability* (pp. 55–68). Oxford University Press.

Marquette, H., & Peiffer, C. (2020). *Corruption functionality framework*. Global Integrity.

Martin, R. C., & Kaufman, H. (1960). The forest ranger: A study in administrative behavior. *Administrative Science Quarterly*, *6*(1), 114.

Mbiti, I., Romero, M., & Schipper, Y. (2019). *Designing effective teacher performance pay programs: Experimental evidence from Tanzania*. National Bureau of Economic Research.

Mbiti, I., & Schipper, Y. (2021). Teacher and parental perceptions of performance pay in education: Evidence from Tanzania. *Journal of African Economies*, *30*(1), 55–80.

McAlpine, K., Kagucia Omsa, N., Semwene, J., & Mbise, A. (2018). *A twist on performance theory*. Twaweza.

McDonald, T. P. (1996). *Assessing the long-term effects of foster care: A research synthesis*. Child Welfare League of America.

McDonnell, E. M. (2020). *Patchwork Leviathan: Pockets of bureaucratic effectiveness in developing states*. Princeton University Press.

McGregor, D. (1960). Theory X and theory Y. *Organization Theory*, *358*(374), 5.

Merkel-Holguin, L. (2004). Sharing power with the people: Family group conferencing as a democratic experiment. *Journal of Sociology and Social Welfare*, *31*(1), 155–173.

Michigan Department of Environmental Quality. (2022). Michigan Department of Environmental Quality. GreeningDetroit.com. https://www.greeningdetroit.com/member/michigan-department-of-environmental-quality/

Michigan Department of Health and Human Services. (2022). Freedom of Information Act (FOIA) Request H015210-041122.

Mikkelsen, K. S., Schuster, C., & Meyer-Sahling, J. H. (2021). A cross-cultural basis for public service? Public service motivation measurement invariance in an original survey of 23,000 public servants in ten countries and four world regions. *International Public Management Journal*, 24(6), 739–761.

Mikkelsen, K. S., Schuster, C., Meyer-Sahling, J. H., & Wettig, M. R. (2022). Bureaucratic professionalization is a contagious process inside government: Evidence from a priming experiment with 3,000 Chilean civil servants. *Public Administration Review*, 82(2), 290–302.

Miller, G. J., & Whitford, A. B. (2016). *Above politics: Bureaucratic discretion and credible commitment.* Cambridge University Press.

Moe, T. M. (1989). The politics of bureaucratic structure. In J. E. Chubb and P. E. Peterson (Eds.), *Can the government govern?* (pp. 267–329). Brookings Institution Press.

Moore, M. H. (2003). *Creating public value: Strategic management in government.* Harvard University Press.

Moore, R. (2019). Strategic choice: A future-focused review of the DFAT-AusAID integration. https://devpolicy.org/publications/reports/DFAT-AusAIDIntegrationReview- FullVersion.pdf

Moynihan, D. P., Baekgaard, M., & Jakobsen, M. L. (2020). Tackling the performance regime paradox: A problem-solving approach engages professional goal-based learning. *Public Administration Review*, 80(6), 1001–1010.

Moynihan, D. P., & Pandey, S. K. (2005). Testing how management matters in an era of government by performance management. *Journal of Public Administration Research and Theory*, 15(3), 421–439.

Moynihan, D. P., & Pandey, S. K. (2007a). The role of organizations in fostering public service motivation (pp. 40–48). *SSRN Electronic Journal*, 67(1).

Moynihan, D. P., & Pandey, S. K. (2007b). The ties that bind: Social networks, person-organization fit and turnover intention. *SSRN Electronic Journal*, 18(2). DOI: https://doi.org/10.2139/ssrn.975270

Moynihan, D., & Roberts, A. (2021). Dysfunction by design: Trumpism as administrative doctrine. *Public Administration Review*, 81(1), 152–156.

Mulgan, R. (2000). "Accountability": An ever-expanding concept? *Public Administration*, 78(3), 555–573.

Mullane, J. V. (2002). The mission statement is a strategic tool: When used properly. *Management Decision 40*(5).

Muller, J. (2018). *The tyranny of metrics.* Princeton University Press.

Muralidharan, K., & Singh, A. (2020). Improving public sector management at scale? Experimental evidence on school governance in India. RISE Working Paper Series 20/056. DOI: https://doi.org/10.35489/BSG-RISE-WP_2020/056

National Institute of Justice. (2022, January 7). Research on body-worn cameras and law enforcement. Retrieved from https://nij.ojp.gov/topics/articles/research-body-worn-cameras-and-law-enforcement

Ndevu, Z. J., & Muller, K. (2018). Operationalising performance management in local government: The use of the balanced scorecard. *SA Journal of Human Resource Management*, 16(1). DOI: https://doi.org/10.4102/sajhrm.v16i0.977

Nesta. (2019). Sparking change in public systems: The 100 day challenge. Nesta. Retrieved from https://media.nesta.org.uk/documents/100_days_to_change_a_system_v8.pdf

Nesta. (2023). People powered results: Reflections on 10 years of People Power in Action. Nesta. Retrieved from https://media.nesta.org.uk/documents/People_Powered_Results_Reflections_on_10_years_of_People_Power_in_Action_dD6ppAv.pdf

Nguyen, C. T. (2022). Transparency is surveillance. *Philosophy and Phenomenological Research*, *105*(2), 331–361.

NYT (New York Times). (2023, June 6). Transcript: Ezra Klein interviews Jennifer Pahlka. *The Ezra Klein Show*.

OECD. (2023). Anti-corruption and integrity in the public sector. OECD. https://www.oecd.org/gov/ethics/

O'Leary, R. (2019). *The ethics of dissent: Managing guerrilla government*. CQ Press.

Pahlka, J. (2023). *Recoding America*. Macmillan.

Peiffer, C., & Armytage, R. (2019). Searching for success: A mixed methods approach to identifying and examining positive outliers in development outcomes. *World Development, 121*, 97–107.

Peiffer, C., Armytage, R., Marquette, H., & Gumisiriza, P. (2021). Lessons from reducing bribery in Uganda's health services. *Development Policy Review, 39*(5), 721–739.

Pepinsky, T. B., Pierskalla, J. H., & Sacks, A. (2017). Bureaucracy and service delivery. *Annual Review of Political Science, 20*(1), 249–268.

Perrow, C. (1986). *Complex organizations: A critical essay*. McGraw-Hill.

Perry, J. L. (2000). Bringing society in: Toward a theory of public-service motivation. *Journal of Public Administration Research and Theory, 10*(2), 471–488.

Perry, J. L. (2020). *Managing organizations to sustain passion for public service*. Cambridge University Press.

Perry, J. L., & Wise, L. R. (1990). Bases of the motivational public service. *Public Administration Review, 50*(3): 367–373.

Pinder, C. C. (2008). *Work motivation in organizational behavior*. Psychology Press.

Pink, D. H. (2011). *Drive: The surprising truth about what motivates us*. Penguin.

Piper, B., Sitabkhan, Y., Mejia, J., & Betts, K. (2018). *Effectiveness of teachers' guides in the Global South: Scripting, learning outcomes, and classroom utilization*. RTI Press.

Piza, C., Zwager, A., Ruzzante, M., Dantas, R., & Loureiro, A. (2020). Supporting teaching, 9857. Autonomy to improve education outcomes: Experimental evidence from Brazil. Work Bank Policy Research Working Paper #9371.

Polanyi, M. (1966). *The tacit dimension*. University of Chicago Press.

Popham, W. J. (2001). Teaching to the test. *Educational Leadership, 58*(6), 16–20.

Pradhan, M., Suryadarma, D., Beatty, A., Wong, M., Gaduh, A., Alisjahbana, A., & Artha, R. P. (2014). Improving educational quality through enhancing community participation: Results from a randomized field experiment in Indonesia. *American Economic Journal: Applied Economics, 6*(2), 105–126.

Prendergast, C. (2001). Selection and oversight in the public sector, with the Los Angeles Police Department as an example. NBER Working Paper.

Prendergast, C. (2007). The motivation and bias of bureaucrats. *American Economic Review, 97*(1), 180–196.

Prendergast, C. (2008). Work incentives, motivation, and identity-intrinsic motivation and incentives. *American Economic Review, 98*(2), 201–205.

Prendergast, C. (2021). "Drive and wave": The response to LAPD police reforms after Rampart. University of Chicago, Becker Friedman Institute for Economics Working Paper.

Prieto, A. I. (2017). The perils of accommodation: Jesuit missionary strategies in the early modern world. *Journal of Jesuit Studies, 4*(3), 395–414.

Pritchett, L. (2013). *The rebirth of education*. Brookings Institution Press.

Pritchett, L., & Murgai, R. (2007). Teacher compensation: Can decentralization to local bodies take India from the perfect storm through troubled waters to clear sailing? In *India Policy Forum 2006–07, 3*, 123–177.

Pyrko, I., Dörfler, V., & Eden, C. (2017). Thinking together: What makes communities of practice work? *Human Relations, 70*(4), 389–409.

Quattrone, P. (2004). Accounting for God: Accounting and accountability practices in the Society of Jesus (Italy, XVI–XVII centuries). *Accounting, Organizations and Society, 29*(7), 647–683.

Quattrone, P. (2009). Books to be practiced: Memory, the power of the visual, and the success of accounting. *Accounting, Organizations and Society, 34*(1), 85–118.

Quattrone, P. (2015). Governing social orders, unfolding rationality, and Jesuit accounting practices: A procedural approach to institutional logics. *Administrative Science Quarterly, 60*(3), 411–445.

Rainey, H. G., & Steinbauer, P. (1999). Galloping elephants: Developing elements of a theory of effective government organizations. *Journal of Public Administration Research and Theory, 9*(1), 1–32.

Rasul, I., & Rogger, D. (2017). Management of bureaucrats and public service delivery: Evidence from the Nigerian civil service. *Economic Journal, 128*(608), 413–446.

Rasul, I., Rogger, D., & Williams, M. J. (2018). *Management and bureaucratic effectiveness: Evidence from the Ghanaian civil service.* World Bank Policy Research Working Paper 8595.

Rasul, I., Rogger, D., & Williams, M. J. (2021). Management, organizational performance, and task clarity: Evidence from Ghana's civil service. *Journal of Public Administration Research and Theory, 31*(2), 259–277.

Reagan, R. (1986, August 12). The president's news conference. National Archives. https://www.reaganlibrary.gov/archives/speech/presidents-news-conference-23

Rein, L. (2017, December 31). How Trump's first year has decimated federal bureaucracy. *The Independent.*

Reinikka, R., & Svensson, J. (2004). Local capture: Evidence from a central government transfer program in Uganda. *Quarterly Journal of Economics, 119*(2), 679–705.

Reinikka, R., & Svensson, J. (2005). Fighting corruption to improve schooling: Evidence from a newspaper campaign in Uganda. *Journal of the European Economic Association, 3*(2–3), 259–267.

Reinikka, R., & Svensson, J. (2011). The power of information in public services: Evidence from education in Uganda. *Journal of Public Economics, 95*(7–8), 956–966.

Resh, W. G., Marvel, J. D., & Wen, B. (2018). The persistence of prosocial work effort as a function of mission match. *Public Administration Review, 78*(1), 116–125.

Riccucci, N. M. (1995). *Unsung heroes: Federal execucrats making a difference.* Georgetown University Press.

Rich, J. A. J. (2022). Outsourcing bureaucracy to evade accountability: How public servants build shadow state capacity. *American Political Science Review, 117*(3), 1–16.

Rothstein, B. (2021a). *Controlling corruption: The social contract approach.* Oxford University Press.

Rothstein, B. (2021b). Three reasons anti-corruption programs fail. *Corruption in Fragile States* (blog). https://www.corruptionjusticeandlegitimacy.org/post/three-reasons-anti-corruption-programs-fail

Ryan, R., & Deci, E. (2000). Self-Determination Theory and the facilitation of intrinsic motivation. *American Psychologist, 55*(1), 68–78.

Sabel, C. F., & Zeitlin, J. (2012). Experimentalist governance. In D. Levi-Faur (Ed.), *The Oxford handbook of governance* (pp. 169–184). Oxford University Press.

Sadiq, M., Usman, M., Zamir, A., Shabbir, M. S., & Arif, A. (2021). Nexus between economic growth and foreign private investment: Evidence from Pakistan economy. *Cogent Economics & Finance, 9*(1). DOI: https://doi.org/10.1080/23322039.2021.1956067

Schein, E. H. (1990). Organizational culture. *American Psychologist, 45*(2), 109–119.

Schleicher, A. (2019, September 23). Building a learning culture for the digital world: Lessons from Moscow. OECD Education and Skills Today. https://oecdedutoday.com/learning-digital-world technology-education-moscow/

Schneider, B. (1987). The people make the place. *Personnel Psychology, 40*(3), 437–453.

Schuster, C., Meyer-Sahling, J., and Mikkelsen, K. S. (2020). (Un)principled principals, (un)principled agents: The differential effects of managerial civil service reforms on corruption in developing and OECD countries. *Governance, 33*(4), 829–848.

Schuster, C., Mikkelsen, K. S., Correa, I., & Meyer-Sahling, J.-H. (2021). Exit, voice, and sabotage: Public service motivation and guerrilla bureaucracy in times of unprincipled political principals. *Journal of Public Administration Research and Theory, 32*(2), 416–435.

Schwartz, B., & Wrzesniewski, A. (2019). Reconceptualizing intrinsic motivation. In K. A. Renninger & S. E. Hidi (Eds.), *The Cambridge handbook of motivation and learning* (pp. 373–396). Cambridge University Press.

Scott, J. C. (1990). *Domination and the arts of resistance: Hidden transcripts.* Yale University Press.

Scott, J. C. (1998). *Seeing like a state: How certain schemes to improve the human condition have failed.* Yale University Press.

Seim, B., Jablonski, R., & Ahlbäck, J. (2020). How information about foreign aid affects public spending decisions: Evidence from a field experiment in Malawi. *Journal of Development Economics, 146,* 102522.

Shook, J. (2010). How to change a culture: Lessons from NUMMI. *MIT Sloan Management Review.* Available at https://sloanreview.mit.edu/article/how-to-change-a-culture-lessons-from-nummi/

Simon, H. A. (1991). Bounded rationality and organizational learning. *Organization Science, 2*(1), 125–134.

Slotnick, D. (2020, August 14). USPS fans are loving a (very unofficial) poster that adds "fascism" to the challenges that can't stop the postal service. *Business Insider.*

Smith, K. A. (2019, January 11). Thinking about filing for unemployment during the government shutdown? Read this first. *Bankrate.com.*

Smith, M. (2022). *Human learning systems: A practical guide for the curious. Case study—Learning as a management strategy: Gateshead Council.* Center for Public Impact, Healthcare Improvement Scotland, Iriss.

Spenkuch, J. L., Teso, E., & Xu, G. (2023). Ideology and performance in public organizations. *Econometrica, 91*(4), 1171–1203.

Stallworth Williams, L. (2008). The mission statement: A corporate reporting tool with a past, present, and future. *Journal of Business Communication (1973), 45*(2), 94–119.

Steijn, B. (2008). Person-environment fit and public service motivation. *International Public Management Journal, 11*(1), 13–27.

Stewart, D. W. (1985). Professionalism vs. democracy: Friedrich vs. Finer revisited. *Public Administration Quarterly, 9*(1), 13–25.

Stillman, J. (2013, Jun3 13). What you can learn about job satisfaction from a janitor. *Inc.*

Stimson, H. L. (1945). Memorandum on the effects of atomic bomb. Available at https://history.state.gov/historicaldocuments/frus1945v02/d13

STiR Education. (2022). *10th Anniversary Celebration Report.* 1–20. STiR Education. Retrieved from https://stireducation.org/stirs-10th-anniversary-report/

Stockard, J., Wood, T. W., Coughlin, C., & Rasplica Khoury, C. (2018). The effectiveness of direct instruction curricula: A meta-analysis of a half century of research. *Review of Educational Research, 88*(4), 479–507.

Strobel, B., & Veit, S. (2021). Incomplete democratisation, system transformations, and the civil service: A case study on the Weimar Republic and the Nazi regime in Germany. In M. W. Bauer, B. G. Peters, J. Pierre, K. Yeşilkağıt, & S. Becker (Eds.), *Liberal Democratic Backsliding and Public Administration* (pp. 22–46). Cambridge University Press.

Szucs, F. Discretion and favoritism in public procurement. *Journal of the European Economic Association,* jvad017. DOI: https://doi.org/10.1093/jeea/jvad017

Szydlowski, G., de Boer, N., & Tummers, L. (2022). Compassion, bureaucrat bashing, and public administration. *Public Administration Review, 82*(4): 619–633.

Tankersley, J., & Kaplan, T. (2019, January 16). Why don't unpaid federal workers walk off the job? *New York Times.*

Taylor, F. (1947). *Scientific management: Comprising Shop management, The principles of scientific management and Testimony before the special House committee.* HarperCollins.

Tendler, J. (1997). *Good government in the tropics.* Johns Hopkins University Press.

Tendler, J., & Freedheim, S. (1994). Trust in a rent-seeking world: Health and government transformed in northeast Brazil. *World Development*, 22(12), 1771–1791.

Thomann, E., van Engen, N., & Tummers, L. (2018). The necessity of discretion: A behavioral evaluation of bottom-up implementation theory. *Journal of Public Administration Research and Theory*, 28(4), 583–601.

Thomson, A. (2022, February 12). Tony Blair: "Voters don't want a situation where women can't talk about being women." *The Times*.

Toral, G. (2023). How patronage delivers: Political appointments, bureaucratic accountability, and service delivery in Brazil. *American Journal of Political Science*. DOI: doi:10.1111/ajps.12758

Transparency International. (2022). *2023 Corruptions Perceptions Index*. Transparency.org. Available at https://www.transparency.org/en/cpi/2022

Tu, W., & Gong, T. (2022). Bureaucratic shirking in China: Is sanction-based accountability a cure? *China Quarterly*, 249, 259–274.

Tummers, L. (2012). Policy alienation of public professionals: The construct and its measurement. *Public Administration Review*, 72(4), 516–525.

Tummers, L., Bekkers, V., & Steijn, B. (2009). Policy alienation of public professionals. *Public Management Review*, 11(5), 685–706.

Tummers, L., Brunetto, Y., & Teo, S. T. (2016). Workplace aggression: Introduction to the special issue and future research directions for scholars. *International Journal of Public Sector Management*, 29(1): 2–10.

UK Department for Education. (2023). Stable homes, built on love: Implementation strategy and consultation. Children's Social Care Reform 2023.

USAID. (2022, October). *Local capacity strengthening policy*. USAID.

US Department of Health and Human Services. (2023). US Public Health Service Commissioned Corps. https://www.hhs.gov/surgeongeneral/corps/index.html#:~:text=The%20U.S.%20Public%20Health%20Service,and%20advancing%20public%20health%20science

Van Loon, N. M., Vandenabeele, W., & Leisink, P. (2015). On the bright and dark side of public service motivation: The relationship between PSM and employee wellbeing. *Public Money & Management*, 35(5), 349–356.

Van Veldhuizen, R. (2013). The influence of wages on public officials' corruptibility: A laboratory investigation. *Journal of Economic Psychology*, 39, 341–356.

Vaughn, R. G. (2012). *The successes and failures of whistleblower laws*. Edward Elgar Publishing.

Vogel, D., & Willems, J. (2020). The effects of making public service employees aware of their prosocial and societal impact: A microintervention. *Journal of Public Administration Research Public Administration*, 86(3), 485–503.

Vox. (2019, June 5). The Ezra Klein show. https://www.vox.com/podcasts/2019/6/5/18654486/michael-lewis-reads-my-mind

Vreeland, J. R. (2006). *The International Monetary Fund (IMF): Politics of conditional lending*. Routledge.

Wagner, Z., Asiimwe, J. B., & Levine, D. I. (2020). When financial incentives backfire: Evidence from a community health worker experiment in Uganda. *Journal of Development Economics*, 144, 102437.

Walker, T. (2020, January 2). Survey: Alarming number of educators may soon leave the profession. *NEA News*.

Walton, A., & Pollock, N. (2022, November 18). Empty classrooms, abandoned kids: Inside America's great teacher resignation. *New York Times*.

Weaver, J. (2021). Jobs for sale: Corruption and misallocation in hiring. *American Economic Review*, 111(10): 3093–3122.

Wenger, E., (2011). *Communities of practice: A brief introduction*. http://hdl.handle.net/1794/11736

Williams, L. S. (2008). The mission statement: A corporate reporting tool with a past, present, and future. *Journal of Business Communication*, 45(2), 94–119.

Williams Jr., M. C., Weil, N., Rasich, E. A., Ludwig, J., Chang, H., & Egrari, S., (2021). Body-worn cameras in policing: Benefits and costs. Working Paper No. 2021-38. Becker Friedman Institute.

Williams, M. J. (2023). *Reform as process: Implementing civil service reform in Africa*. Unpublished book manuscript.

Williams, M. J., & Yecalo-Tecle, L. (2020). Innovation, voice, and hierarchy in the public sector: Evidence from Ghana's civil service. *Governance, 33*(4), 789–807.

Williamson, O. E. (1981). The economics of organization: The transaction cost approach. *American Journal of Sociology, 87*(3), 548–577.

Wilson, J. Q. (1989). *Bureaucracy: What government agencies do and why they do it*. Basic Books.

World Bank. (2004). *World development report 2004: Making services work for poor people*. World Bank.

World Bank. (2021, May). *Thailand overview*. World Bank.

World Bank. (2022). *Worldwide Bureaucracy Indicators (WWBI)*. Available from https://datacatalog.worldbank.org/search/dataset/0038132

Wright, B. E., Moynihan, D. P., & Pandey, S. K. (2012). Pulling the levers: transformational leadership, public service motivation, and mission valence. *Public Administration Review, 72*(2), 206–215. DOI: https://doi.org/10.1111/j.1540-6210.2011.02496.x

Wright, B. E., & Pandey, S. K. (2008). Public service motivation and the assumption of person-organization fit. *Administration & Society, 40*(5), 502–521. DOI: https://doi.org/10.1177/0095399708320187

Wrzesniewski, A., & Dutton, J. E. (2001). Crafting a job: Revisioning employees as active crafters of their work. *Academy of Management Review, 26*(2), 179–201.

Yeşilkağıt, K. (2018). Bureaucracy under authoritarian rule: Autonomy and resilience of administrative institutions in divided times (pp. 1–30). *Structure and organization of government*. Working paper, University of Potsdam.

Yesilkagit, K., & Christensen, J. 2022. Political and administrative elites under authoritarian rule: Elite transformations and economic policymaking in Italy and Germany during the Interbellum. Paper prepared for IPPA Workshop, Budapest, June 28–30. Online at: https://www.ippapublicpolicy.org/file/paper/629eed81214fd.pdf

Zacka, B. (2017). *When the state meets the street: Public service and moral agency*. Harvard University Press.

Zak, P. J. (2014, October). Why your brain loves good storytelling. Harvard Business Review.

Zarychta, A., Grillos, T., & Andersson, K. P. (2020). Public sector governance reform and the motivation of street-level bureaucrats in developing countries. *Public Administration Review, 80*(1), 75–91.

INDEX

For the benefit of digital users, indexed terms that span two pages (e.g., 52–53) may, on occasion, appear on only one of those pages.

Tables, figures, and boxes are indicated by an italic *t*, *f*, and *b* following the para ID.

239